Textbook
3B

Maths —
No Problem!

Singapore Maths
English National Curriculum 2014

Consultant and Author
Dr. Yeap Ban Har

UK Consultant
Dr. Anne Hermanson

Authors
Dr. Foong Pui Yee
Lim Li Gek Pearlyn
Wong Oon Hua

shinglee

Published by Maths — No Problem!
Copyright © 2017 by Maths — No Problem!

Printed in the United Kingdom
First Printing, 2015
Reprinted twice in 2016 and once in 2017

ISBN 978-1-910504-10-9

Maths — No Problem!
Dowding House, Coach & Horses Passage
Tunbridge Wells, UK TN2 5NP
www.mathsnoproblem.co.uk

Acknowledgements

This Maths — No Problem! series, adapted from the New Syllabus
Primary Mathematics series, is published in collaboration with
Shing Lee Publishers. Pte Ltd.

Design and Illustration by Kin

Preface

Maths — No Problem! is a comprehensive series that adopts a spiral design with carefully built-up mathematical concepts and processes adapted from the maths mastery approaches used in Singapore. The Concrete-Pictorial-Abstract (C-P-A) approach forms an integral part of the learning process through the materials developed for this series.

Maths — No Problem! incorporates the use of concrete aids and manipulatives, problem-solving and group work.

In Maths — No Problem! Primary 3, these features are exemplified throughout the chapters:

Chapter Opener

Familiar events or occurrences that serve as an introduction for pupils.

In Focus

Includes questions related to various lesson objectives as an introductory activity for pupils.

Let's Learn

Introduces new concepts through a C-P-A approach with the use of engaging pictures and manipulatives. Guided examples are provided for reinforcement.

Activity Time

Provides pupils with opportunities to work as individuals or in small groups to explore mathematical concepts or to play games.

by foot   by bus   by train   by car   by bicycle

Guided Practice

Comprises questions for further consolidation and for the immediate evaluation of pupils' learning.

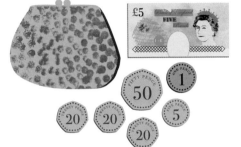

Mind Workout

Challenging non-routine questions for pupils to apply relevant heuristics and to develop higher-order thinking skills.

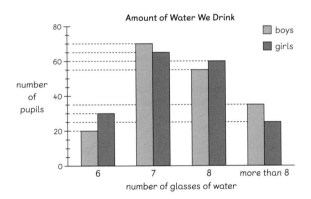

Maths Journal

Provides pupils with opportunities to show their understanding of the mathematical concepts learnt.

sport	How are angles used?
javelin throw	The athlete uses angles to help him throw the javelin as far as possible.

Self Check

Allows pupils to assess their own learning after each chapter.

I know how to...

Self Check

☐ draw picture graphs and bar graphs.
☐ read and interpret bar graphs.
☐ dolve problems using information from bar graphs.

Contents

Chapter 10

Picture Graphs and Bar Graphs

Chapter 11

Fractions

Chapter 12 — Angles

| Chapter 13 | Lines and Shapes | Page |

| Chapter 14 | Perimeter of Figures | |

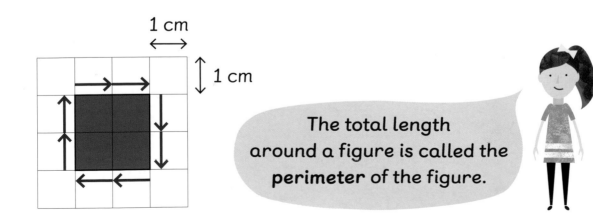

The total length around a figure is called the **perimeter** of the figure.

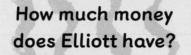

How much money
does Elliott have?

Chapter 8
Money

Naming Amounts of Money

In Focus

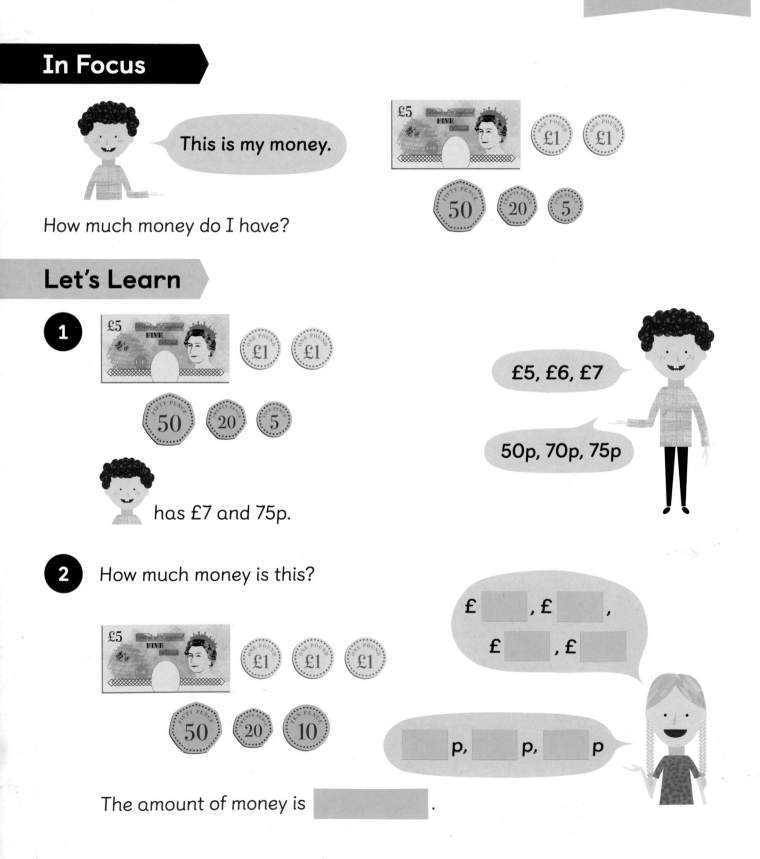

This is my money.

How much money do I have?

Let's Learn

1   has £7 and 75p.

£5, £6, £7

50p, 70p, 75p

2   How much money is this?

£ ___, £ ___, £ ___, £ ___

___ p, ___ p, ___ p

The amount of money is ___.

Guided Practice

How much money does each child have?

(a)

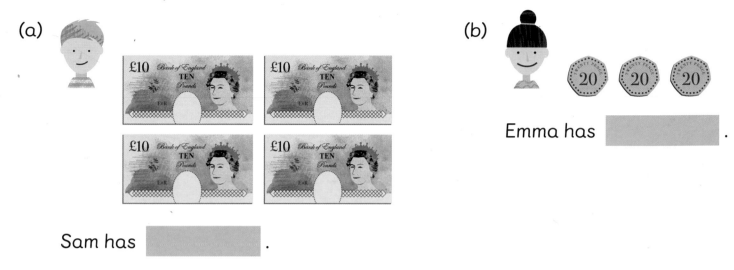

Sam has [   ].

(b)

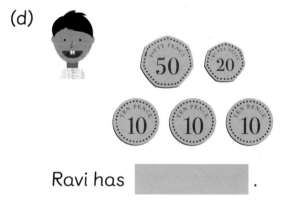

Emma has [   ].

(c)

Holly has [   ].

(d)

Ravi has [   ].

(e)

Lulu has [   ].

(f)

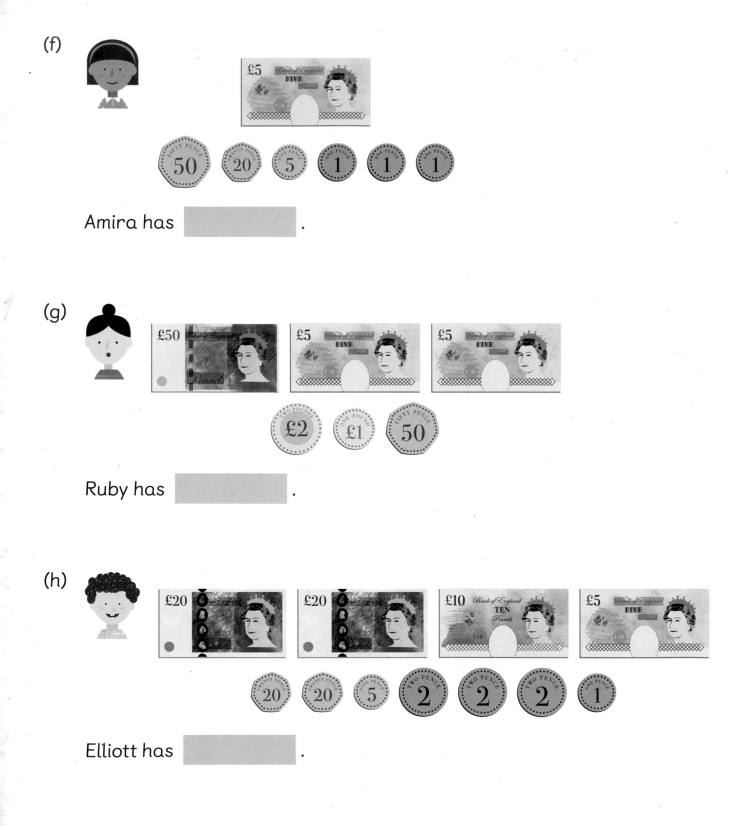

Amira has ⬜⬜⬜ .

(g)

Ruby has ⬜⬜⬜ .

(h)

Elliott has ⬜⬜⬜ .

Complete Worksheet **1** – Page **1** - **2**

Naming Amounts of Money

In Focus

Is 🧑 correct?

There is more than £10 but less than £11.

Let's Learn

1. How much is this?

This is £1.

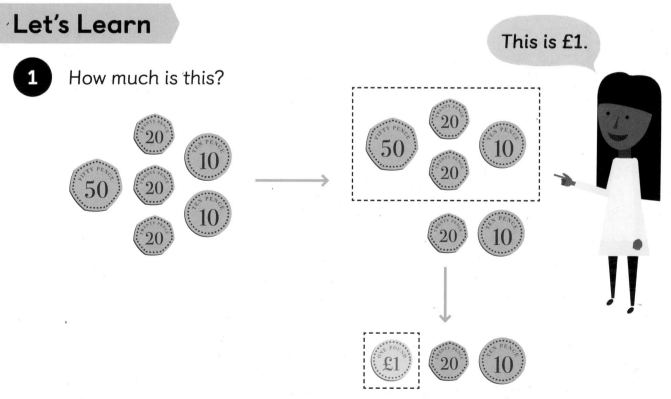

This is £1 and 30p.

2 Find the amount of money shown.

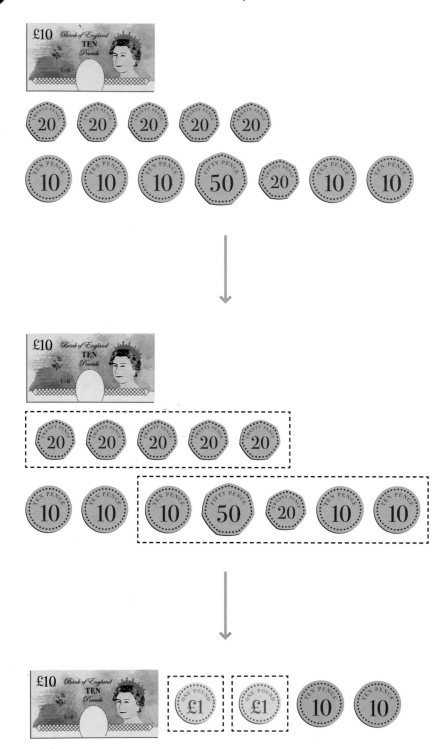

The amount of money is £12 and 20p.

Guided Practice

These wallets and purses have been emptied.
How much money did each one contain?

(a)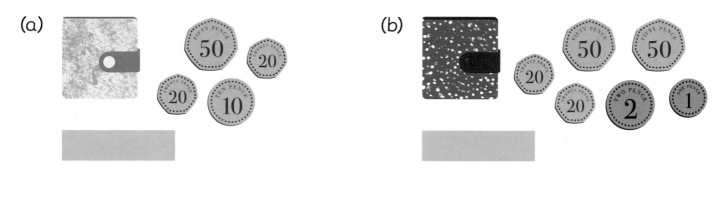

(b)

(c)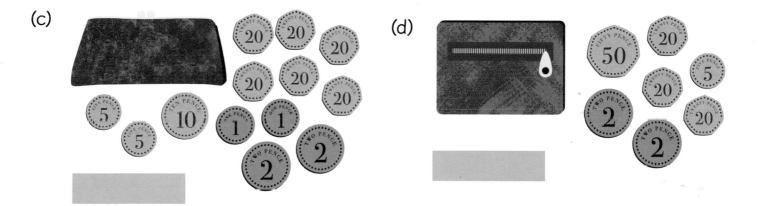

(d)

(e)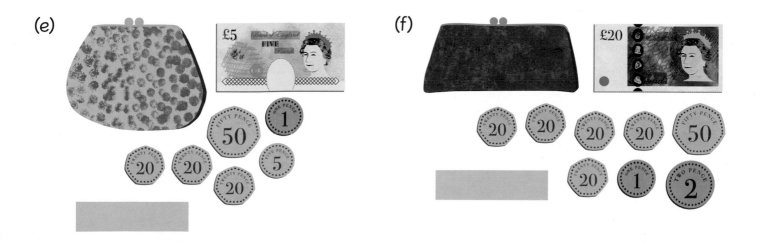

(f)

Complete Worksheet 2 – Page 3 – 4

Showing Amounts of Money

In Focus

This smoothie costs £2 and 80p.
In what ways can Sam pay for it?

Let's Learn

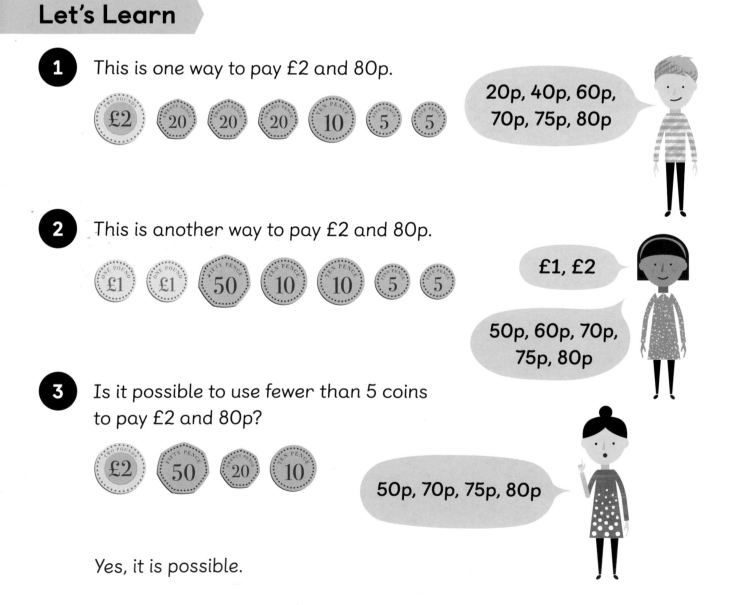

1 This is one way to pay £2 and 80p.

£2 20 20 20 10 5 5

20p, 40p, 60p,
70p, 75p, 80p

2 This is another way to pay £2 and 80p.

£1 £1 50 10 10 5 5

£1, £2

50p, 60p, 70p,
75p, 80p

3 Is it possible to use fewer than 5 coins
to pay £2 and 80p?

£2 50 20 10

50p, 70p, 75p, 80p

Yes, it is possible.

Work in pairs.

What you need:

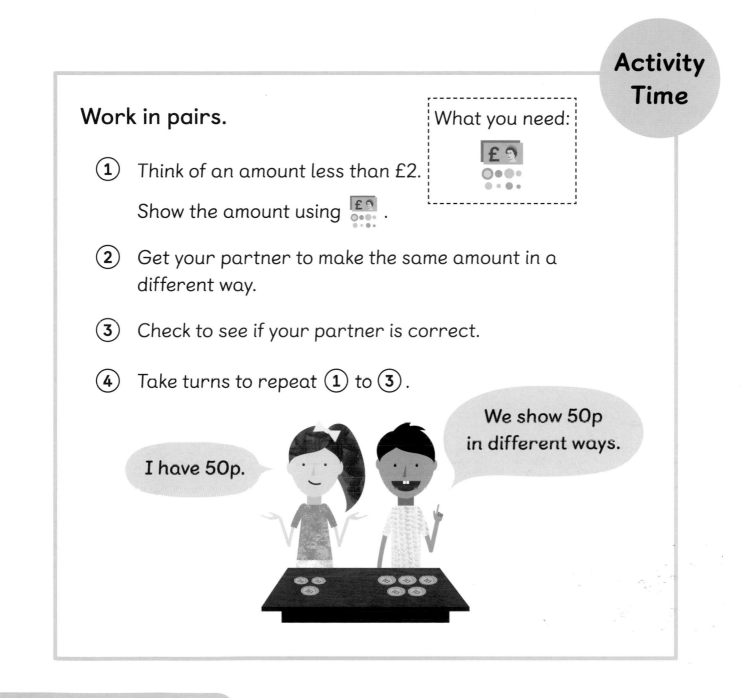

① Think of an amount less than £2.
Show the amount using 💷.

② Get your partner to make the same amount in a different way.

③ Check to see if your partner is correct.

④ Take turns to repeat ① to ③.

I have 50p.

We show 50p in different ways.

Guided Practice

1 Show two different ways to pay exactly £1.
Select from these coins.

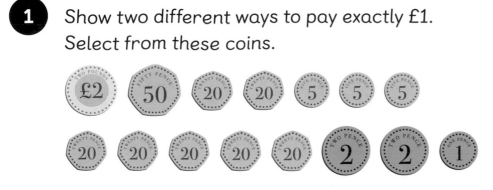

2

£ 1 and 10p

100 ml

(a) Use 2 coins to pay for the carton of orange juice.

(b) Use 3 coins to pay for the carton of orange juice.

3 Use as few coins as possible to pay for the can of juice.

79p

330ml

Complete Worksheet 3 – Page 5 - 6

Adding Money

In Focus

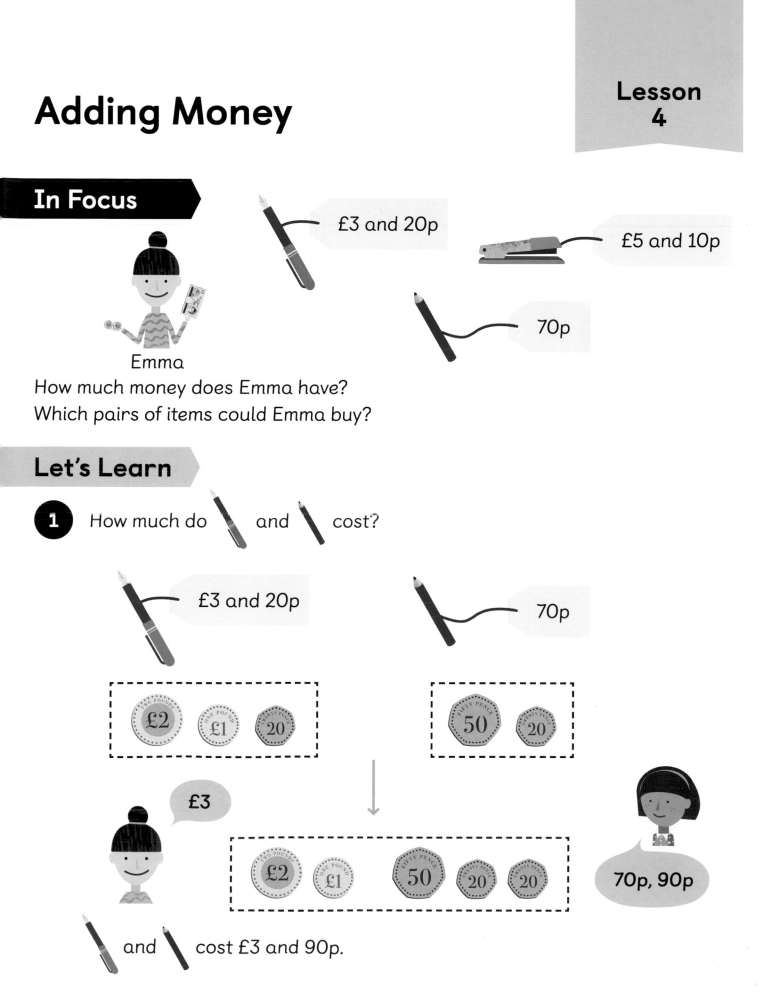

£3 and 20p

£5 and 10p

70p

Emma

How much money does Emma have?
Which pairs of items could Emma buy?

Let's Learn

1 How much do and cost?

£3 and 20p

70p

£2 £1 20

50 20

£3

£2 £1 50 20 20

70p, 90p

and cost £3 and 90p.

These cost £5 and 80p.

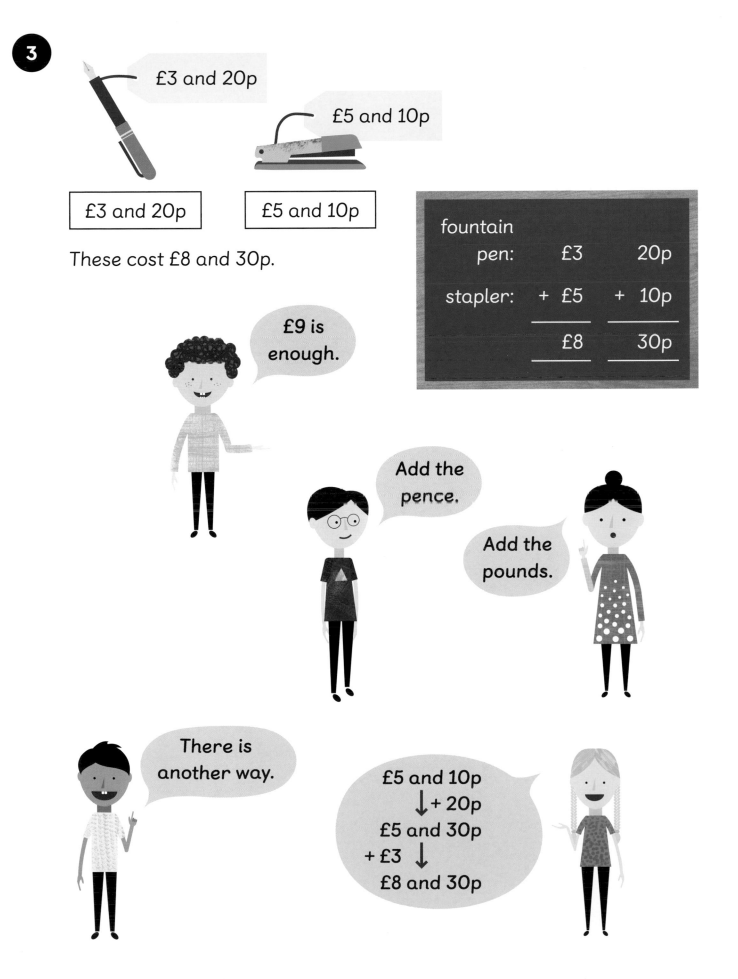

Guided Practice

Find the total price.

(a)

£1 and 30p

65p

300ml

(b)

£7 and 90p

10 Colours

Notes

£2

(c)

£10 and 25p

£7 and 10p

(d)

£17 and 50p

£18 and 30p

Complete Worksheet 4 – Page 7 - 8

Adding Money

In Focus

In what different ways can you find the total price?

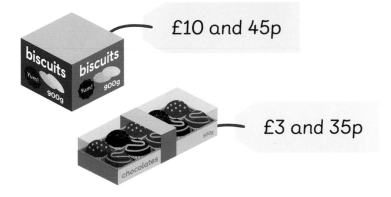

£10 and 45p

£3 and 35p

Let's Learn

 1 Add £10 and 45p and £3 and 35p.

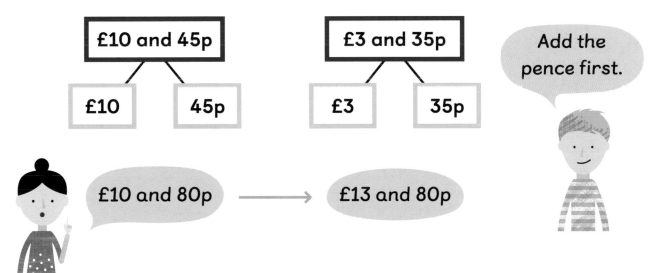

| £10 and 45p |
| £10 | 45p |

| £3 and 35p |
| £3 | 35p |

Add the pence first.

£10 and 80p ⟶ £13 and 80p

The total price is £13 and 80p.

2 Find the sum of £10 and 45p and £3 and 35p.

Add the £: £10 + £3 = £13
Add the p: 45p + 35p = 80p

The sum is £13 and 80p.

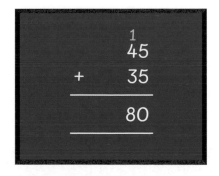

$$\begin{array}{r} \ \ ^{1}45 \\ +\ \ \ 35 \\ \hline 80 \\ \hline \end{array}$$

1 Find the total price.

(a)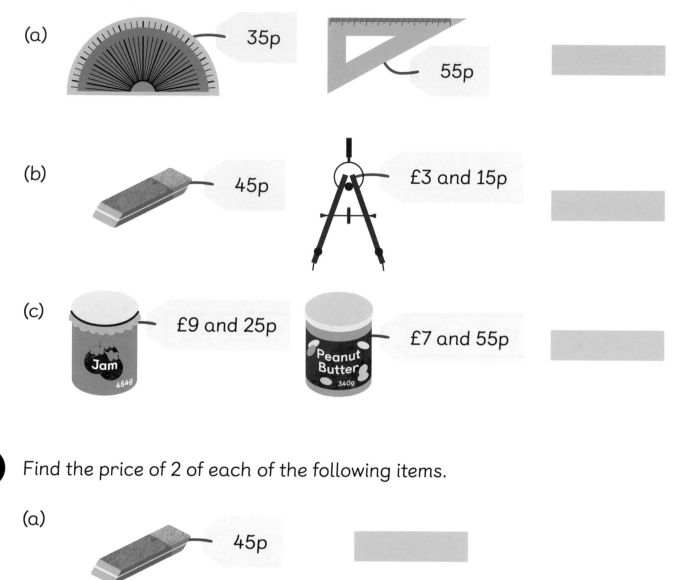

35p

55p

(b)

45p

£3 and 15p

(c)

£9 and 25p

£7 and 55p

Jam
454g

Peanut Butter
340g

2 Find the price of 2 of each of the following items.

(a)

45p

(b)

£3 and 15p

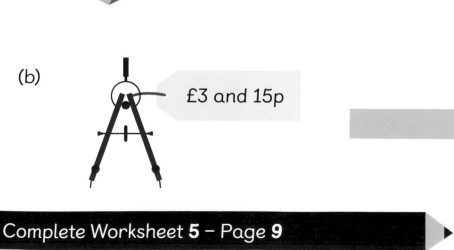

Complete Worksheet **5** – Page **9**

Adding Money

In Focus

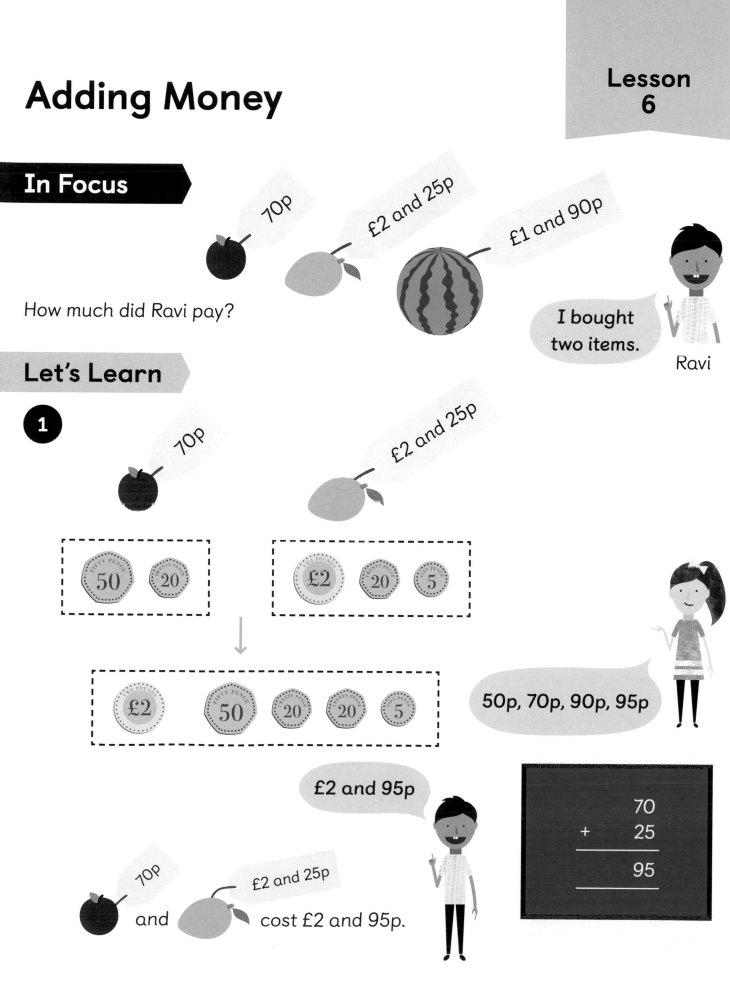

How much did Ravi pay?

70p

£2 and 25p

£1 and 90p

I bought two items.

Ravi

Let's Learn

1

70p

£2 and 25p

| 50 | 20 |

| £2 | 20 | 5 |

| £2 | 50 | 20 | 20 | 5 |

50p, 70p, 90p, 95p

£2 and 95p

70p and £2 and 25p cost £2 and 95p.

$$\begin{array}{r} 70 \\ +25 \\ \hline 95 \end{array}$$

2

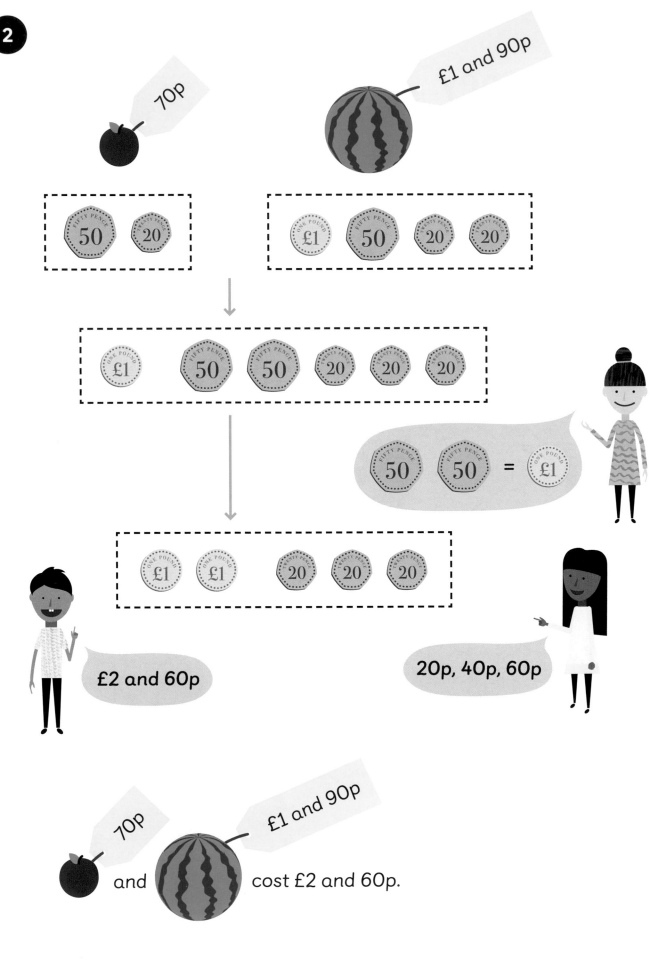

70p

£1 and 90p

£2 and 60p

20p, 40p, 60p

and cost £2 and 60p.

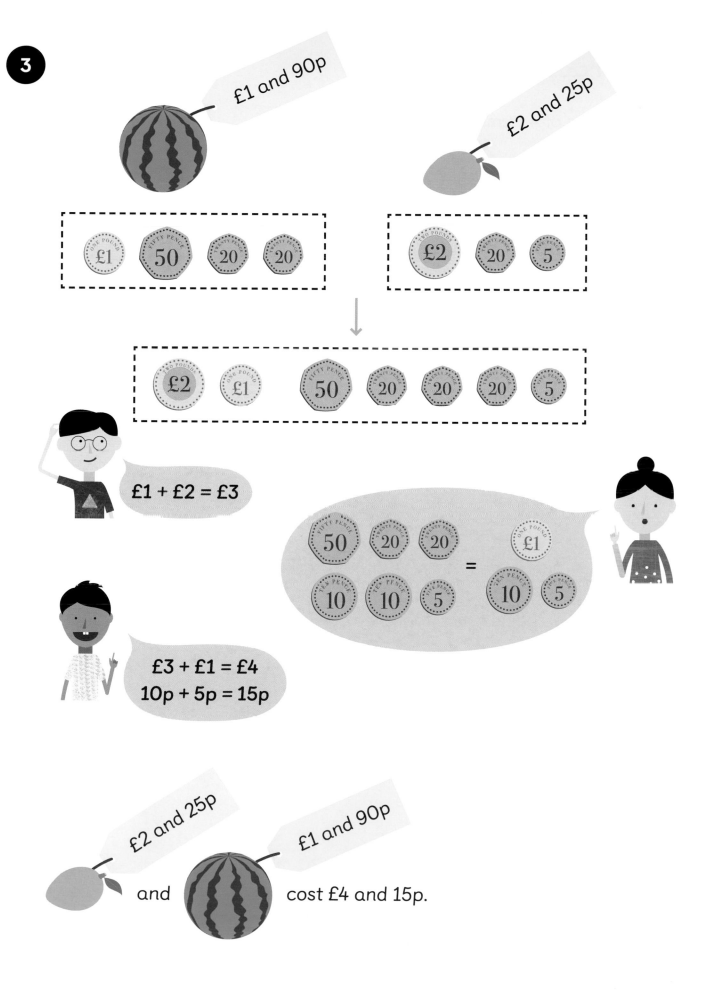

Guided Practice

1 The prices of 4 items are shown.

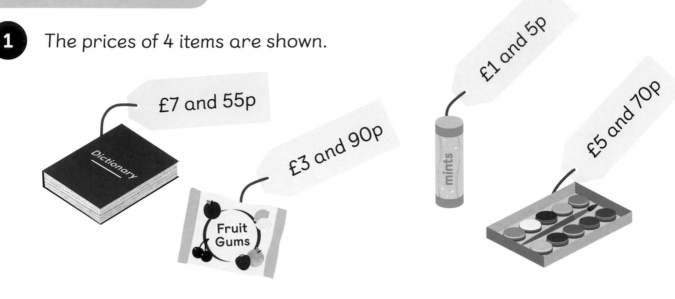

£7 and 55p

£3 and 90p

£1 and 5p

£5 and 70p

Dictionary

Fruit Gums

mints

(a) Pick two items which together cost less than £10.
Use two different methods to find the total.

(b) Find the total price of  and .

(c) Pick two items which together cost more than £10 but less than £12.

2 Add £34 and 60p and £17 and 60p.

Complete Worksheet **6** – Page **10 – 13** ▶

Adding Money

In Focus

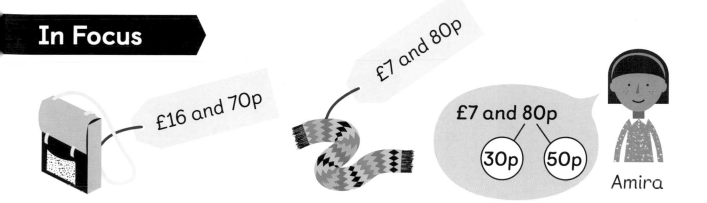

How does Amira find the total of the two amounts?

Let's Learn

1 Add £16 and 70p and £7 and 80p.

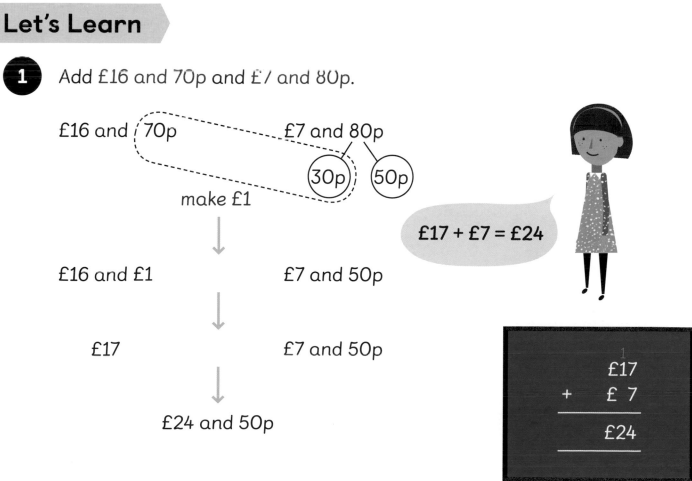

£16 and (70p) £7 and 80p

(30p) (50p)

make £1

£17 + £7 = £24

£16 and £1   £7 and 50p

£17   £7 and 50p

£24 and 50p

```
        1
      £17
  +   £ 7
  _____
      £24
```

The two items cost £24 and 50p.

2 Find the sum of £16 and 70p and £7 and 80p.

Add the £.

£16 + £7 = ▢

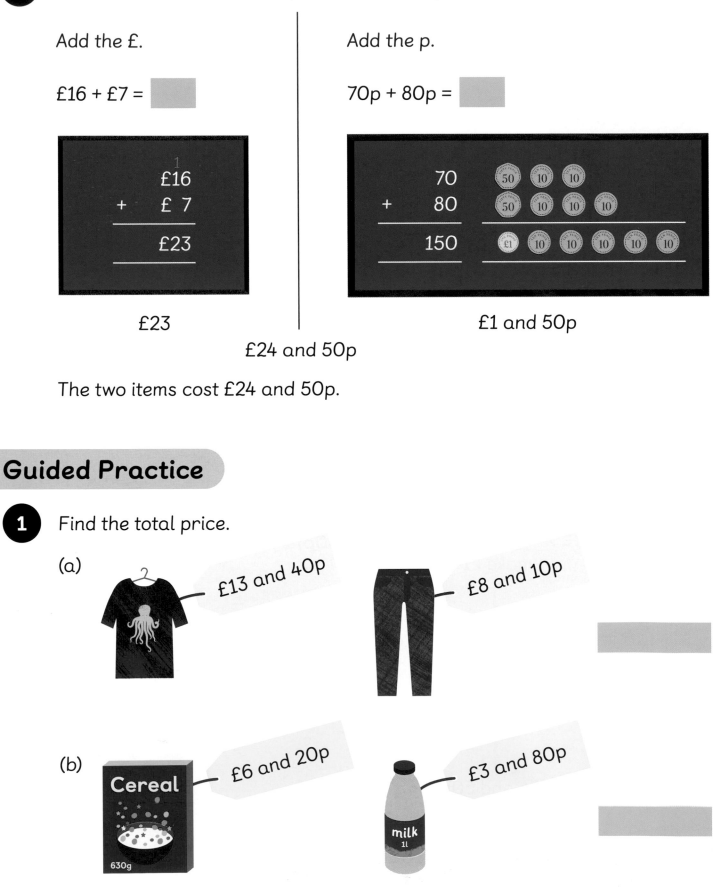

Add the p.

70p + 80p = ▢

£23

£1 and 50p

£24 and 50p

The two items cost £24 and 50p.

Guided Practice

1 Find the total price.

(a) £13 and 40p   £8 and 10p   ▢

(b) Cereal £6 and 20p   £3 and 80p   ▢

2 Find the total price.

(a)

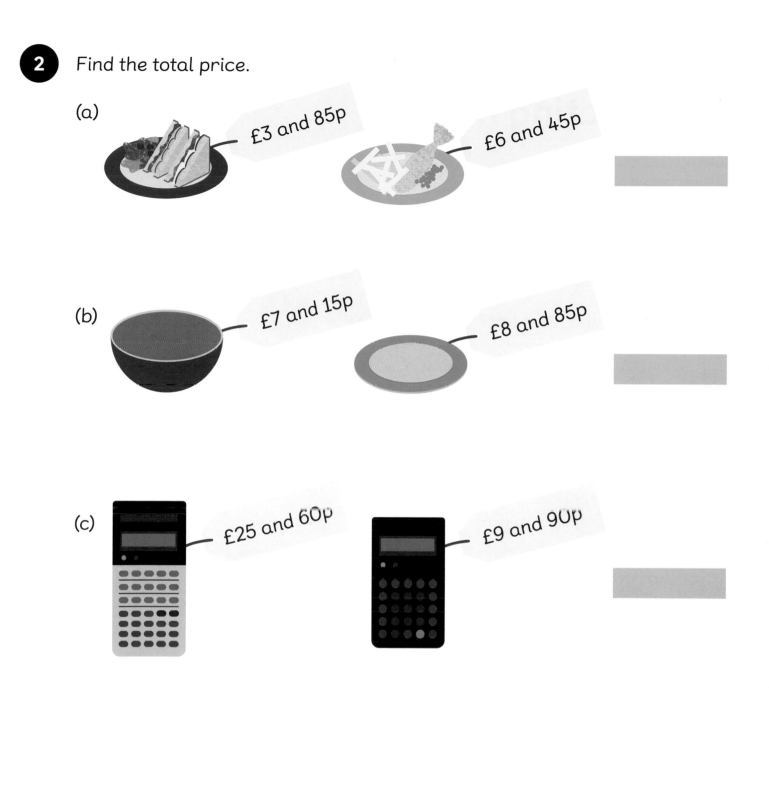

£3 and 85p

£6 and 45p

(b)

£7 and 15p

£8 and 85p

(c)

£25 and 60p

£9 and 90p

Complete Worksheet 7 – Page **14 - 15**

Subtracting Money

In Focus

Emma had £8 and 50p.
She bought a book.

How much did she have left?

£5 and 10p

Let's Learn

 1 Emma spent £5 and 10p.
How much did she have left?

£5 and 10p

Emma had £3 and 40p left.

2 Subtract 60p from £4 and 80p.

£4 and 80p

↓ subtract 60p

£4 and 20p

80p − 60p = 20p

60p subtracted from £4 and 80p is £4 and 20p.

3 Find the difference between £4 and 80p and £3 and 60p.

Subtract the £: £4 – £3 = £1

Subtract the p: 80p – 60p = 20p

The difference is £1 and 20p.

> £4 and 80p
> ↓ – 60p
> £4 and 20p
> – £3 ↓
> £1 and 20p

Guided Practice

1  costs 30p less than  .

Find the price of  .

£9 and 70p

2 How much cheaper is  than  ?

£5 and 30p

£9 and 70p

3 Ravi had £5 and 80p.

Then he bought  .

£2 and 30p

How much did Ravi have left?

Complete Worksheet 8 – Page 16 – 17

Subtracting Money

Which costs more?
How much more does it cost?

£3 and 25p

£5 and 65p

Let's Learn

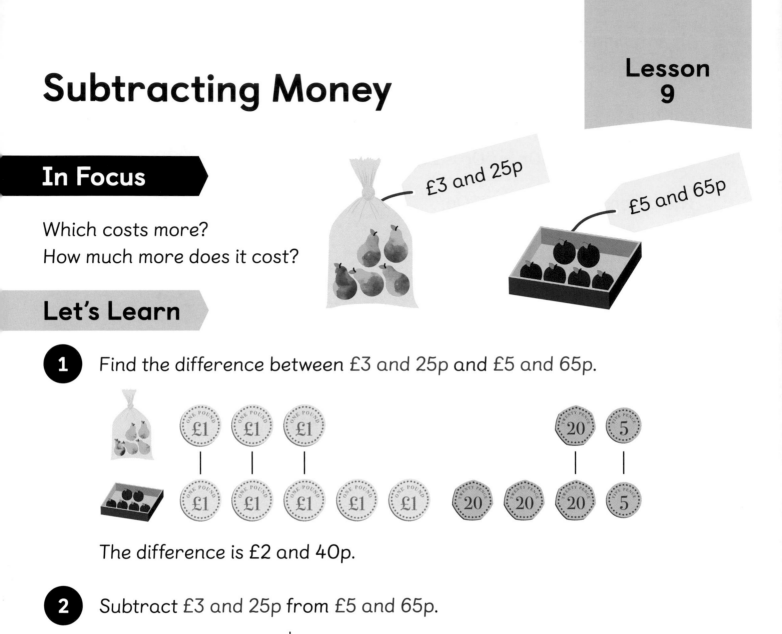

1 Find the difference between £3 and 25p and £5 and 65p.

The difference is £2 and 40p.

2 Subtract £3 and 25p from £5 and 65p.

Subtract the £. | Subtract the p.
£5 − £3 = £2 | 65p − 25p = 40p

```
    65
 -  25
 ─────
    40
 ─────
```

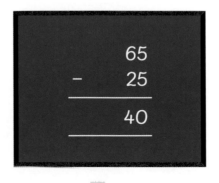 costs £2 and 40p more than .

Guided Practice

1 Subtract £1 and 25p from £5 and 85p.

2 Find the difference between £10 and 75p and £6 and 15p.

3 Which pair costs more?
How much more?

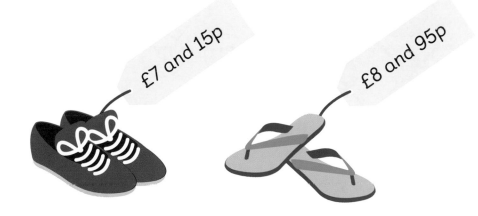

£7 and 15p

£8 and 95p

Lesson 10

Subtracting Money

In Focus

In a sale, 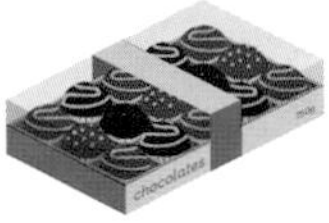 is 40p cheaper than usual.

How much does it cost during the sale?

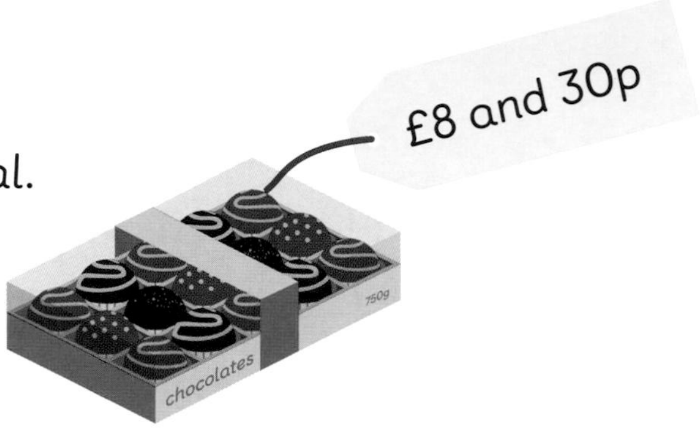

£8 and 30p
chocolates
750g

Let's Learn

1 What is 40p less than £8 and 30p?

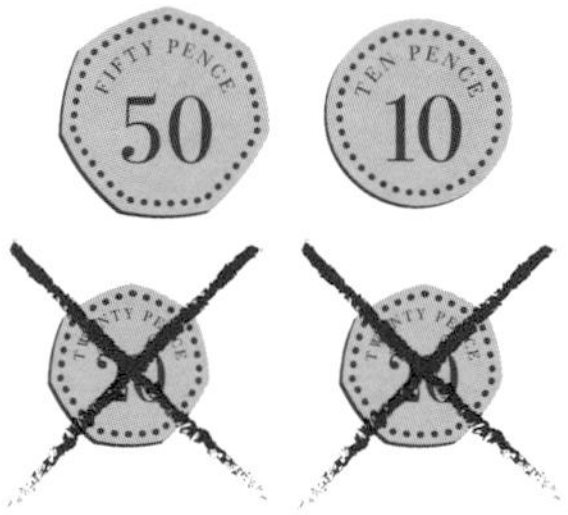

50
10

£8 and [30p]

(£1) (£7)

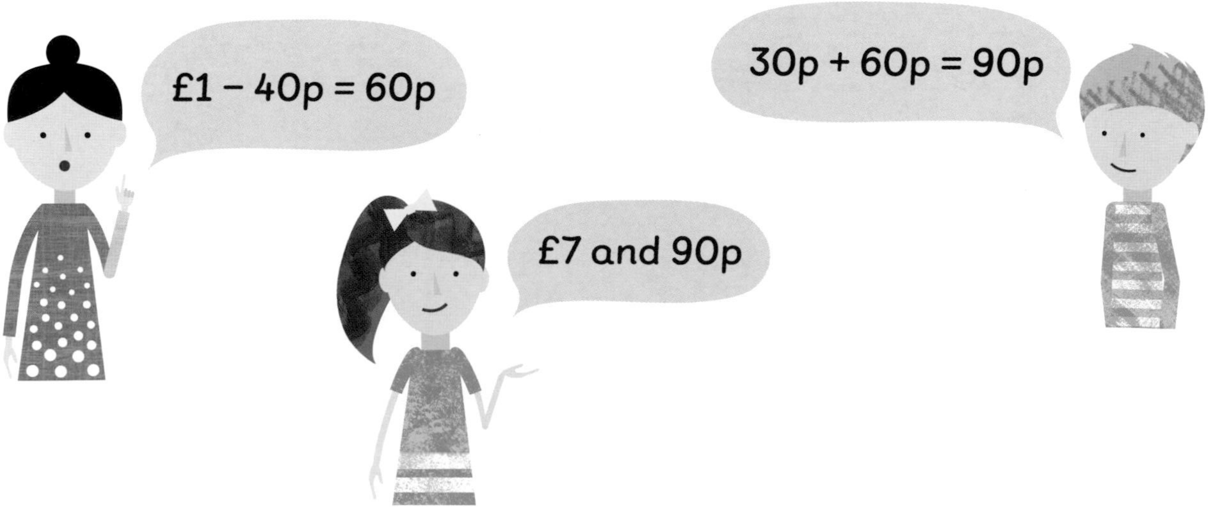

£1 – 40p = 60p
30p + 60p = 90p
£7 and 90p

40p less than £8 and 30p is £7 and 90p.

2 Subtract 40p from £8 and 30p.

£8 and 30p
   ↓ subtract 30p
£8
   ↓ subtract 10p
£7 and 90p

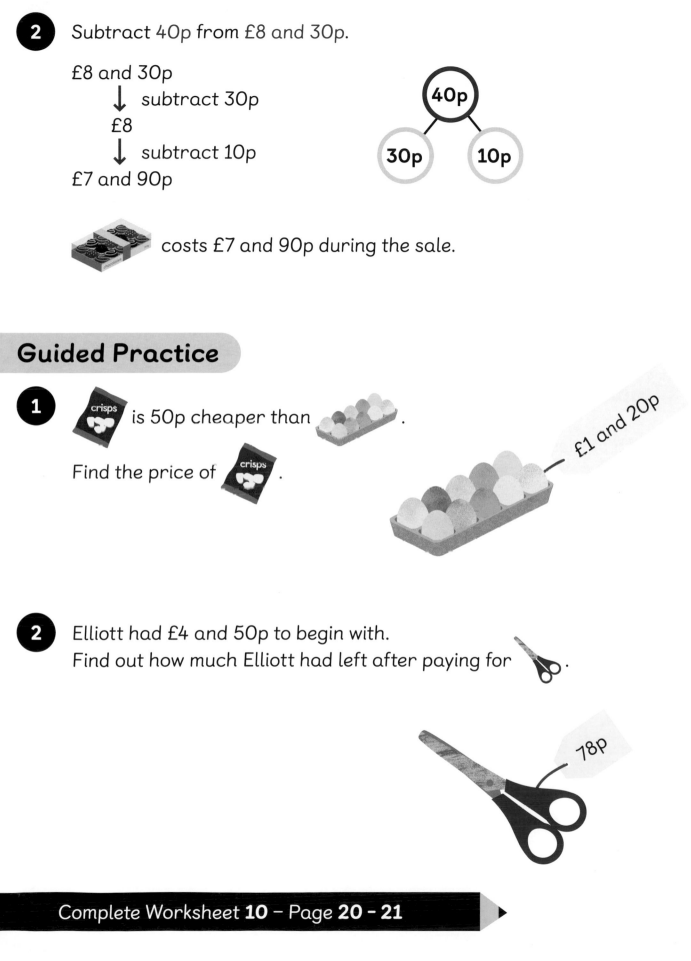

40p

30p   10p

 costs £7 and 90p during the sale.

Guided Practice

1 is 50p cheaper than .

Find the price of .

£1 and 20p

2 Elliott had £4 and 50p to begin with.
Find out how much Elliott had left after paying for .

78p

Complete Worksheet **10** – Page **20 - 21**

Subtracting Money

In Focus

£6 and 50p

£3 and 90p

£10 and 80p

Which item costs the most?

Let's Learn

1 Which of these two items costs more? How much more?

£10 and 80p

£6 and 50p

£10 − £6 = £4

80p − 50p = 30p

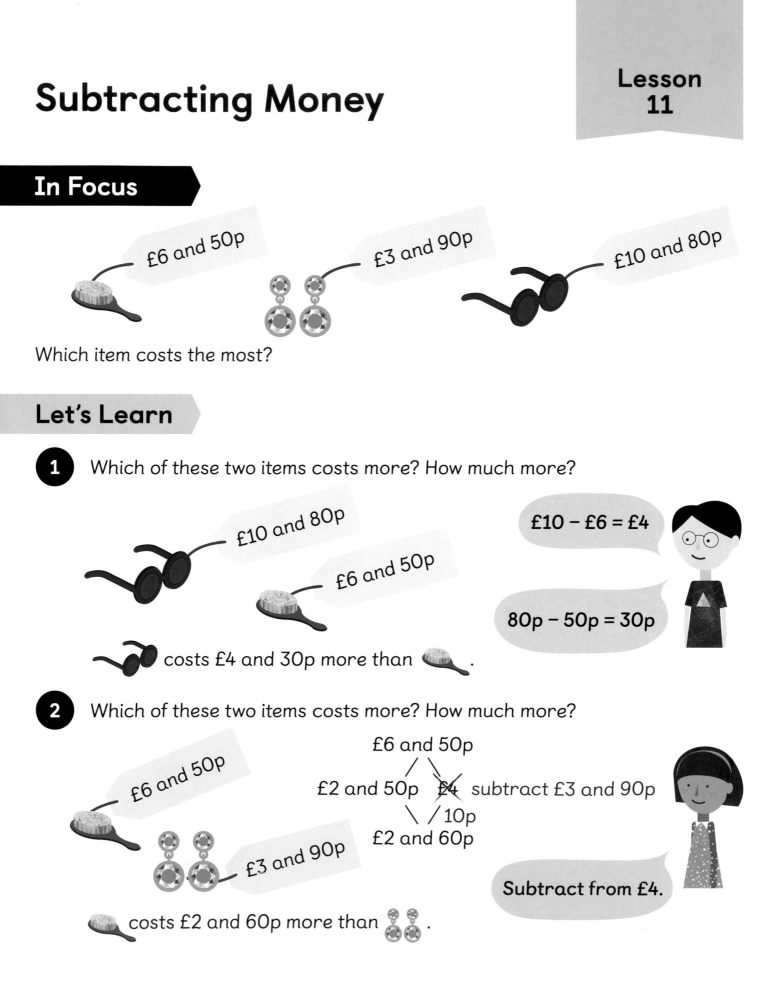 costs £4 and 30p more than 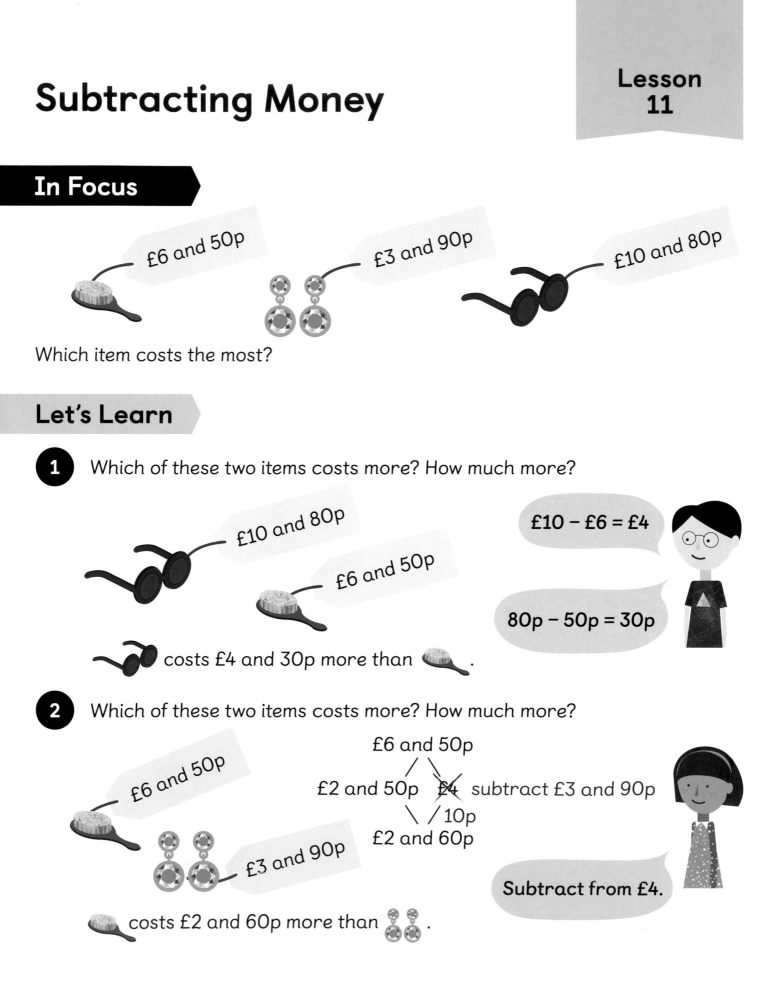.

2 Which of these two items costs more? How much more?

£6 and 50p

£6 and 50p
/   \
£2 and 50p   £4   subtract £3 and 90p
\   /10p
£2 and 60p

£3 and 90p

Subtract from £4.

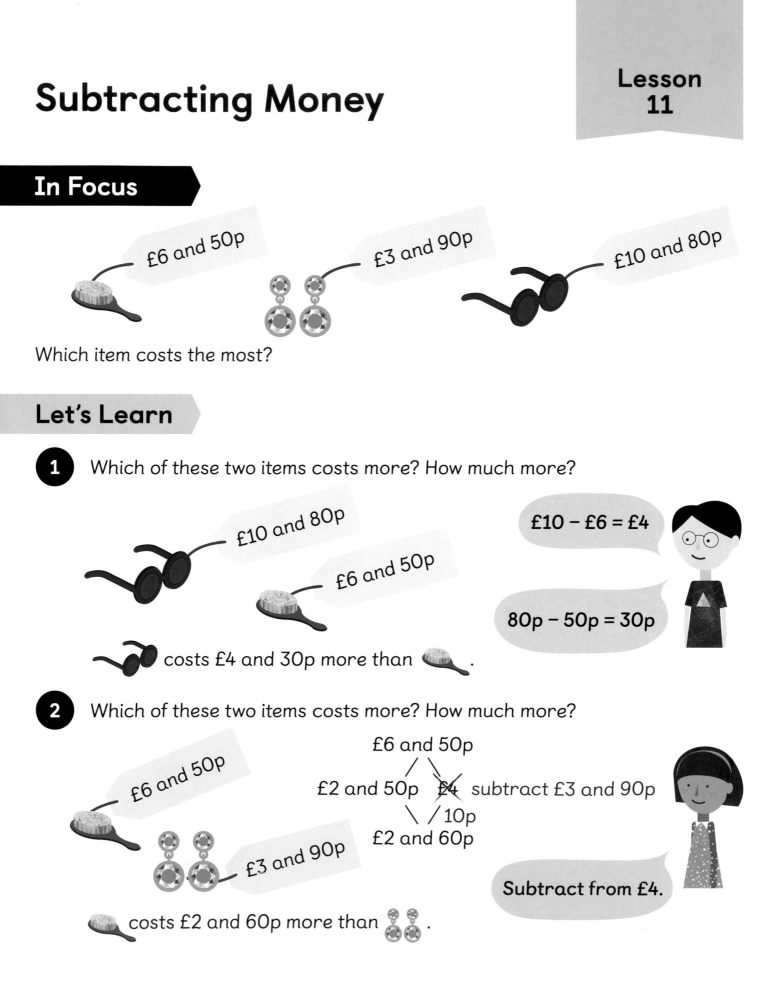 costs £2 and 60p more than 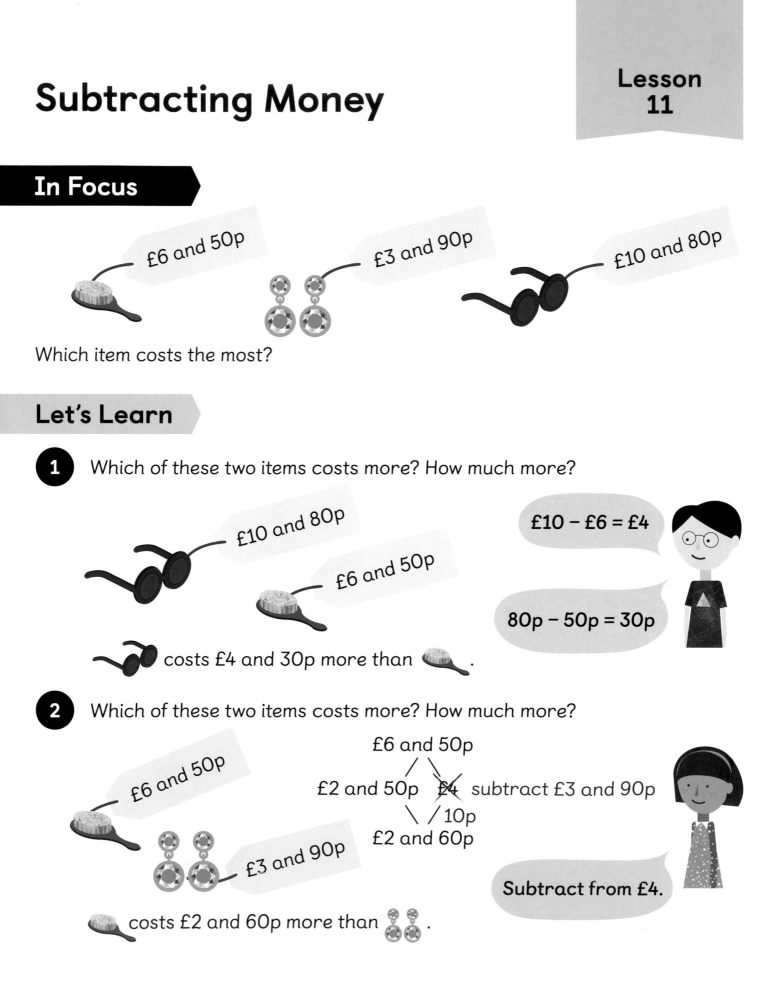.

3 Find the difference between £10 and 80p
and £3 and 90p.

£10 and 80p

£6 and 80p   £4   subtract £3 and 90p
                    10p
£6 and 90p

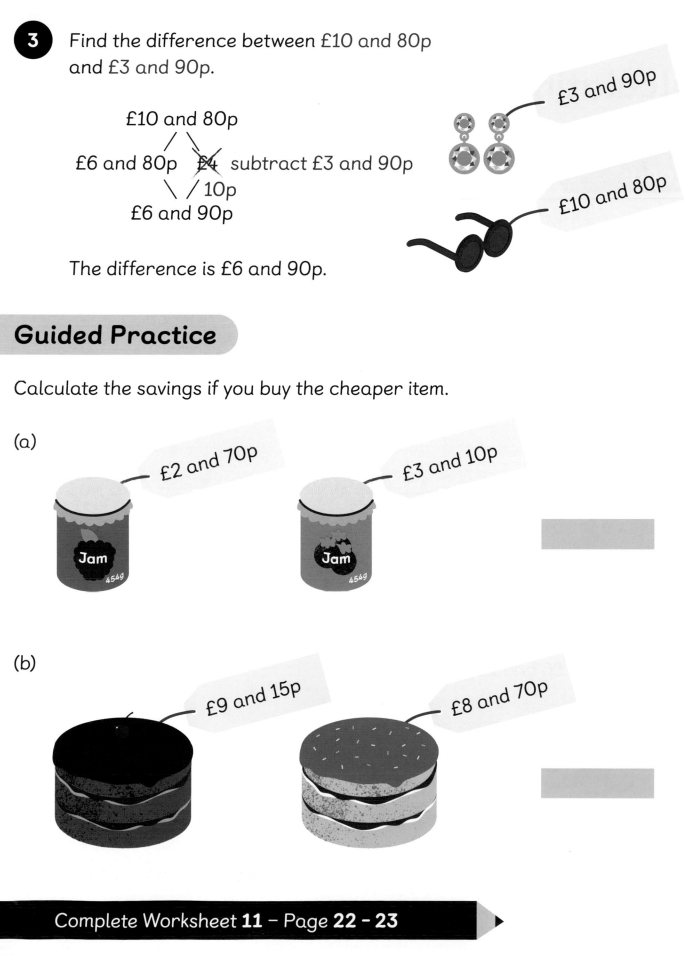

£3 and 90p

£10 and 80p

The difference is £6 and 90p.

Guided Practice

Calculate the savings if you buy the cheaper item.

(a)

£2 and 70p

£3 and 10p

Jam
454g

Jam
454g

(b)

£9 and 15p

£8 and 70p

Complete Worksheet **11** – Page **22 - 23**

Calculating Change

In Focus

£3 and 80p

£5 and 30p

£6 and 20p

Emma

Ravi

Amira

How much change does each of them get?

Let's Learn

1 How much change does Emma get?

£3 and 80p
↓ 20p
£4
↓ £6
£10

Emma gets £6 and 20p change.

2 How much change does Ravi get?

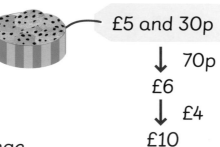

£5 and 30p
↓ 70p
£6
↓ £4
£10

Ravi gets £4 and 70p change.

3 How much change does Amira get?

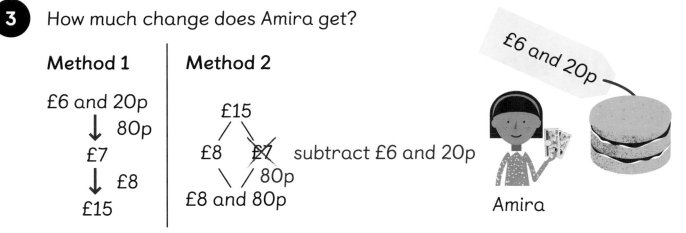

£6 and 20p

Amira

Method 1	Method 2
£6 and 20p	£15
↓ 80p	£8 ~~£7~~ subtract £6 and 20p
£7	80p
↓ £8	£8 and 80p
£15	

Amira gets £8 and 80p change.

Guided Practice

Calculate the change.

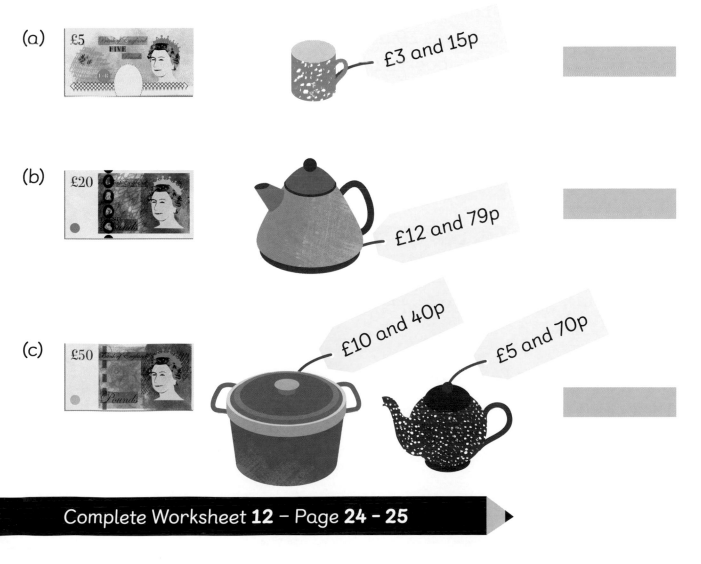

(a) £5   £3 and 15p

(b) £20   £12 and 79p

(c) £50   £10 and 40p   £5 and 70p

Complete Worksheet **12** – Page **24 – 25**

Solving Word Problems

In Focus

The price of a book is reduced.
How much cheaper is the sale price?

sale! now £5.00 ~~£9.50~~

Let's Learn

1 A book is reduced to £5.
Its price before the sale was £9 and 50p.
How much cheaper is the book in the sale?

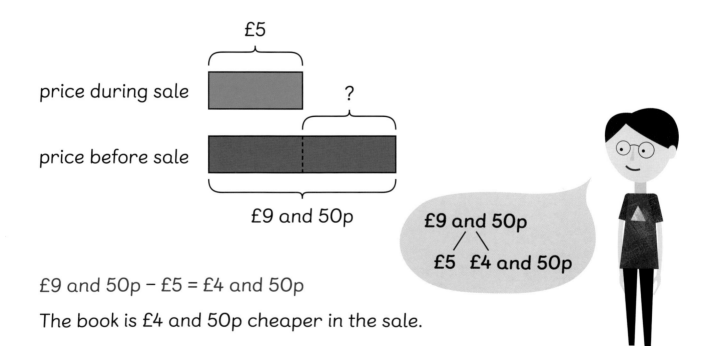

£5

price during sale

?

price before sale

£9 and 50p

£9 and 50p
/ \
£5 £4 and 50p

£9 and 50p – £5 = £4 and 50p

The book is £4 and 50p cheaper in the sale.

2 Ruby saved £24 and 50p in May.
She saved £6 and 80p more in June than she did in May.
How much money did she save in June?

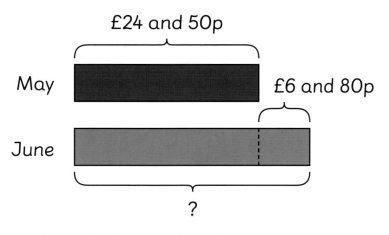

Add the £: £24 + £6 = £30
Add the p: 50p + 80p = £1 and 30p

£30 + £1 and 30p = £31 and 30p

Ruby saved £31 and 30p in June.

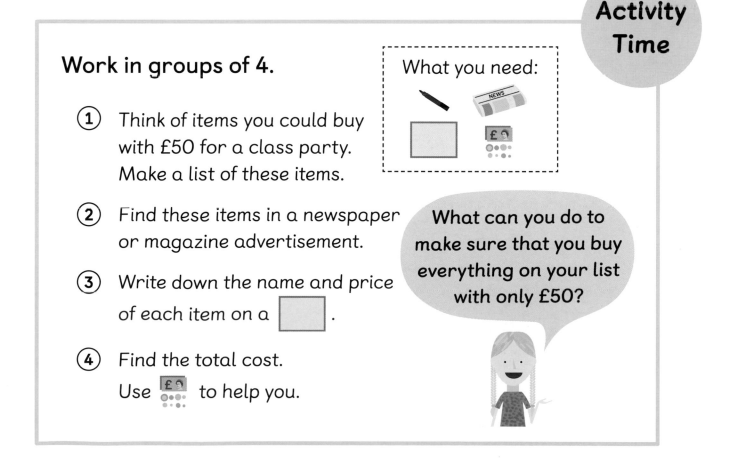

Guided Practice

Solve.

1 Sam wants to buy a train set which costs £25 and 60p.
He needs to save £6 and 80p more than he has now.
How much does he have now?

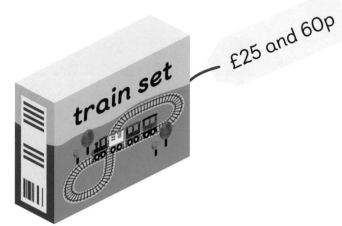

£25 and 60p

2 A box of chocolates costs £12 and 80p.
A box of crackers is £4 and 20p cheaper than the box of chocolates.

(a) How much does the box of crackers cost?

(b) What is the total cost of the box of chocolates and
the box of crackers?

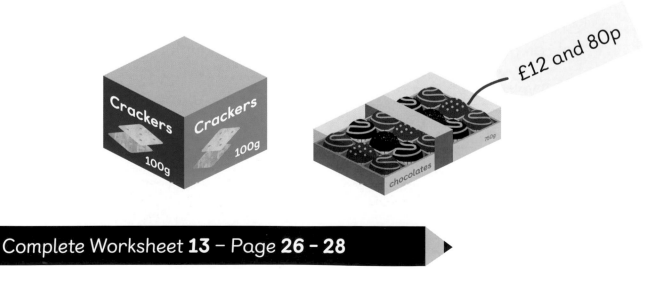

£12 and 80p

Complete Worksheet **13** – Page **26 – 28**

Solving Word Problems

In Focus

Elliott bought both shirts with a fifty-pound note. How much change did he get?

£20 and 50p

£27 and 90p

Let's Learn

1 Add £20 and 50p and £27 and 90p.

£50

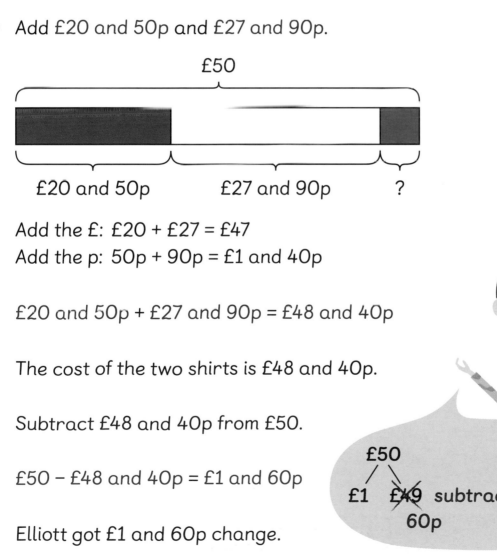

£20 and 50p   £27 and 90p   ?

Add the £: £20 + £27 = £47
Add the p: 50p + 90p = £1 and 40p

£20 and 50p + £27 and 90p = £48 and 40p

The cost of the two shirts is £48 and 40p.

Subtract £48 and 40p from £50.

£50 – £48 and 40p = £1 and 60p

Elliott got £1 and 60p change.

£50
/   \
£1   ~~£49~~   subtract £48 and 40p
        60p

2 Lulu bought a box of chocolates for £4 and 5p and a box of cookies for £5 and 30p.
She had £15 left.

(a) How much did she spend altogether?

(b) How much did she have to begin with?

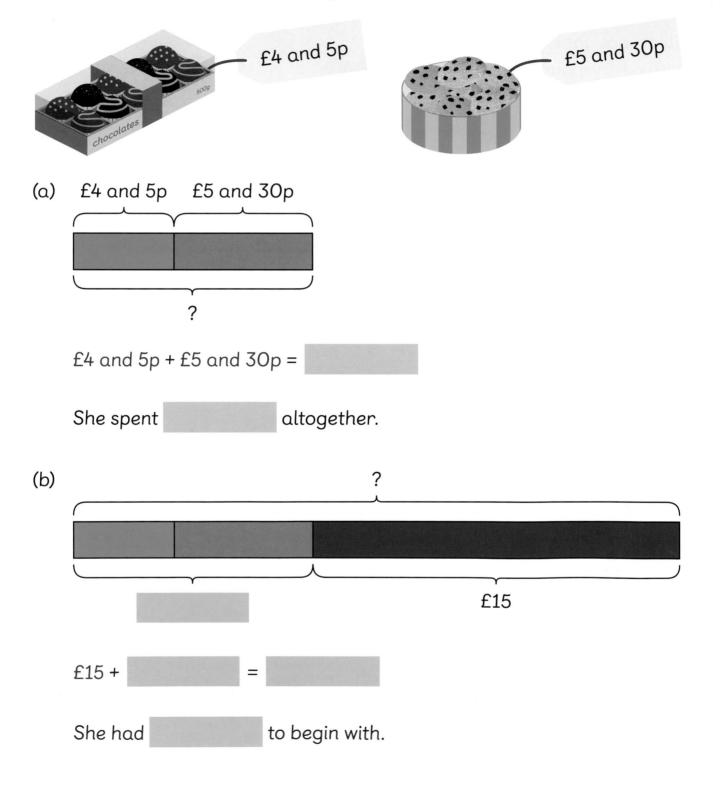

(a) £4 and 5p   £5 and 30p

?

£4 and 5p + £5 and 30p =

She spent _____ altogether.

(b) ?

£15

£15 + _____ = _____

She had _____ to begin with.

Guided Practice

1 Hannah saved a total of £75 in June, July and August.
She saved £18 and 25p in June and £28 and 65p in August.
How much did she save in July?

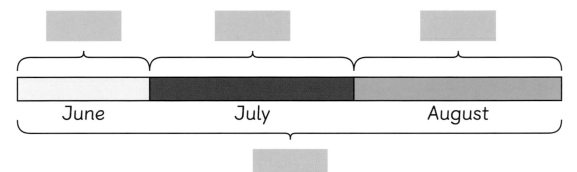

2 Sam bought a pair of shoes and a shirt.
The pair of shoes cost £46 and 90p and the shirt cost £15 and 60p.
After buying the items, he had £29 and 70p left.
How much did he have to begin with?

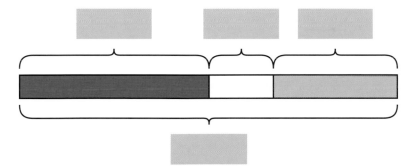

Complete Worksheet **14** – Page **29 - 30** ▶

Mind Workout ▶

Emma, Charles and Amira spent less than £30 altogether.
Amira spent the most and Charles spent the least.
Charles says that he spent £10.
Do you believe him? Why or why not?

Draw a model to help you.

Maths Journal

Go to the local store.
Look for things that you can buy for lunch.
The total price must be less than £5.
Draw what you plan to buy and write down its price.

Ravi's Journal

£2.50   80p   £1.00

I know how to...

☐ name the amount of money in pounds and pence.

☐ use different ways to show the same amount of money.

☐ add money in pounds and pence.

☐ subtract money in pounds and pence.

☐ calculate change in pounds and pence.

☐ solve word problems on money.

Self Check

What is the time now?

Chapter 9
Time

Telling the Time

In Focus

Sam asked Ravi where he was at 9:30 and
Ravi said he was in school.
Later, he said he was at home at 9:30.

Could Ravi have been telling the truth?

Let's Learn

1

Ravi was in class at half past nine in the morning.
We write the time as **9:30 a.m.**

We use **a.m.** to tell the time from just after
12 midnight to just before 12 noon.

2

Ravi was at home at half past nine at night.
We write the time as **9:30 p.m.**

We use **p.m.** to tell the time from just after
12 noon to just before 12 midnight.

3

Sam brushes his teeth at 8:15 in the morning.
We write the time as **8:15 a.m.**

The hour hand is just after 8.

4

Emma finishes reading her book at 1:30 in the afternoon.

We write the time as 1:30 ⬜ .

Where is the hour hand?

5

The programme ends at 6:55 in the evening.
We write the time as 6:55 ⬜ .

The hour hand is almost at 7.

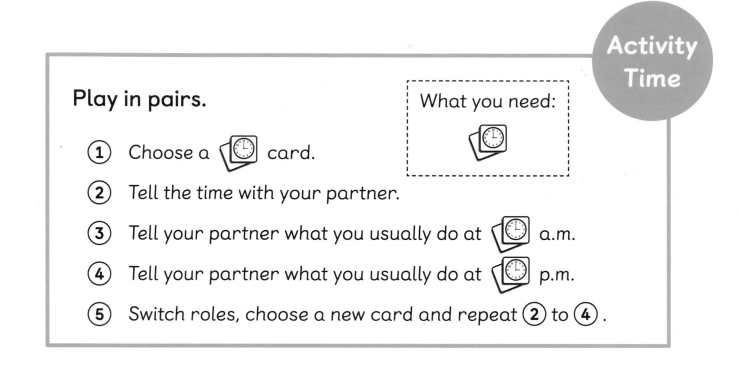

Activity Time

Play in pairs.

What you need:

① Choose a ⏰ card.

② Tell the time with your partner.

③ Tell your partner what you usually do at ⏰ a.m.

④ Tell your partner what you usually do at ⏰ p.m.

⑤ Switch roles, choose a new card and repeat ② to ④.

Guided Practice

Tell the time using **a.m.** or **p.m.**

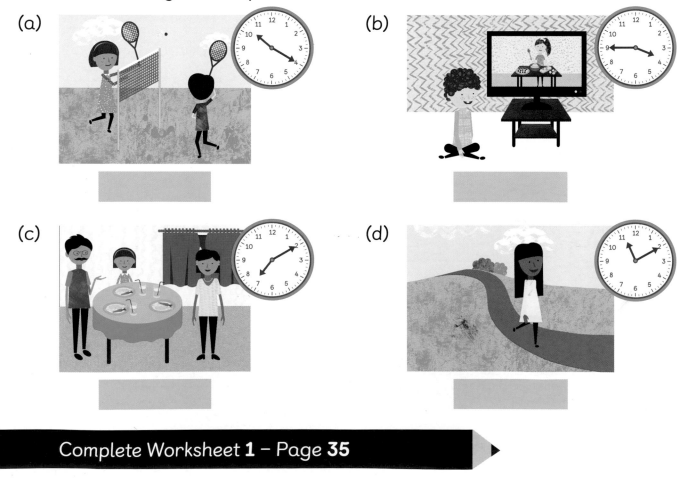

(a)

(b)

(c)

(d)

Complete Worksheet 1 – Page 35

Telling the Time

In Focus

What time does the clock show?

Using a clock, turn the minute hand to show one hour. What do you notice about the hour hand?

Let's Learn

1

0 1 minute

Each small marking on the clock face stands for 1 minute.
The minute hand shows 1 minute after the hour, so the time is 12:01.

2

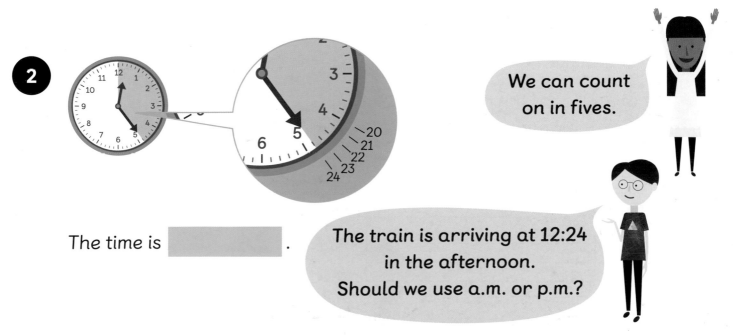

The time is ⬚ .

We can count on in fives.

The train is arriving at 12:24 in the afternoon. Should we use a.m. or p.m.?

3

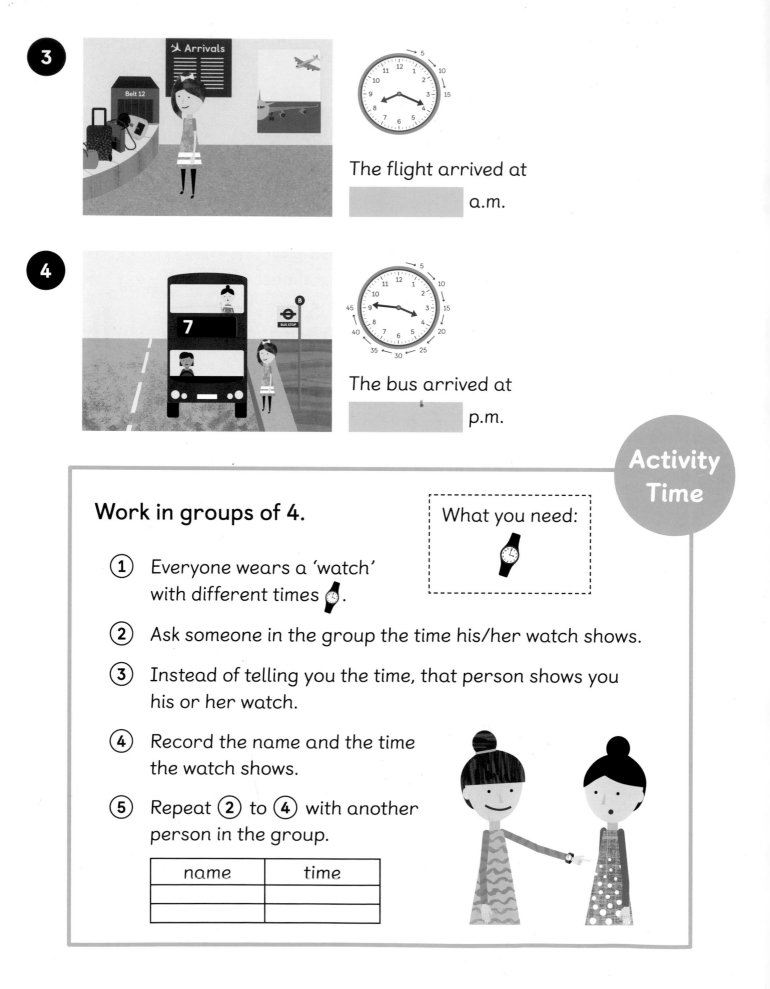

The flight arrived at

_____ a.m.

4

The bus arrived at

_____ p.m.

Work in groups of 4.

What you need:

① Everyone wears a 'watch' with different times.

② Ask someone in the group the time his/her watch shows.

③ Instead of telling you the time, that person shows you his or her watch.

④ Record the name and the time the watch shows.

⑤ Repeat ② to ④ with another person in the group.

name	time

Guided Practice

Write the time.

(a)

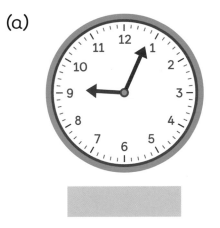

(b)

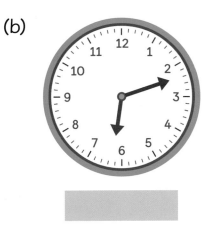

(c)

(d)

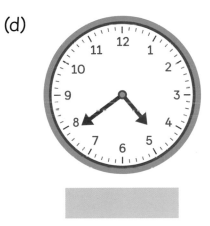

What do we need to do to tell time to the minute?

Complete Worksheet **2** – Page **36**

Telling the Time

Charles leaves school at 1:30 p.m.
Can you tell the time in other ways?

Let's Learn

1 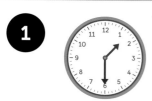 It is 1:30 p.m.
It is 1:30 in the afternoon.

2  It is half past one in the afternoon.

3  It is 30 minutes past one in the afternoon.

4 Charles arrives in school at  every school day.

8:25 a.m.

8:25 in the morning.

25 minutes past 8 in the morning.

Guided Practice

1 Tell the time in as many ways as you can.

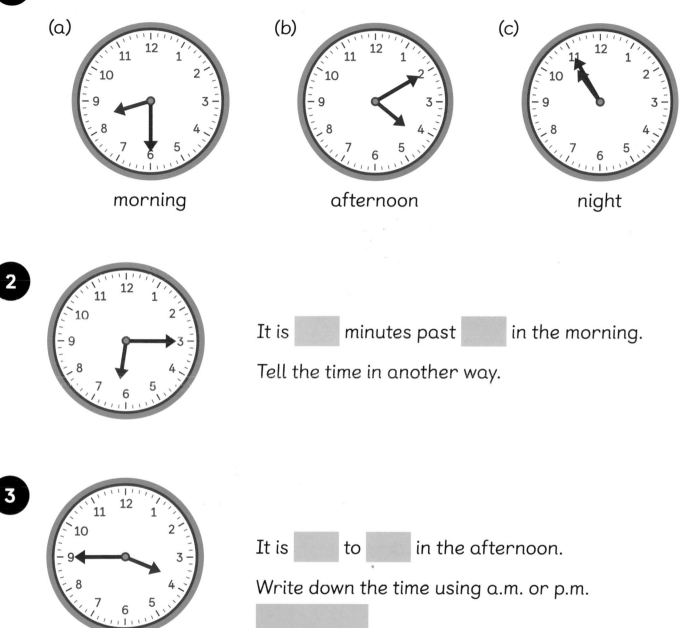

(a)

morning

(b)

afternoon

(c)

night

2

It is [ ] minutes past [ ] in the morning.

Tell the time in another way.

3

It is [ ] to [ ] in the afternoon.

Write down the time using a.m. or p.m.

Complete Worksheet **3** – Page **37**

Telling the Time

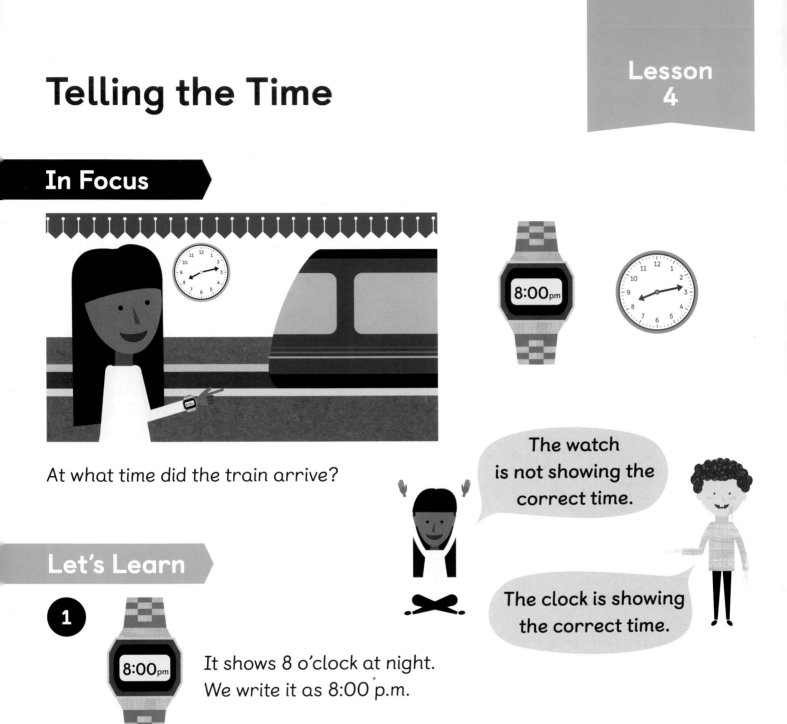

At what time did the train arrive?

The watch is not showing the correct time.

The clock is showing the correct time.

Let's Learn

1.
   It shows 8 o'clock at night.
   We write it as 8:00 p.m.

2. It shows 13 minutes past 8 at night.
   We write it as 8:13 p.m.

   The train arrived at 8:13 p.m.

Match the clocks that show the same time.

The time is ☐ minutes past ☐ .

Can you suggest something that might happen at each of these times?

Complete Worksheet 4 – Page 38

Telling the Time

In Focus

It is 8:45 a.m.

Charles

No, it is 9:45 a.m.

Emma

Who is correct? Why?

Let's Learn

1

It is past 8 o'clock.
It is before 9 o'clock.

It is 15 minutes before 9 o'clock.

It is 15 minutes to 9 in the morning.
It is 8:45 a.m.

2 What time does each clock show?

It is noon.

It leaves at 11 minutes to noon.

The plane leaves at 11:49 a.m. The plane leaves at 11 minutes to 12 in the morning.

3 What time does each clock show?

It is midnight.

It arrives at 9 minutes to midnight.

The flight arrives at 11:51 p.m. The flight arrives at 9 minutes to 12 at night.

Guided Practice

1 Tell the time.

It could be [   ] or [   ].

2 Tell the time. Write in a.m. or p.m.

(a)

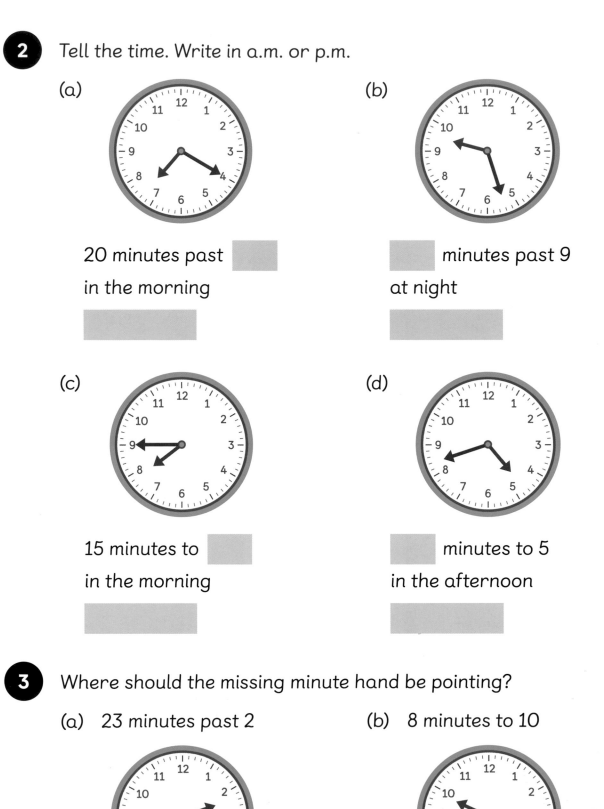

20 minutes past ☐
in the morning

☐

(b)

☐ minutes past 9
at night

☐

(c)

15 minutes to ☐
in the morning

☐

(d)

☐ minutes to 5
in the afternoon

☐

3 Where should the missing minute hand be pointing?

(a) 23 minutes past 2

(b) 8 minutes to 10

Complete Worksheet **5** – Page **39 – 40**

Telling the Time

In Focus

✈ Departures				
Time	Flight	Destination	Gate	Status
12:20	CA 9234	Sydney	06	Departed
13:00	EZ 67	Sydney	10	Gate closed
13:25	AL 089	Perth	09	Final call
13:40	BA 2909	Hong Kong	11	Boarding now
14:50	SA 100	Bangkok	08	
15:45	VA 4017	Melbourne	01	
17:20	EZ 081	Brisbane	15	

What time is it now?

What time is the flight to Bangkok?

Let's Learn

 1 What time it is now?

 11 o'clock in the morning   **11:00**

 12 o'clock at noon   **12:00**

13:00

 1 o'clock in the afternoon   **13:00**

 13 00 is 1 o'clock in the afternoon.

2 What time is the flight to Bangkok? `14:50`

2 o'clock
in the afternoon `14:00`

The flight is at 10 minutes to 3 in the afternoon.

14 50 is 2:50 p.m.
The flight to Bangkok is at 2:50 p.m.

3 What is the boarding time?

FlyAirlines	Boarding Pass	
Travel Date	From	
23 Jan	London Heathrow	
Flight Number	To	
LQ 321	Singapore	67FR S26B
	Passenger	Seat
	Sam Barrow	26a
Boarding Time Gate		
10 15 11	Gates close 15 minutes before departure	

`10:15`

It is at 10:15 a.m.

It is at 15 minutes past 10 in the morning.

4

SkyAirlines	Boarding Pass	
Travel Date	From	
23 Jan	London Heathrow	
Flight Number	To	
SA 456	New York	67FR S26B
	Passenger	Seat
	Hannah Rogers	12b
Boarding Time Gate		
16 55 04	Gates close 15 minutes before departure	

`16:55`

It is at 4:55 p.m.

It is at 5 minutes to 5 in the afternoon.

Guided Practice

	Tell the time shown.	Write it.	Say it.

1 `08:20` — 8:20 a.m. — 20 minutes past 8 in the morning

2 `10:40` — ☐ — ☐ minutes to ☐ in the ☐

3 `12:00` — ☐ — ☐ in the ☐

4 `13:30` — ☐ — ☐ minutes past ☐ in the ☐

5 `18:24` — ☐ — ☐ minutes past ☐ in the ☐

6 `23:59` — ☐ — ☐ minute to ☐

Complete Worksheet **6** – Page **41**

Telling the Time

In Focus

What time is it now?

IV is often shown as IIII on clocks.

Let's Learn

The time is 16 00.

1 What time is it now?

It is 4 o'clock in the afternoon.
We write it as 4:00 p.m.

2

It is half past 7 in the morning.
We write it as 7:30 a.m.

3

It is 15 minutes to 1 in the afternoon.
We write it as 12:45 p.m.

It is past noon.

4

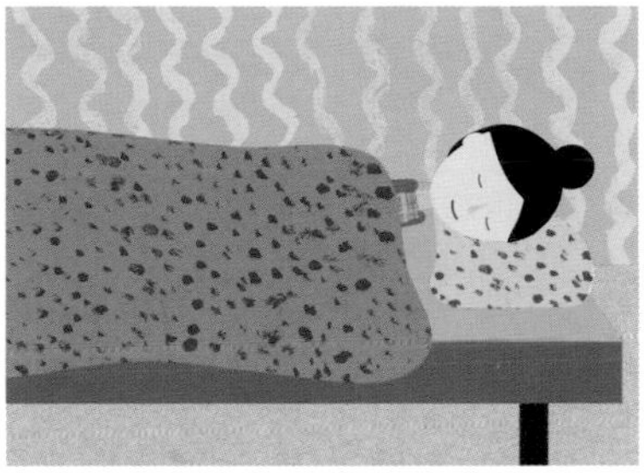

It is 5 minutes to midnight.
We write it to 11:55 p.m.

It is almost midnight.

Guided Practice

Tell the time.

(a)

(b)

(c)

(d)

Complete Worksheet 7 – Page 42

Measuring and Comparing Time in Seconds

In Focus

How many times can you clap in 15 seconds?

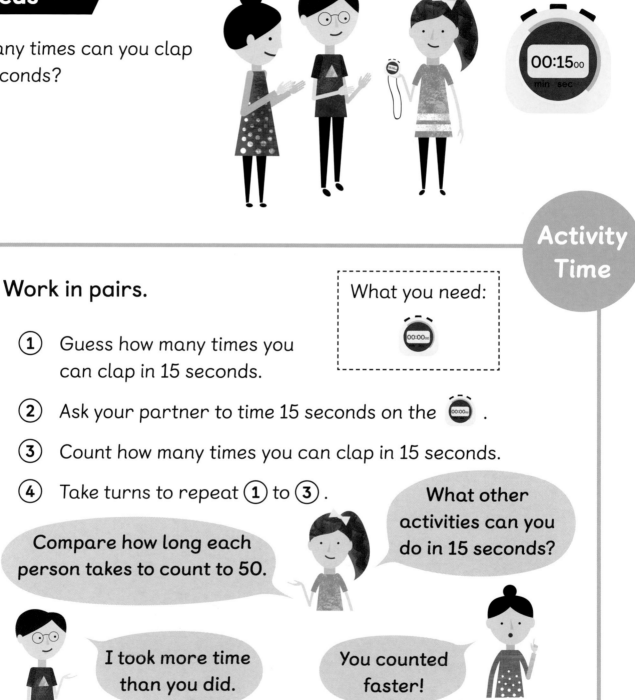

Activity Time

Work in pairs.

What you need:

① Guess how many times you can clap in 15 seconds.

② Ask your partner to time 15 seconds on the ⏱.

③ Count how many times you can clap in 15 seconds.

④ Take turns to repeat ① to ③.

Compare how long each person takes to count to 50.

What other activities can you do in 15 seconds?

I took more time than you did.

You counted faster!

1 Do a countdown from 10 to 0.
How many seconds is that?

10, 9, 8, 7, 6, 5, 4, 3, 2, 1, 0

The countdown takes about ▢ seconds.

We can measure short amounts of time using seconds.

2 Do a count for a game of Hide-and-Seek.
How long did that take?

1, 2, 3, 4, 5, 6, 7, 8, 9, 10. Ready or not, here I come!

The count took about ▢ seconds.

3 Watch a 100 m race on a video.
How long did the winner take to complete the race?

100m Finish

The winner took about ▢ seconds.

4 These British runners have run the 100-metre race in under 10 seconds.

We write 10 seconds like this.

10 s

I ran 100 m in less than 10 s twice.

James Dasaolu

I ran it in less than 10 s once.

Jason Gardner

I ran it in less than 10 s in 2014.

Chijudu Ujah

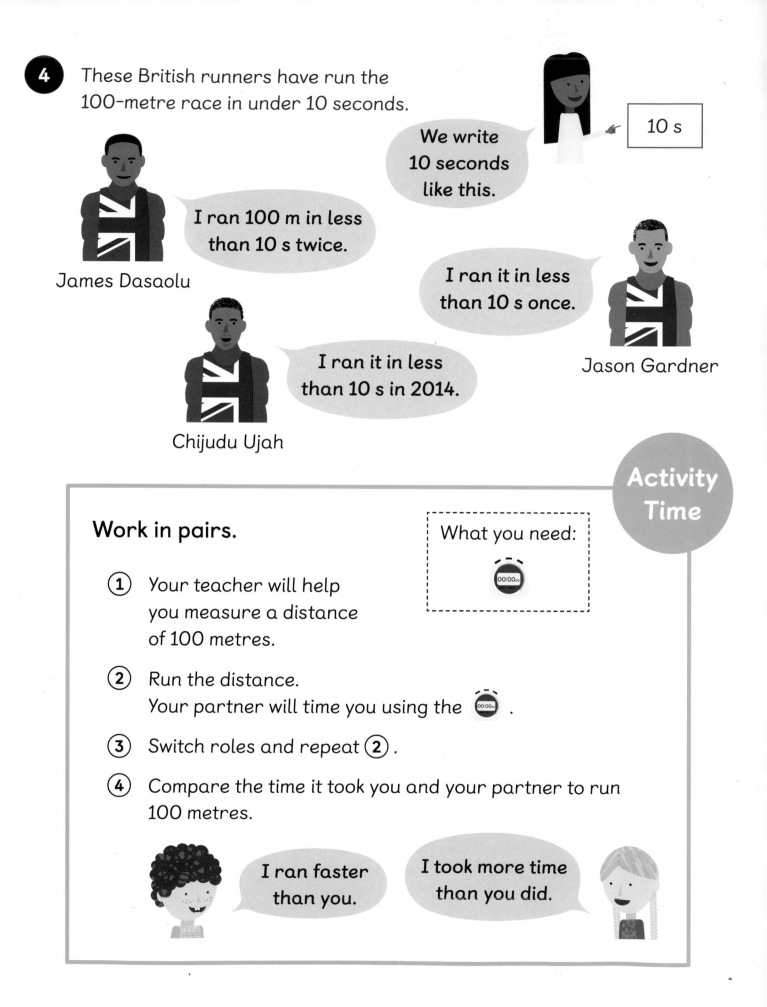

Activity Time

Work in pairs.

What you need:

① Your teacher will help you measure a distance of 100 metres.

② Run the distance. Your partner will time you using the 🕐.

③ Switch roles and repeat ②.

④ Compare the time it took you and your partner to run 100 metres.

I ran faster than you.

I took more time than you did.

Guided Practice

Fill in each blank with a whole number.

(a)

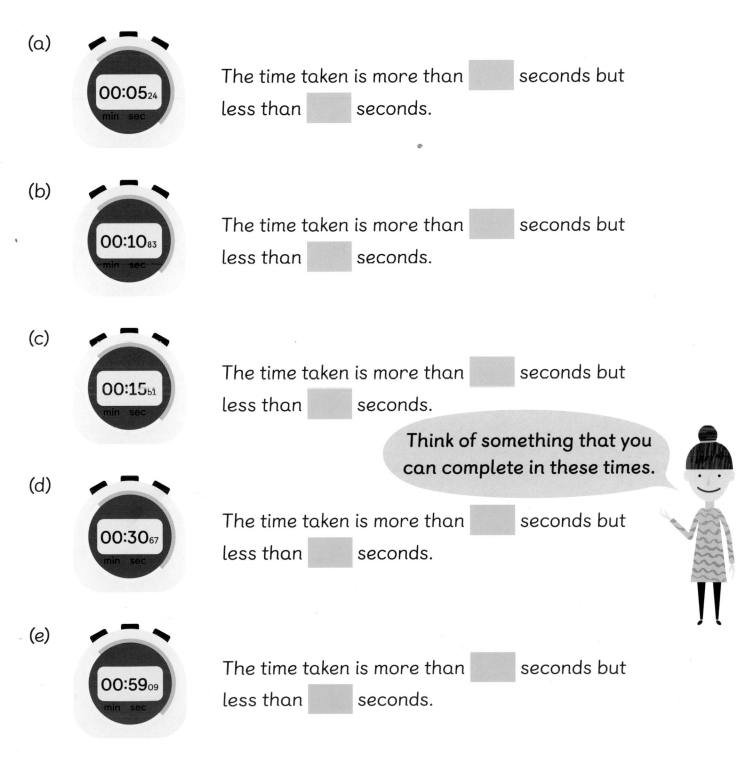

00:05₂₄
min   sec

The time taken is more than ☐ seconds but less than ☐ seconds.

(b)

00:10₈₃
min   sec

The time taken is more than ☐ seconds but less than ☐ seconds.

(c)

00:15₆₁
min   sec

The time taken is more than ☐ seconds but less than ☐ seconds.

Think of something that you can complete in these times.

(d)

00:30₆₇
min   sec

The time taken is more than ☐ seconds but less than ☐ seconds.

(e)

00:59₀₉
min   sec

The time taken is more than ☐ seconds but less than ☐ seconds.

Complete Worksheet 8 – Page 43

Measuring Time in Seconds

In Focus

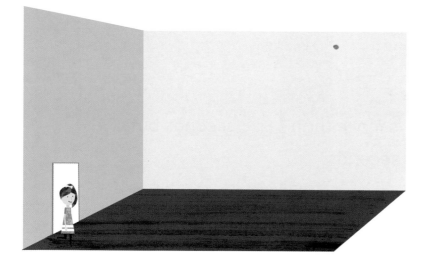

Use a stopwatch to measure the time.

How long does it take to walk from one end of the room to the other?

Let's Learn

1 How much time did each child take?

8 seconds > 6 seconds

  took about 8 seconds.

 took about 6 seconds.

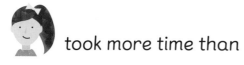 took more time than .

2 Can you guess the number of seconds you might take to run 50 metres?

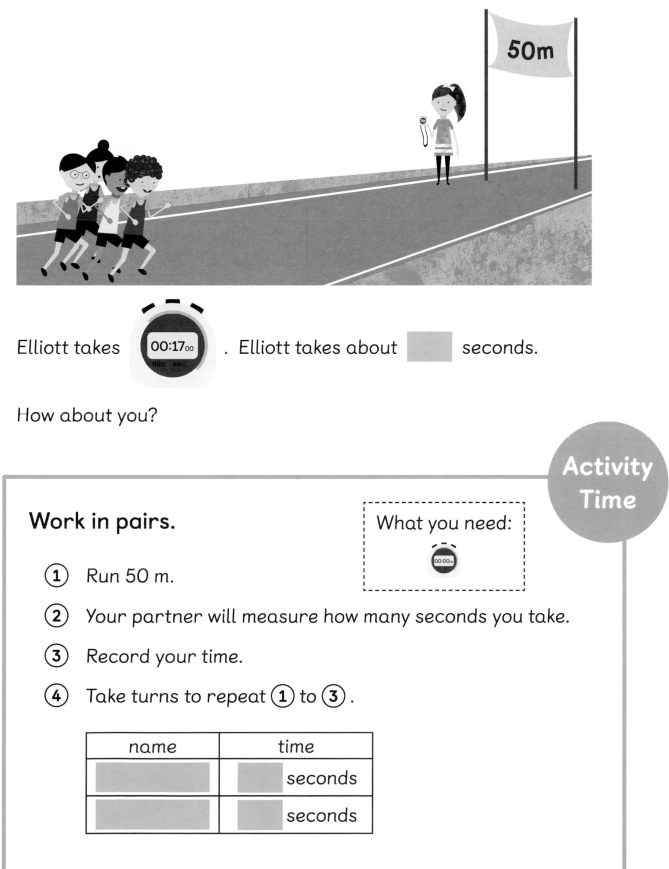

Elliott takes 00:17₀₀ . Elliott takes about ⬜ seconds.

How about you?

Activity Time

Work in pairs.

What you need:

① Run 50 m.

② Your partner will measure how many seconds you take.

③ Record your time.

④ Take turns to repeat ① to ③ .

name	time
	seconds
	seconds

1 Emma used a stopwatch to find out how many seconds her friend took to run 100 metres.

Emma's friend took about [ ] seconds.

2 Sam used his phone's stopwatch to find out how many seconds his dog took to find a hidden ball.

Sam's dog took about [ ] seconds.

Complete Worksheet 9 – Page 44

Measuring Time in Seconds

In Focus

 The second hand moves rather fast.

Look at the second hand on a clock.
Let's use a clock in an experiment with a pendulum.

 Pull the pendulum to one side.

 Let the pendulum go.

 We count this as one swing (across and back).

Count how many swings the pendulum makes in 20 seconds.

1 How long is 20 seconds?

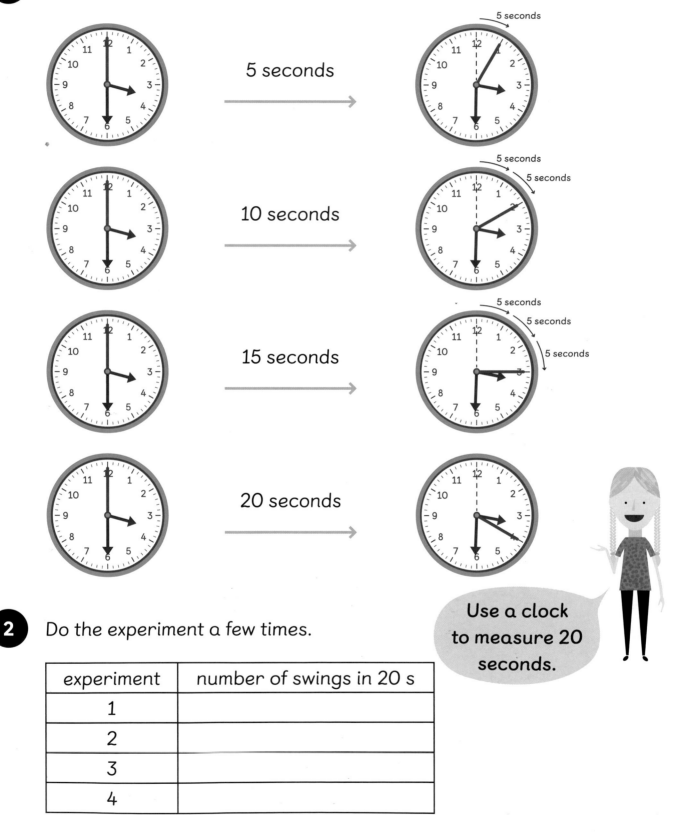

5 seconds

10 seconds

15 seconds

20 seconds

2 Do the experiment a few times.

experiment	number of swings in 20 s
1	
2	
3	
4	

Use a clock to measure 20 seconds.

3 How many seconds went by?

start   stop

5 seconds
5 seconds
5 seconds
5 seconds
5 seconds
5 seconds
5 seconds
5 seconds

[   ] seconds went by.

We can write
s for second.

4 How many seconds went by?

start   stop

15 seconds
15 seconds   15 seconds

[   ] seconds went by.

Guided Practice

Sam burns a small strip of metal in an experiment.
He uses a clock to measure the time it takes to burn the metal.
He did the experiment 4 times.

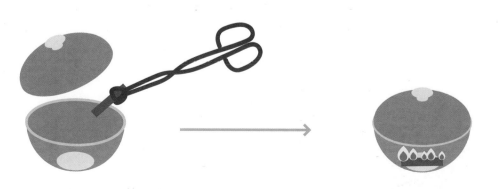

Experiment A

Experiment B

Experiment C

Experiment D

(a) Compare the times taken in experiment A and experiment B.
     What do you observe?

(b) Compare the times taken in experiment C and experiment D.
     What do you observe?

(c) In which experiment did the metal take the longest time to burn?

Complete Worksheet **10** – Page **45**

Measuring Time in Hours

Lesson 11

In Focus

A man started his car journey at  in the morning.

He ended the journey at  in the afternoon.

How long was his journey?

Let's Learn

1 Lulu did the following.

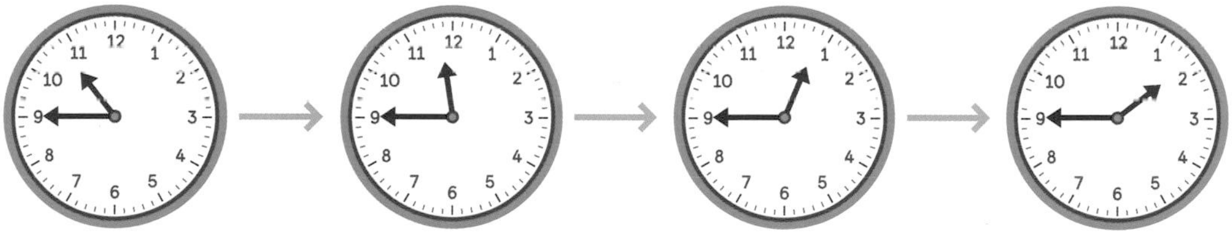

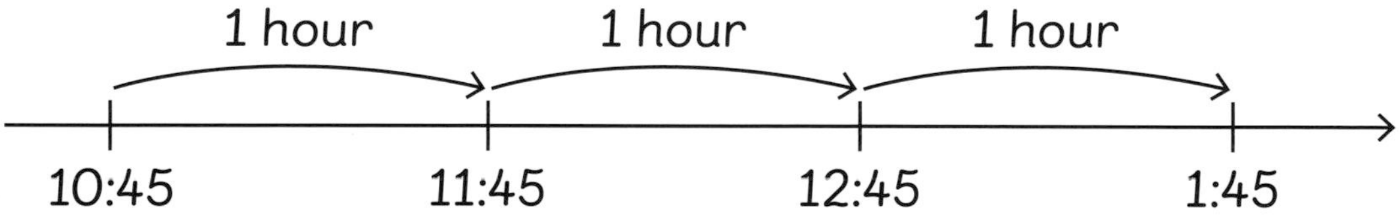
1 hour
1 hour
1 hour
10:45
11:45
12:45
1:45

The journey was 3 hours.

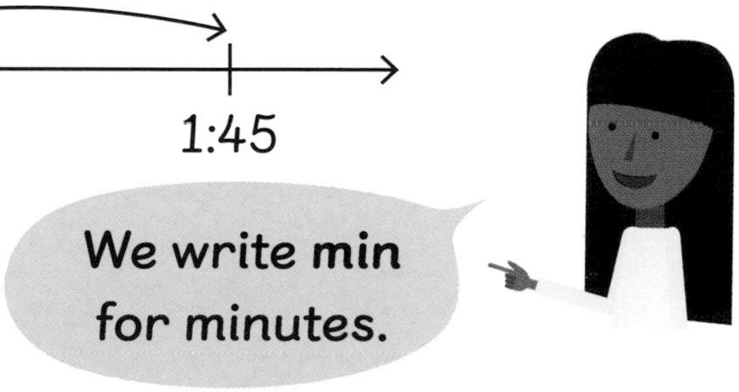
We write min for minutes.

2 Ravi did the following.

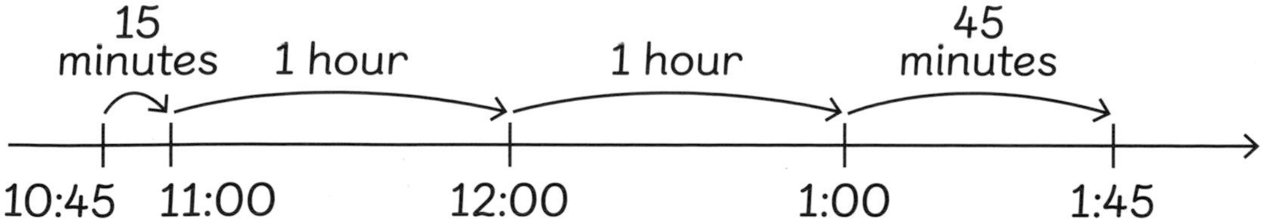
15 minutes
1 hour
1 hour
45 minutes
10:45
11:00
12:00
1:00
1:45

The journey was 3 hours.

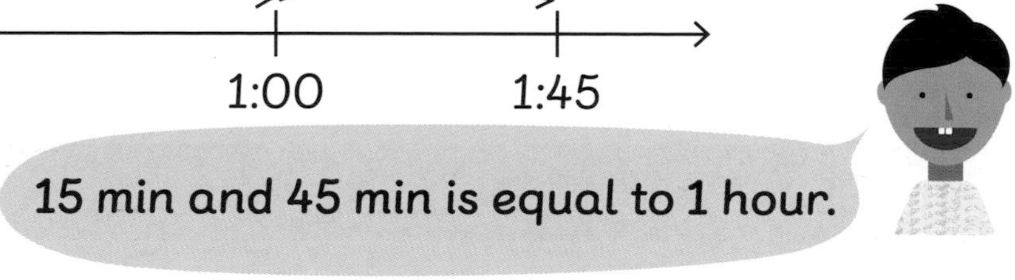
15 min and 45 min is equal to 1 hour.

Guided Practice

The following activities started in the morning and ended in the afternoon. How long was each activity?

Suggest what each activity could be.

(a)

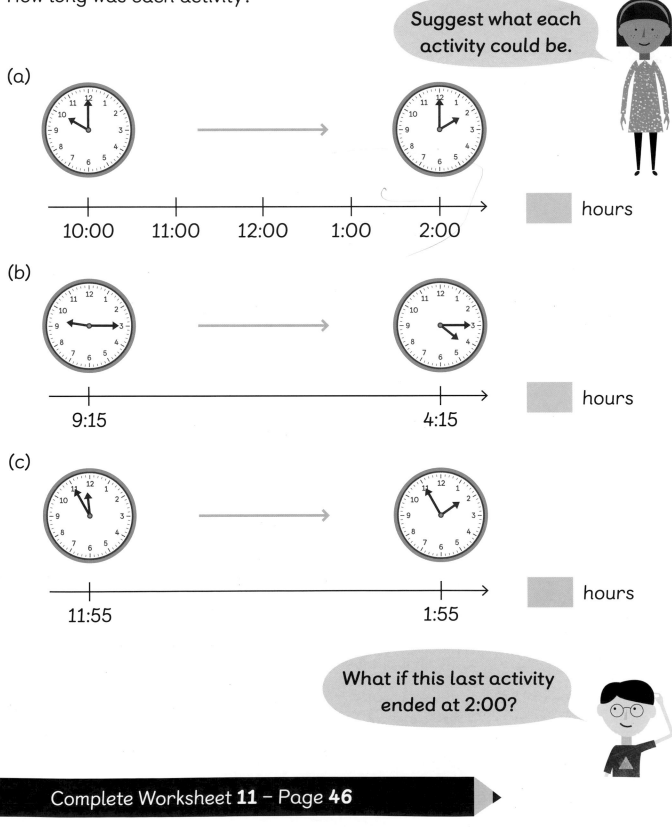

10:00   11:00   12:00   1:00   2:00

[ ] hours

(b)

9:15   4:15

[ ] hours

(c)

11:55   1:55

[ ] hours

What if this last activity ended at 2:00?

Complete Worksheet **11** – Page **46**

Measuring Time in Hours

In Focus

The art class started at 3:00 p.m.
It ended 1 hour later.
At what time did the art class end?

Let's Learn

1 What is 1 hour after 3:00 p.m?

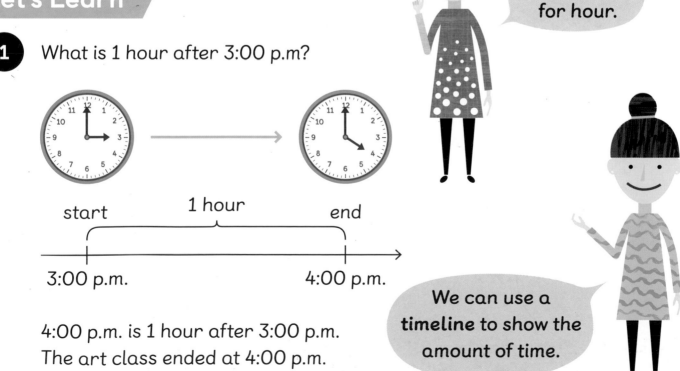

We write **h** for hour.

We can use a **timeline** to show the amount of time.

4:00 p.m. is 1 hour after 3:00 p.m.
The art class ended at 4:00 p.m.

2 If the class started at 3:30 p.m. and ended 1 hour later, what time did it end?

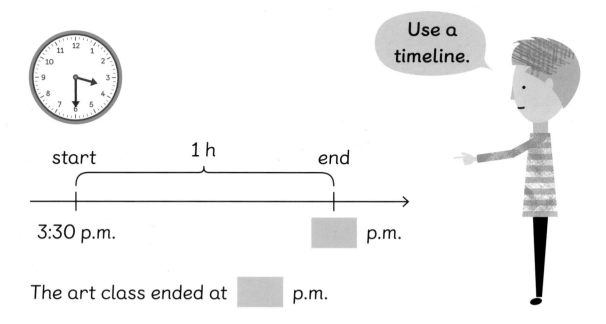

start   1 h   end

3:30 p.m.   p.m.

The art class ended at   p.m.

3 If the class started at 2:15 p.m. and ended 2 hours later, what time did it end?

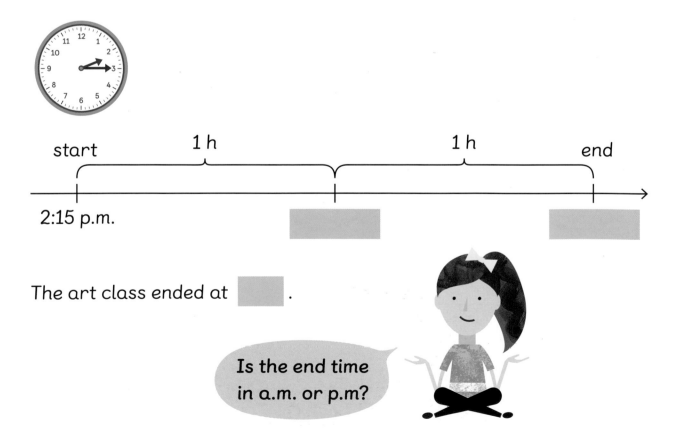

start   1 h   1 h   end

2:15 p.m.

The art class ended at   .

Is the end time in a.m. or p.m?

Guided Practice

1 What is the time 1 hour later?

(a)

(b)

(c)

(d) `08:31`

(e) `11:54`

2 What is the time 5 hours later?

(a)

(b)

(c)

(d) `04:36`

(e) `12:08`

Complete Worksheet **12** – Page **47**

Measuring Time in Hours

In Focus

We have been here for 5 hours!

Emma

At what time did Emma arrive?

Let's Learn

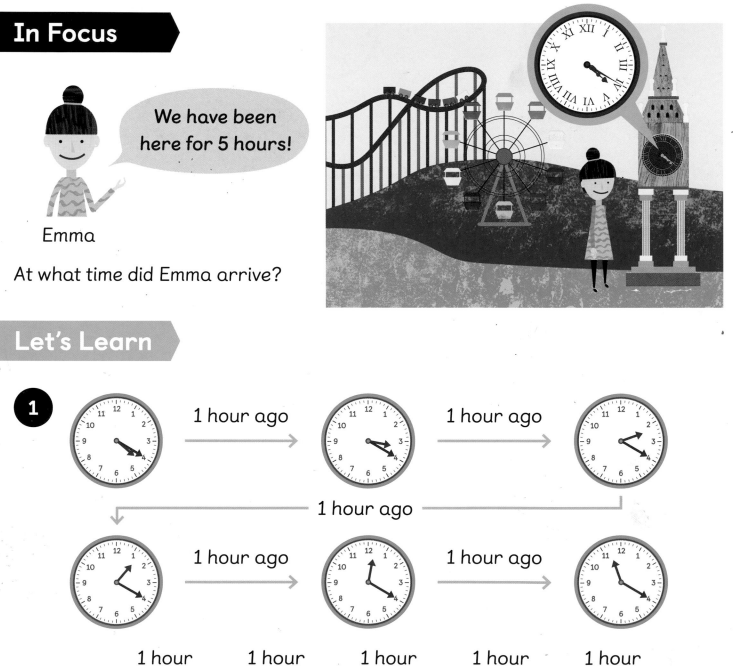

1

1 hour ago → 1 hour ago →

1 hour ago

1 hour ago → 1 hour ago →

| 1 hour | 1 hour | 1 hour | 1 hour | 1 hour |

11:20   12:20   1:20   2:20   3:20   4:20

Emma arrived at 11:20 in the morning.

2 What if Emma had been there for 4 hours and 30 minutes?

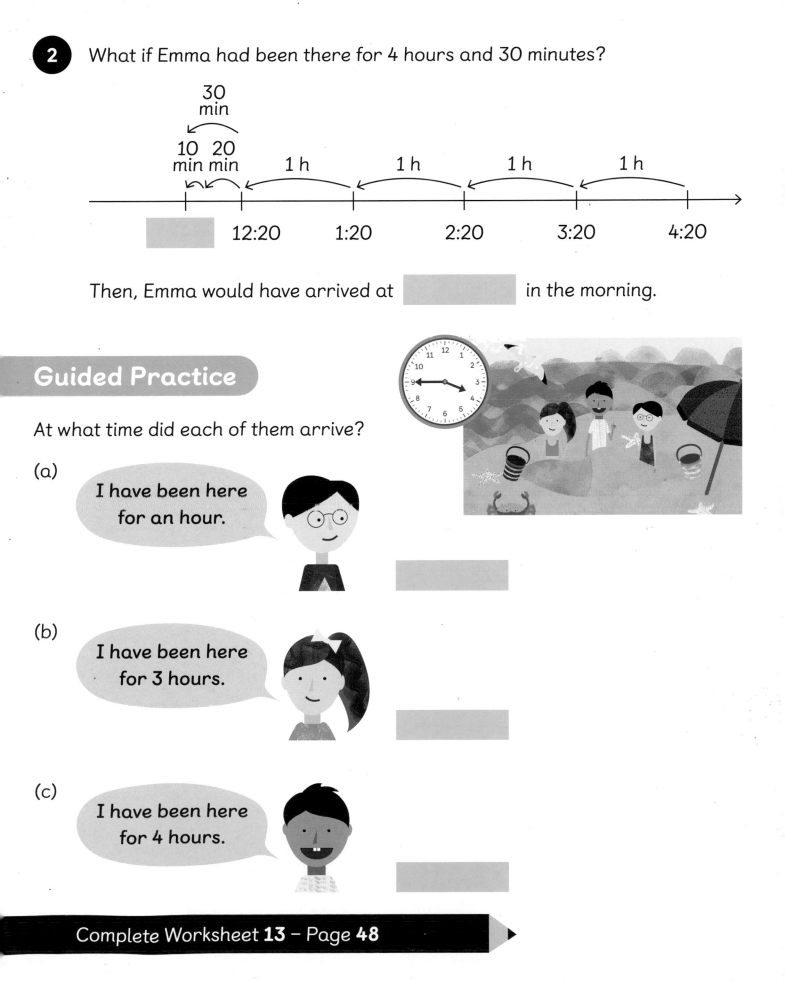

30 min

10 min 20 min

1 h 1 h 1 h 1 h

12:20 1:20 2:20 3:20 4:20

Then, Emma would have arrived at [   ] in the morning.

Guided Practice

At what time did each of them arrive?

(a)

I have been here for an hour.

(b)

I have been here for 3 hours.

(c)

I have been here for 4 hours.

Complete Worksheet **13** – Page **48**

Measuring Time in Minutes

In Focus

How long did Elliott take to finish the painting?

Let's Learn

1 Find the number of minutes Elliott took to paint.

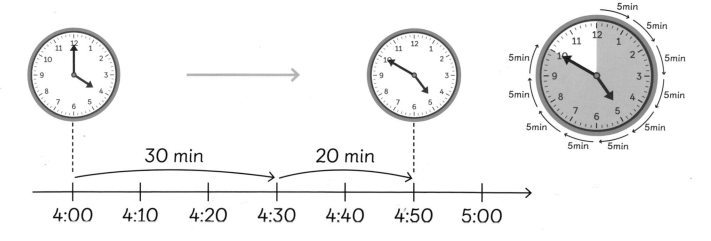

Elliott took 50 minutes to finish the painting.

2 If Elliott started at 4:05 p.m, at what time would he finish the painting?

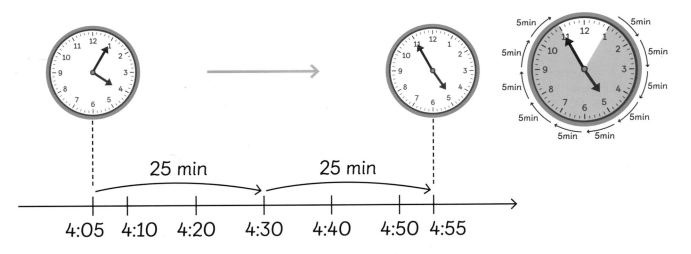

Elliott would finish the painting at 4:55 p.m.

3 If Elliott started at 4:30 p.m, at what time would he finish the painting?

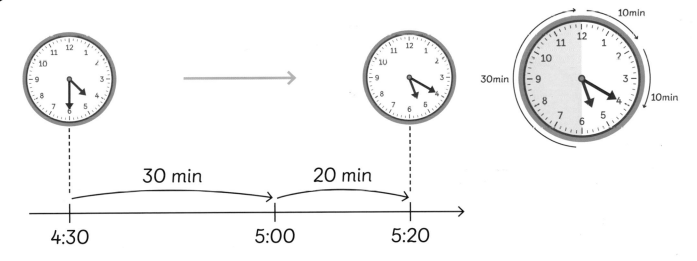

Elliott would finish the painting at 5:20 p.m.

4 Lulu wants to watch "Eastenders". How long is the programme?

☐ min

|———————————————————→
7:30 p.m.   8:00 p.m.

The programme lasts for ☐ minutes.

SMTV ONE
7.00pm   The One Show
7.30pm   Eastenders
8.00pm   Holby City

We can also ask "What is the duration of the programme?"

Guided Practice

1 Write down how long each activity took.

start   end

Suggest what each activity could be.

(a) ☐ minutes

(b) ☐ minutes

(c) ☐ minutes

2 Write down how long each activity took.

(a) start → end
11:06 → 11:40
☐ minutes

(b) start → end
09:54 → 10:17
☐ minutes

Complete Worksheet **14** – Page **49**

Measuring Time in Minutes

In Focus

A game of football started at 11:20 a.m.
It lasted for 45 minutes.
At what time did the game end?

Let's Learn

1 What is 45 minutes after 11:20 a.m.?

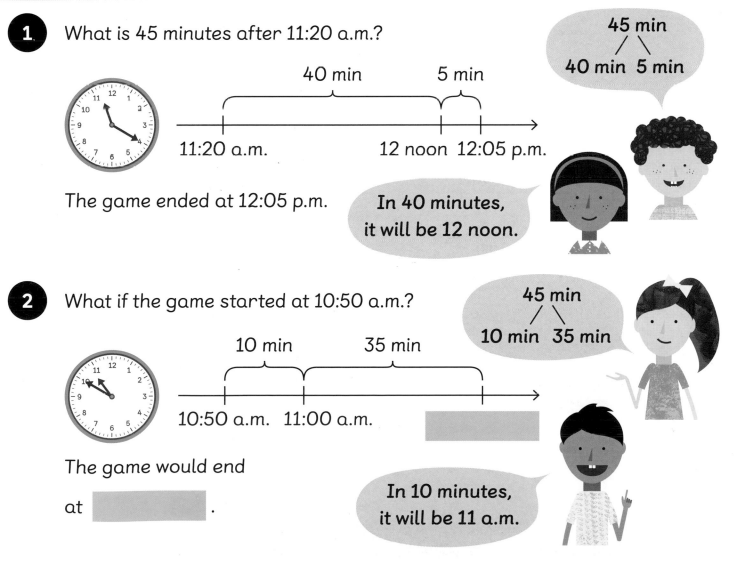

The game ended at 12:05 p.m.

In 40 minutes, it will be 12 noon.

45 min
40 min   5 min

2 What if the game started at 10:50 a.m.?

10 min   35 min

10:50 a.m.   11:00 a.m.

The game would end

at _____.

In 10 minutes, it will be 11 a.m.

45 min
10 min   35 min

Guided Practice

1 Find the time each activity ended.

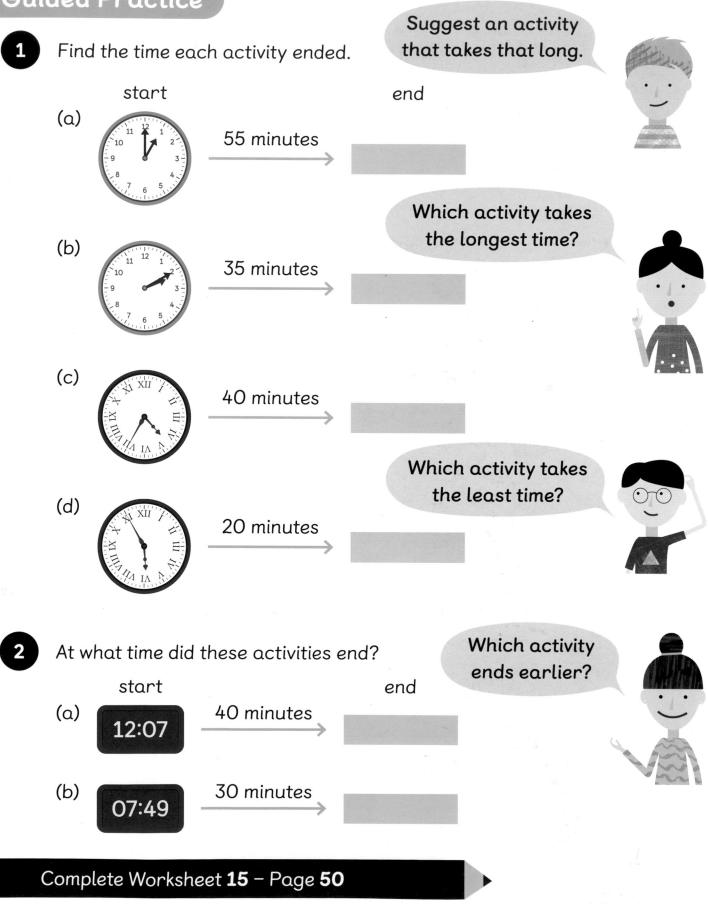

Suggest an activity that takes that long.

Which activity takes the longest time?

Which activity takes the least time?

start		end
(a)	55 minutes	
(b)	35 minutes	
(c)	40 minutes	
(d)	20 minutes	

2 At what time did these activities end?

Which activity ends earlier?

start		end
(a) 12:07	40 minutes	
(b) 07:49	30 minutes	

Complete Worksheet **15** – Page **50**

Measuring Time in Minutes

In Focus

Elliott and Lulu are meeting at the park at ⏰ .

What time should they leave home?

I take 25 minutes.

Elliott

Lulu

I take 45 minutes.

Let's Learn

1

25 minutes ➔

| 5 min | 5 min | 5 min | 5 min | 5 min |

7:05   7:10   7:15   7:20   7:25   7:30

Elliott should leave at 7:05.

2

45 minutes ➔

45 min

30 min   **15 min**

| 5 min | 5 min | 5 min | 30 min |

7:00   7:30

Lulu should leave at ▢ .

Guided Practice

Find the time each activity started.

1 (a)

start   end

[   ] → 35 minutes →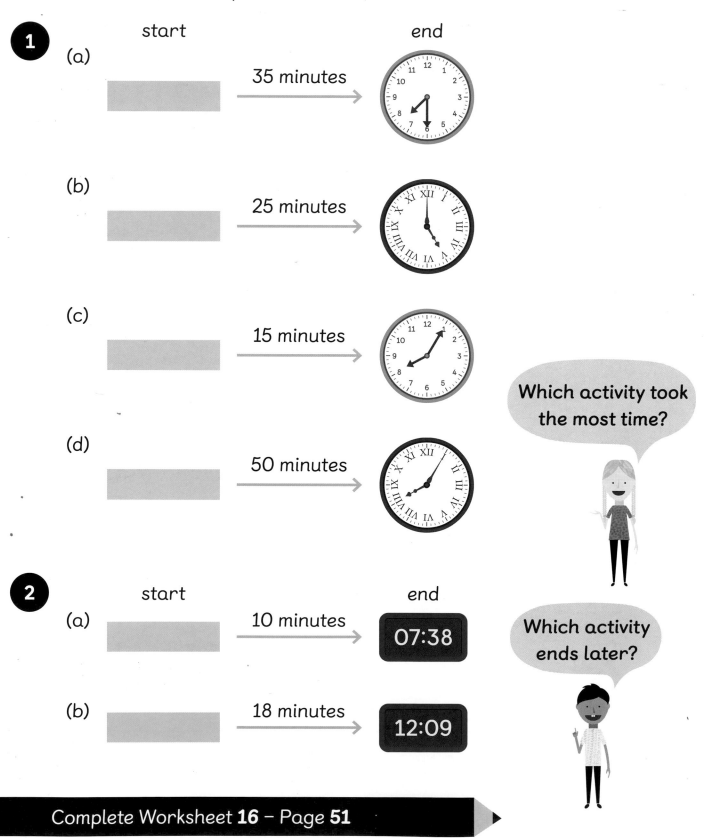

(b)

[   ] → 25 minutes →

(c)

[   ] → 15 minutes →

Which activity took the most time?

(d)

[   ] → 50 minutes →

2

start   end

(a) [   ] → 10 minutes → 07:38

Which activity ends later?

(b) [   ] → 18 minutes → 12:09

Complete Worksheet 16 – Page 51

Changing Minutes to Seconds

In Focus

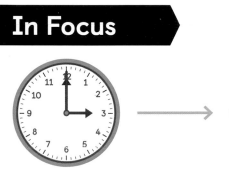

How much does the second hand move in a minute?

Let's Learn

1 Observe the second hand for 1 minute.

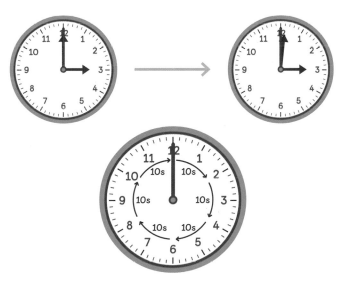

The second hand moves 1 complete turn in 1 minute.
In 1 minute, there are 60 seconds.

$$1 \text{ min} = 60 \text{ s}$$

2 Observe the second hand for 5 minutes.

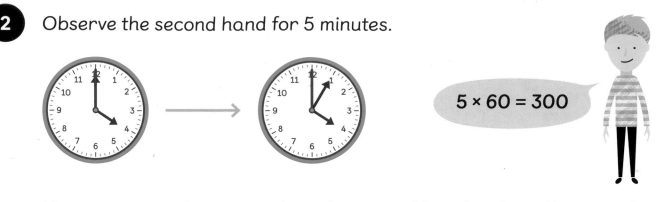

5 × 60 = 300

How many complete turns does the second hand make in 5 minutes?
In 5 minutes, there are 5 × 60 seconds.

Guided Practice

Solve.

1 How many seconds have passed between 4:30 p.m. and 4:40 p.m.?

2 Charles took 2 minutes to swim the length of a pool.
How many seconds is that?

1 minute   = 60 seconds

2 minutes = [   ] × 60 seconds

        = [   ] seconds

3 Class 3B won a relay race.
The class took 3 minutes.
How many seconds is that?

Complete Worksheet 17 – Page 52

Changing Seconds to Minutes

In Focus

In a puzzle-solving competition, a team took 120 seconds to complete the task.

Is that more than a minute?

Let's Learn

1 How many minutes is 120 seconds?

60 seconds = 1 minute
120 seconds = 2 minutes

120 s
60 s 60 s

2 Another team took 100 seconds.

100 seconds = 1 minute 40 seconds

100 s
60 s 40 s

3 A third team took 200 seconds.

200 seconds = 3 minutes 20 seconds

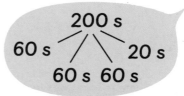

200 s
60 s   20 s
60 s 60 s

1   180 seconds = [ ] minutes [ ] seconds

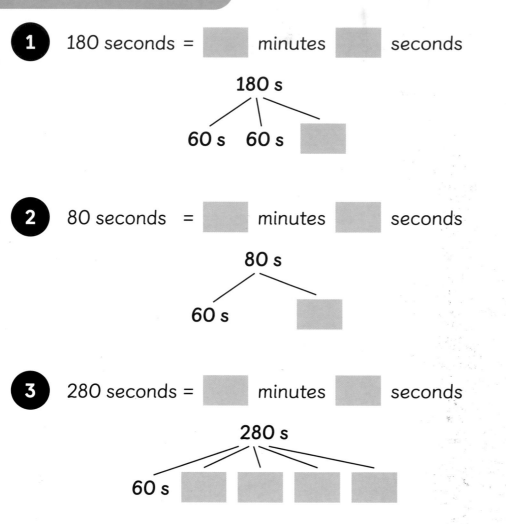

2   80 seconds = [ ] minutes [ ] seconds

3   280 seconds = [ ] minutes [ ] seconds

4   Which is longer, 150 seconds or 2 minutes 30 seconds? [ ]

Complete Worksheet 18 – Page 53

Finding Number of Days

In Focus

January

M	T	W	T	F	S	S
			1	2	3	4
5	6	7	8	9	10	11
12	13	14	15	16	17	18
19	20	21	22	23	24	25
26	27	28	29	30	31	

February

M	T	W	T	F	S	S
						1
2	3	4	5	6	7	8
9	10	11	12	13	14	15
16	17	18	19	20	21	22
23	24	25	26	27	28	

March

M	T	W	T	F	S	S
						1
2	3	4	5	6	7	8
9	10	11	12	13	14	15
16	17	18	19	20	21	22
23	24	25	26	27	28	29
30	31					

April

M	T	W	T	F	S	S
	1	2	3	4	5	
6	7	8	9	10	11	12
13	14	15	16	17	18	19
20	21	22	23	24	25	26
27	28	29	30			

May

M	T	W	T	F	S	S
				1	2	3
4	5	6	7	8	9	10
11	12	13	14	15	16	17
18	19	20	21	22	23	24
25	26	27	28	29	30	31

June

M	T	W	T	F	S	S
1	2	3	4	5	6	7
8	9	10	11	12	13	14
15	16	17	18	19	20	21
22	23	24	25	26	27	28
29	30					

July

M	T	W	T	F	S	S
	1	2	3	4	5	
6	7	8	9	10	11	12
13	14	15	16	17	18	19
20	21	22	23	24	25	26
27	28	29	30	31		

August

M	T	W	T	F	S	S
					1	2
3	4	5	6	7	8	9
10	11	12	13	14	15	16
17	18	19	20	21	22	23
24	25	26	27	28	29	30
31						

September

M	T	W	T	F	S	S
	1	2	3	4	5	6
7	8	9	10	11	12	13
14	15	16	17	18	19	20
21	22	23	24	25	26	27
28	29	30				

October

M	T	W	T	F	S	S
			1	2	3	4
5	6	7	8	9	10	11
12	13	14	15	16	17	18
19	20	21	22	23	24	25
26	27	28	29	30	31	

November

M	T	W	T	F	S	S
						1
2	3	4	5	6	7	8
9	10	11	12	13	14	15
16	17	18	19	20	21	22
23	24	25	26	27	28	29
30						

December

M	T	W	T	F	S	S
	1	2	3	4	5	6
7	8	9	10	11	12	13
14	15	16	17	18	19	20
21	22	23	24	25	26	27
28	29	30	31			

Ravi: Each month has 30 days.

Ruby: I don't think that's correct.

Who is correct?

1 There are 30 days in some months.

April

M	T	W	T	F	S	S
			1	2	3	4	5
6	7	8	9	10	11	12
13	14	15	16	17	18	19
20	21	22	23	24	25	26
27	28	29	30			

June

M	T	W	T	F	S	S
1	2	3	4	5	6	7
8	9	10	11	12	13	14
15	16	17	18	19	20	21
22	23	24	25	26	27	28
29	30					

September

M	T	W	T	F	S	S
	1	2	3	4	5	6
7	8	9	10	11	12	13
14	15	16	17	18	19	20
21	22	23	24	25	26	27
28	29	30				

November

M	T	W	T	F	S	S
						1
2	3	4	5	6	7	8
9	10	11	12	13	14	15
16	17	18	19	20	21	22
23	24	25	26	27	28	29
30						

2 There are 31 days in other months.

January

M	T	W	T	F	S	S
			1	2	3	4
5	6	7	8	9	10	11
12	13	14	15	16	17	18
19	20	21	22	23	24	25
26	27	28	29	30	31	

March

M	T	W	T	F	S	S
						1
2	3	4	5	6	7	8
9	10	11	12	13	14	15
16	17	18	19	20	21	22
23	24	25	26	27	28	29
30	31					

May

M	T	W	T	F	S	S
				1	2	3
4	5	6	7	8	9	10
11	12	13	14	15	16	17
18	19	20	21	22	23	24
25	26	27	28	29	30	31

July

M	T	W	T	F	S	S
			1	2	3	4	5
6	7	8	9	10	11	12
13	14	15	16	17	18	19
20	21	22	23	24	25	26
27	28	29	30	31		

August

M	T	W	T	F	S	S
					1	2
3	4	5	6	7	8	9
10	11	12	13	14	15	16
17	18	19	20	21	22	23
24	25	26	27	28	29	30
31						

October

M	T	W	T	F	S	S
			1	2	3	4
5	6	7	8	9	10	11
12	13	14	15	16	17	18
19	20	21	22	23	24	25
26	27	28	29	30	31	

December

M	T	W	T	F	S	S
	1	2	3	4	5	6
7	8	9	10	11	12	13
14	15	16	17	18	19	20
21	22	23	24	25	26	27
28	29	30	31			

3 In February, there are 28 days or 29 days.

year	number of days in February	year	number of days in February
2012	29	2017	28
2013	28	2018	28
2014	28	2019	28
2015	28	2020	29
2016	29	2021	28

What do you notice?

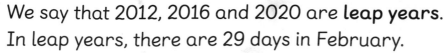

We say that 2012, 2016 and 2020 are **leap years**.
In leap years, there are 29 days in February.

4 How many days are in a year that is not a leap year?

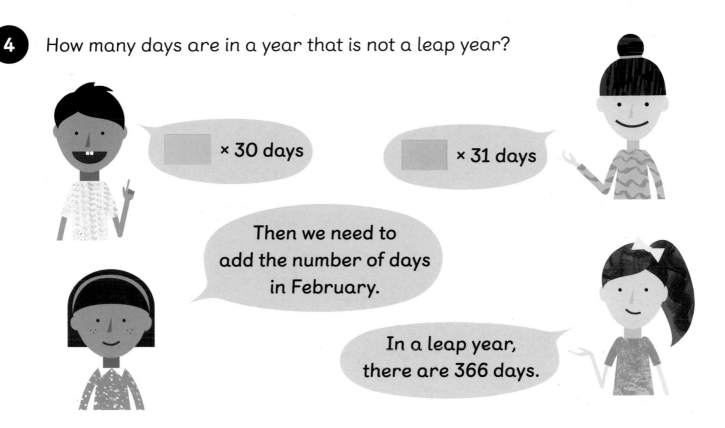

☐ × 30 days

☐ × 31 days

Then we need to add the number of days in February.

In a leap year, there are 366 days.

In a year that is not a leap year, there are 365 days.

Guided Practice

Solve.

1 Charles took the entire month of March to complete a project. How many days did he take?

2 Lulu took two months to read a collection of 8 books. How many days did she take?

Does it matter which two months it was?

Complete Worksheet **19** – Page **54 – 55** ▶

Finding Number of Days

In Focus

Lulu started her holiday on 3rd March.
The holiday ended on 17th March.
How many days was Lulu's holiday?

			March			
M	T	W	T	F	S	S
						1
2	3	4	5	6	7	8
9	10	11	12	13	14	15
16	17	18	19	20	21	22
23	24	25	26	27	28	29
30	31					

Let's Learn

1

			March			
M	T	W	T	F	S	S
						1
2	3	4	5	6	7	8
9	10	11	12	13	14	15
16	17	18	19	20	21	22
23	24	25	26	27	28	29
30	31					

Lulu's holiday lasted for 15 days.

2 What if the holiday started on 3rd March and lasted for 10 days?

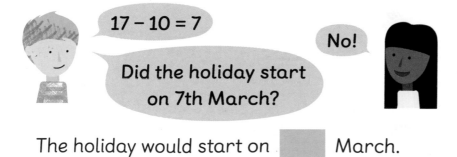

The holiday would end on 13th March.

That is not correct.

The holiday would end on 12th March.

			March			
M	T	W	T	F	S	S
						1
2	3	4	5	6	7	8
9	10	11	12	13	14	15
16	17	18	19	20	21	22
23	24	25	26	27	28	29
30	31					

3 What if the holiday ended on 17th March and lasted for 10 days?

17 – 10 = 7

Did the holiday start on 7th March?

No!

The holiday would start on ☐ March.

			March			
M	T	W	T	F	S	S
						1
2	3	4	5	6	7	8
9	10	11	12	13	14	15
16	17	18	19	20	21	22
23	24	25	26	27	28	29
30	31					

Guided Practice

April						
M	T	W	T	F	S	S
		1	2	3	4	5
6	7	8	9	10	11	12
13	14	15	16	17	18	19
20	21	22	23	24	25	26
27	28	29	30			

May						
M	T	W	T	F	S	S
			1	2	3	
4	5	6	7	8	9	10
11	12	13	14	15	16	17
18	19	20	21	22	23	24
25	26	27	28	29	30	31

Solve using the calendars above.

1 A book festival started on 5th April.
It ended on 9th April.
How many days was the festival?

2 A music festival started on 28th April.
It lasted for 7 days.
On what date did the festival end?

3 A food festival closed on 1st May.
It lasted for 9 days.
On what date did the festival open?

Complete Worksheet 20 – Page 56

Mind Workout

London time is 8 hours behind Singapore.
London time is 5 hours ahead of New York.
It is Tuesday, 24th March, 6:00 p.m. in London.
What day and time is it in Singapore and New York?
Explain your answer.

Use a timeline to help you.

Maths Journal

How do you spend your Sunday?
Describe the activities you do,
starting from the time you wake up.

At what time does each activity start and end?

How long does each activity last?

Self Check

I know how to...

☐ tell and write time in a.m. and in p.m.

☐ tell and write time using "past" and "to".

☐ tell and write time shown on different types of clocks.

☐ measure time in seconds, hours and minutes.

☐ find starting time, ending time and duration.

☐ change minutes to seconds, and seconds to minutes.

☐ know the number of days in each month, year and leap year.

☐ find the number of days using a calendar.

How can Emma draw a graph to show
the number of each type of fruit?

Chapter 10
Picture Graphs and
Bar Graphs

Drawing Picture Graphs

In Focus

Emma uses a tally chart to show the number of fruits in the baskets.

orange	ⵏⵏⵏⵏ |||
pear	ⵏⵏⵏⵏ	
strawberry	ⵏⵏⵏⵏ ⵏⵏⵏⵏ

How else can she show the number of each type of fruit?

Let's Learn

1 Emma uses a table.

	oranges	pears	strawberries
number of fruits	8	6	10

2 She also uses a picture graph or a pictogram.

Number of Fruits in the Baskets

orange		🔴🔴🔴🔴🔴🔴🔴🔴
pear		🔴🔴🔴🔴🔴🔴
strawberry		🔴🔴🔴🔴🔴🔴🔴🔴🔴🔴

Each stands for 1 fruit.

3 She draws a different picture graph.

Number of Fruits in the Baskets

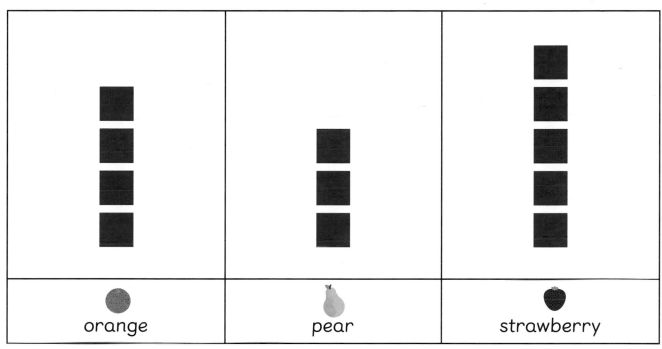

| orange | pear | strawberry |

Each ■ stands for 2 fruits.

Guided Practice

The graph shows the number of pupils who joined the football club.

Number of Pupils in Football Club

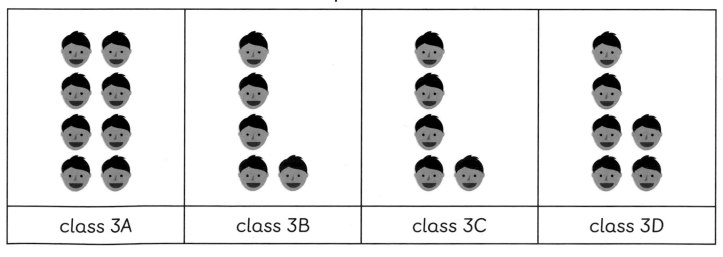

| class 3A | class 3B | class 3C | class 3D |

Each 😊 stands for 1 pupil.

(a) Complete the table.

class	number of pupils in football club
3A	
3B	
3C	
3D	

(b) Draw another picture graph to show the number of pupils in each class who joined the football club.

Number of Pupils in Football Club

3A	
3B	
3C	
3D	

Each ⬤ stands for 2 pupils.

Complete Worksheet 1 – Page 61 - 64 ▶

Drawing Bar Graphs

In Focus

Ravi draws a picture graph to show the number of fruits in three baskets.

Number of Fruits in the Baskets

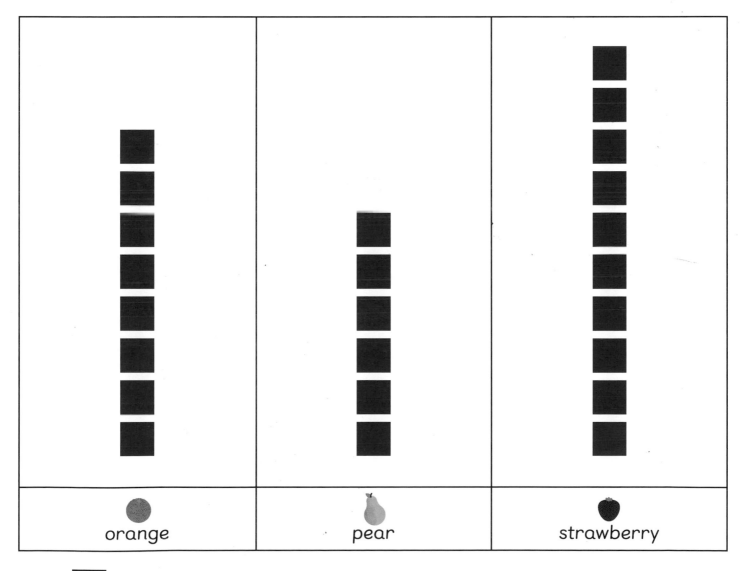

| orange | pear | strawberry |

Each ■ stands for 1 fruit.

How can Ravi draw another graph to show the same information?

Let's Learn

We can use a **bar graph** to show the number of each type of fruit.

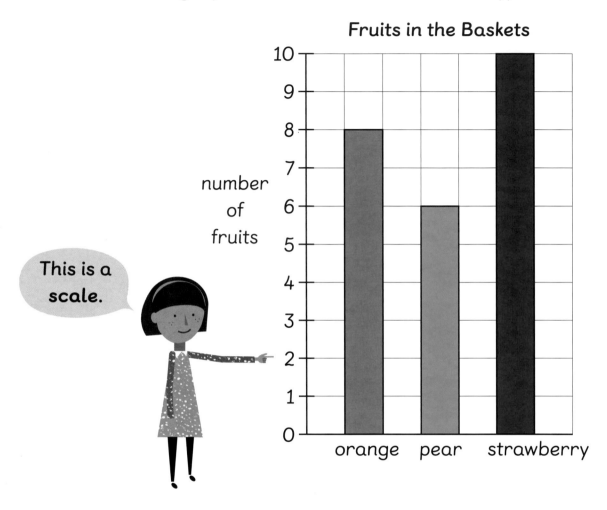

This is a scale.

Fruits in the Baskets

There are 6 pears.
There are 2 more oranges than pears.
The largest group is the strawberries.

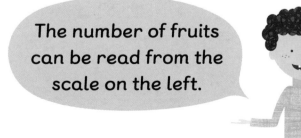

The number of fruits can be read from the scale on the left.

Guided Practice

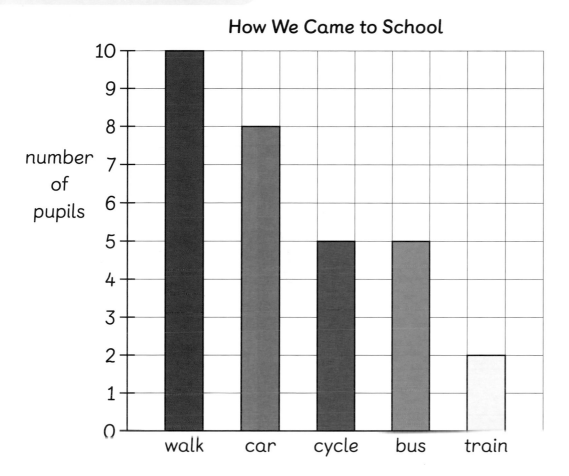

How We Came to School

Pupils in a class were asked how they came to school that day.

(a) How many pupils walked to school?

(b) The number of pupils who came by car is ☐ less than the number of pupils who walked.

(c) Is Hannah correct? Explain.

> There were more pupils who walked to school than those who did not.

(d) There were ☐ pupils in the class that day.

Complete Worksheet 2 – Page 65 – 68

Reading Bar Graphs

In Focus

Ravi and Lulu asked the pupils in a class to name their favourite type of book.

Favourite Type of Book

type of book	number of pupils
mystery	~~////~~ ~~////~~ //
science fiction	////
comic	~~////~~ ~~////~~
fairy tale	//

This bar graph shows the same information.

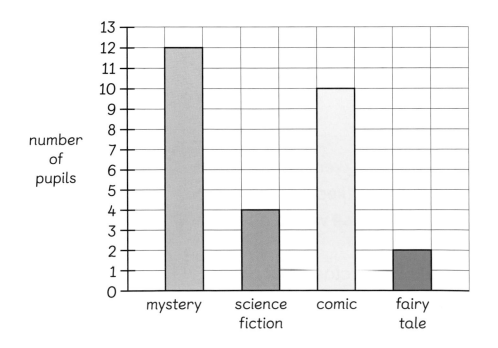

Let's Learn

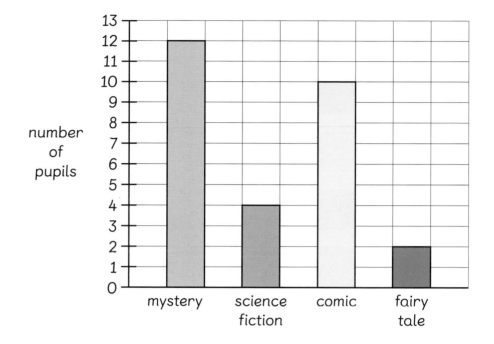

number of pupils

mystery   science   comic   fairy
           fiction   tale

The bar graph shows the number of pupils in a class who like to read different types of books.

1 Which type of book is the most popular?

Mystery books are the most popular.

The most popular type of book is the one chosen by the most pupils.

2 How many more pupils like to read comic books than science fiction books?

10 pupils like to read comic books.
4 pupils like to read science fiction books.

$10 - 4 = 6$

6 more pupils like to read comic books than science fiction books.

Guided Practice

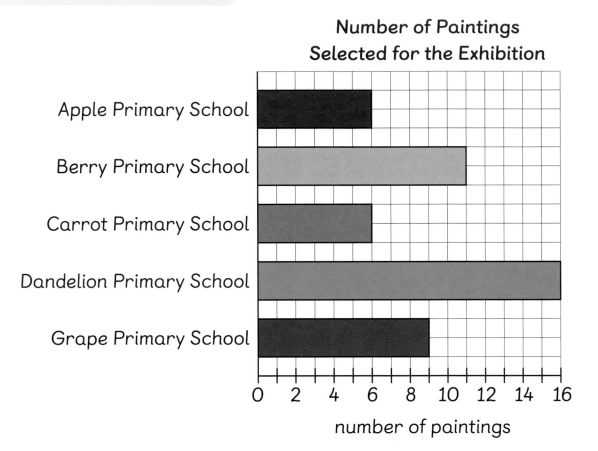

Number of Paintings Selected for the Exhibition

Answer each of the following questions.

(a) Which school has the most paintings at the exhibition?

(b) How many paintings does Carrot Primary School have at the exhibition?

(c) How many paintings does Grape Primary School have at the exhibition?

(d) Berry Primary School has _____ more paintings than Apple Primary School has at the exhibition.

Complete Worksheet 3 – Page 69 – 72 ▶

Reading Bar Graphs

In Focus

Different types of pastry are sold at a bakery each day.
The baker draws a bar graph to show the number of each type of pastry
he sold in one day.

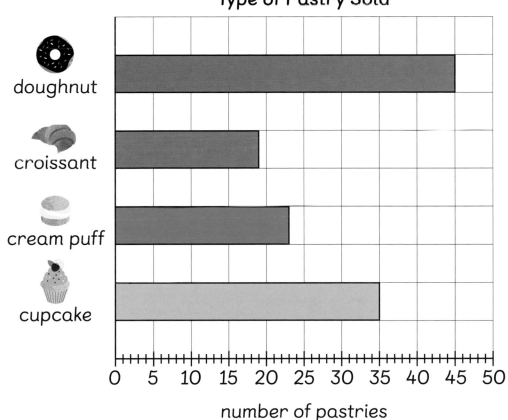

How many doughnuts did the baker sell?

Let's Learn

1 How many doughnuts did the baker sell?

The baker sold 45 doughnuts.

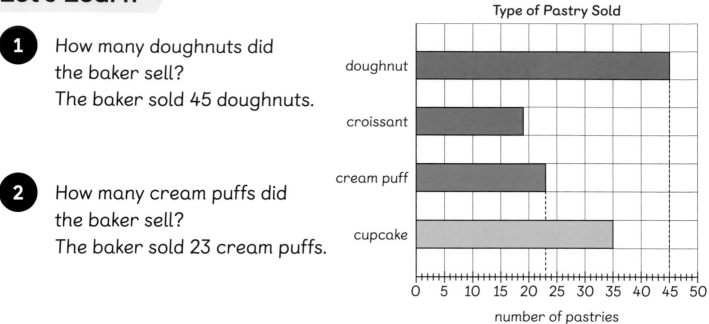

Type of Pastry Sold

2 How many cream puffs did the baker sell?

The baker sold 23 cream puffs.

3 Which type of pastry was the least popular?

The least popular pastry is the pastry that sold the least.

Croissants were the least popular.

4 Did the baker sell more cream puffs or cupcakes?

How many more?

The baker sold more cupcakes than cream puffs.

The baker sold 35 cupcakes and 23 cream puffs.

35 − 23 = 12

The baker sold 12 more cupcakes than cream puffs.

35   23

Guided Practice

The bar graph shows the number of children who like each type of food.

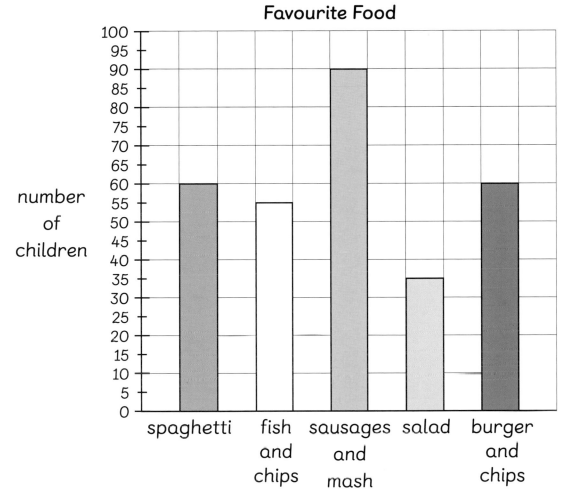

(a) Which type of food is the least popular?

(b) How many children like fish and chips?

(c) Do more children like spaghetti or sausages and mash?

How many more?

(d) Which two types of food do the same number of children like?

and

Complete Worksheet 4 – Page 73 - 76

Reading Bar Graphs

In Focus

The bar graph shows the number of pupils who like different sports.

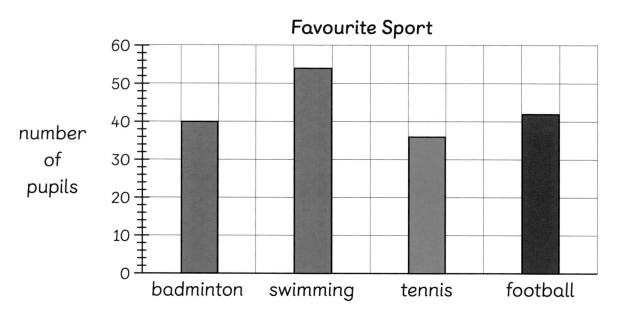

Three pupils are talking about the graph.

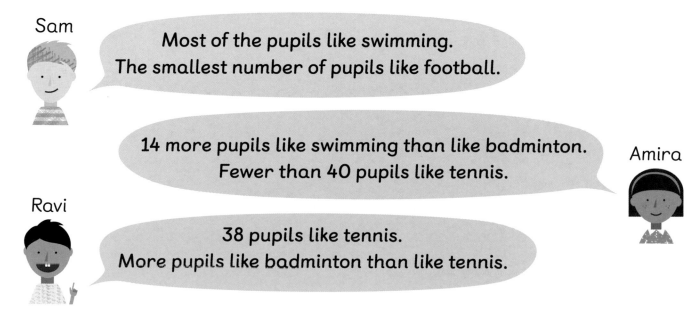

Sam

Most of the pupils like swimming.
The smallest number of pupils like football.

Amira

14 more pupils like swimming than like badminton.
Fewer than 40 pupils like tennis.

Ravi

38 pupils like tennis.
More pupils like badminton than like tennis.

Whose statements are all correct?

Let's Learn

1 For Sam :

> Most of the pupils like swimming.

> The number of pupils who like football is not the smallest.

> The smallest number of pupils like tennis.

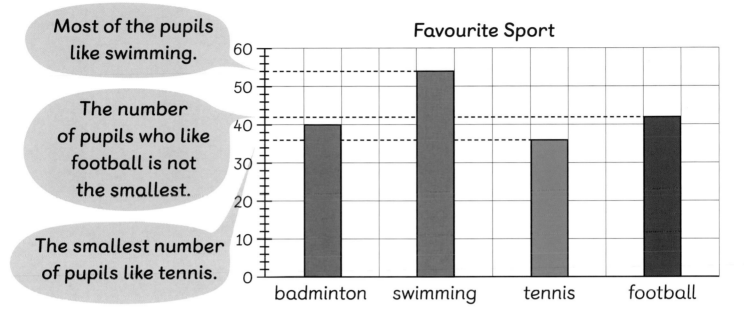

Favourite Sport

Sam's statements are not all correct.

2 For Amira :

> 54

> 40

> Fewer than 40 pupils like tennis.

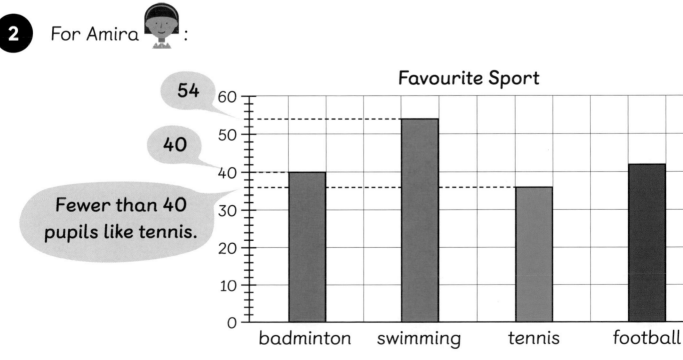

Favourite Sport

54 – 40 = 14

14 more pupils like swimming than like badminton.

Amira's statements are all correct.

For Ravi :

Favourite Sport

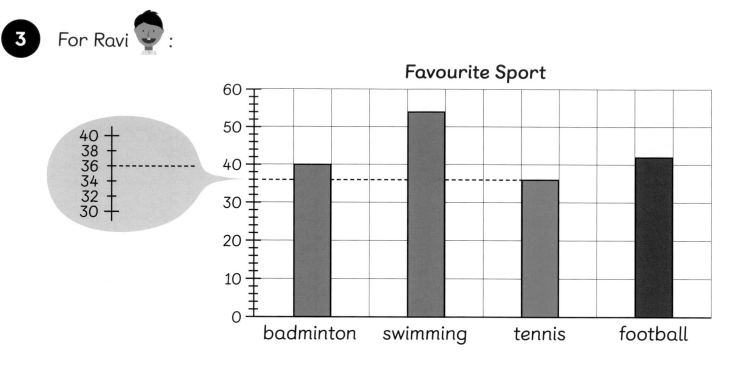

40
38
36
34
32
30

36 pupils like tennis, not 38.

Favourite Sport

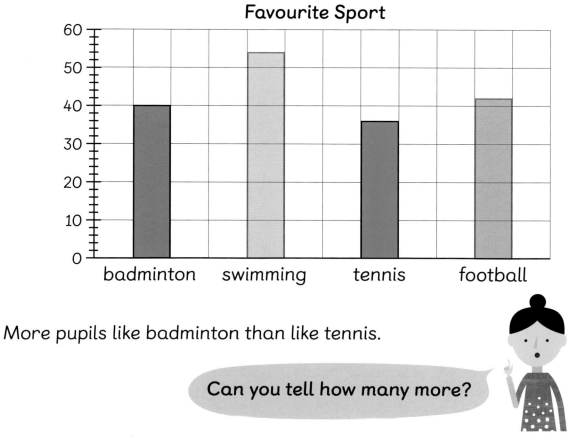

More pupils like badminton than like tennis.

Can you tell how many more?

Ravi's statements are not all correct.

Work in groups of 4.

① Here are some different types of transport.

by foot   by bus   by train   by car   by bicycle

How do your classmates get to school every day?
Discuss some ways you can collect the information.

> We can ask them to raise their hands.

② Your teacher will teach you to use a spreadsheet.

③ Type in the number of pupils next to each type of transport to create a bar graph.

Example

type of transport	number of pupils
by foot	15
by bus	11
by train	5
by car	3
by bicycle	5

④ Write five sentences to describe the information given by the bar graph.
Compare your sentences with your classmates.

Guided Practice

The bar graph shows the number of children who visited the library over five days.

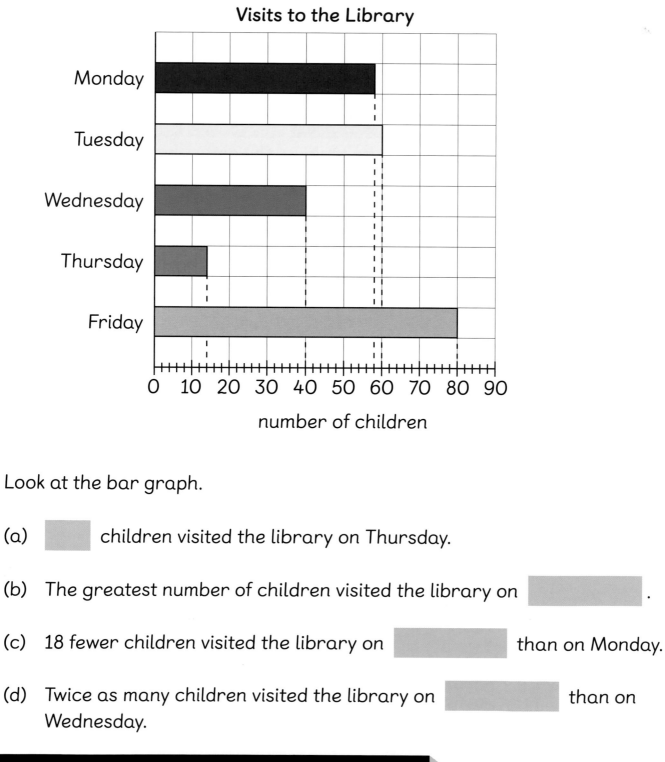

Visits to the Library

number of children

Look at the bar graph.

(a) [   ] children visited the library on Thursday.

(b) The greatest number of children visited the library on [   ].

(c) 18 fewer children visited the library on [   ] than on Monday.

(d) Twice as many children visited the library on [   ] than on Wednesday.

Complete Worksheet 5 – Page 77 - 80 ▶

Mind Workout

Elliott carried out a survey to find out the number of glasses of water pupils drink in a day. He drew a bar graph to show the results.

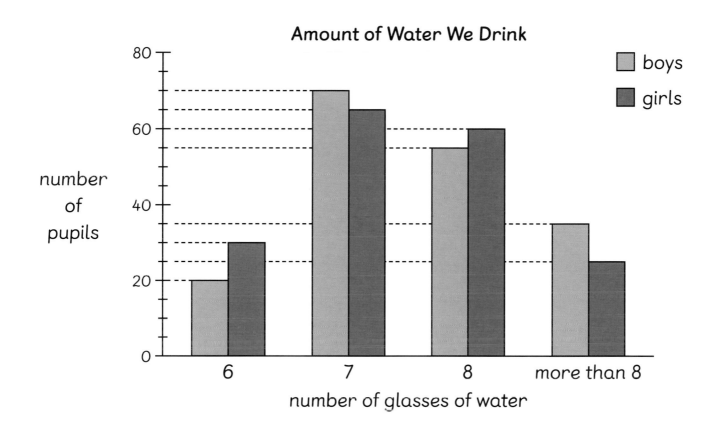

Look at the bar graph and answer the questions.

(a) Do more boys or girls drink 6 glasses of water a day?

How many more?

(b) Do fewer pupils drink 7 glasses of water or 8 glasses of water a day?

(c) We should drink 8 glasses or more of water every day. How many boys do not drink enough water?

Maths Journal

The bar graph shows the number of pupils in a class who like different colours.

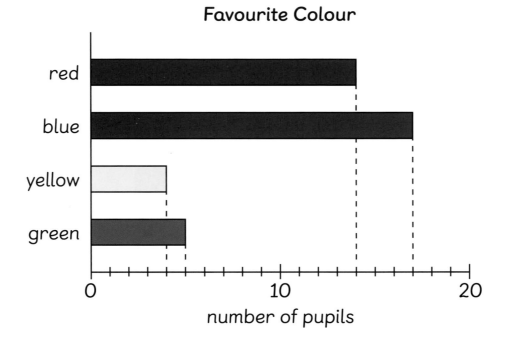

Favourite Colour

number of pupils

Study the graph.

Write three sentences to tell a story from the information.

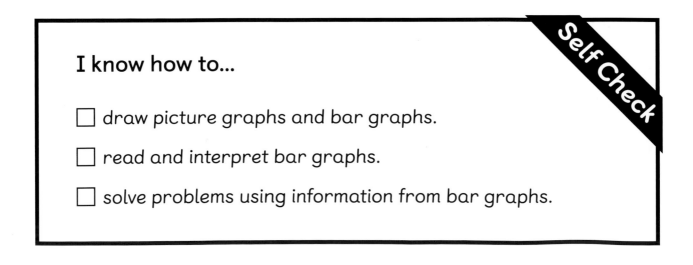

Do you prefer picture graphs or bar graphs? Why?

I know how to...

☐ draw picture graphs and bar graphs.

☐ read and interpret bar graphs.

☐ solve problems using information from bar graphs.

Self Check

What are some examples of fractions that
you can find around you?

Chapter 11
Fractions

Counting in Tenths

In Focus

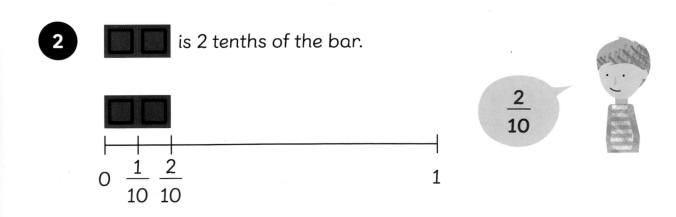

How much of the chocolate bar does each child get?

Let's Learn

1 The chocolate bar is cut into 10 pieces.

 is 1 tenth of the bar.

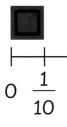

0   $\dfrac{1}{10}$ 1

$\dfrac{1}{10}$

2  is 2 tenths of the bar.

0   $\dfrac{1}{10}$ $\dfrac{2}{10}$ 1

$\dfrac{2}{10}$

3 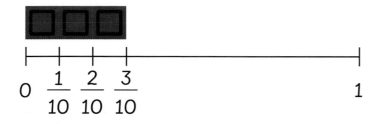 is 3 tenths.

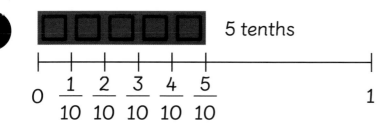

 $\frac{3}{10}$

4  is 4 tenths.

 $\frac{4}{10}$

5 5 tenths

 $\frac{5}{10}$

6 tenths

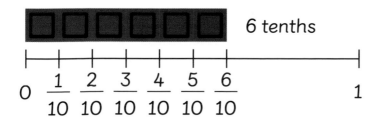

 $\frac{6}{10}$

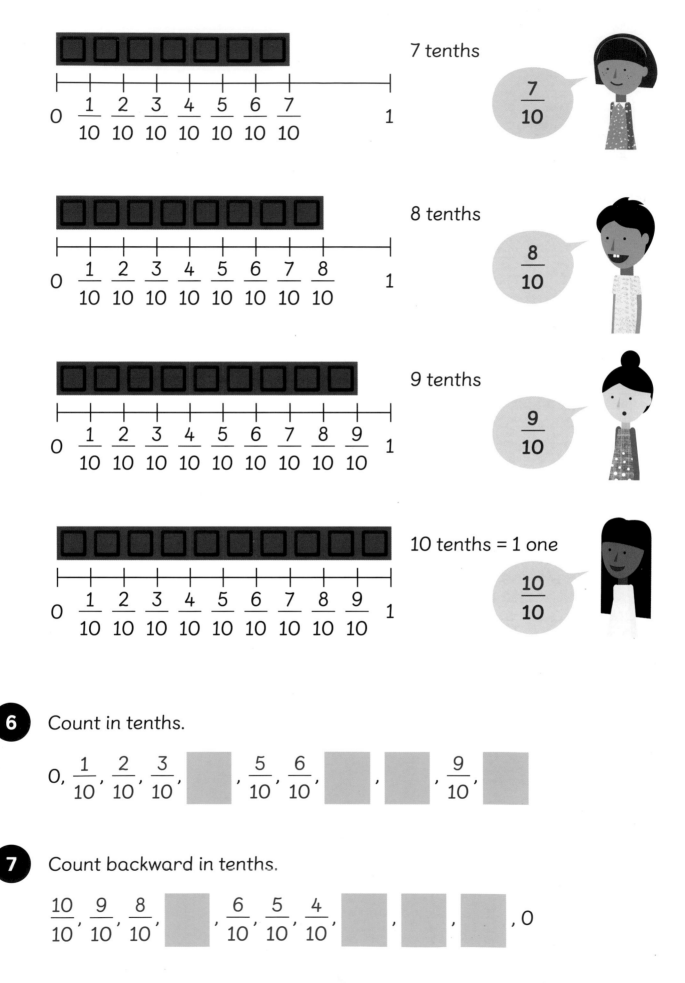

7 tenths

$\dfrac{7}{10}$

8 tenths

$\dfrac{8}{10}$

9 tenths

$\dfrac{9}{10}$

10 tenths = 1 one

$\dfrac{10}{10}$

6 Count in tenths.

$0, \dfrac{1}{10}, \dfrac{2}{10}, \dfrac{3}{10}, \boxed{}, \dfrac{5}{10}, \dfrac{6}{10}, \boxed{}, \boxed{}, \dfrac{9}{10}, \boxed{}$

7 Count backward in tenths.

$\dfrac{10}{10}, \dfrac{9}{10}, \dfrac{8}{10}, \boxed{}, \dfrac{6}{10}, \dfrac{5}{10}, \dfrac{4}{10}, \boxed{}, \boxed{}, \boxed{}, 0$

Guided Practice

1 This is 1.

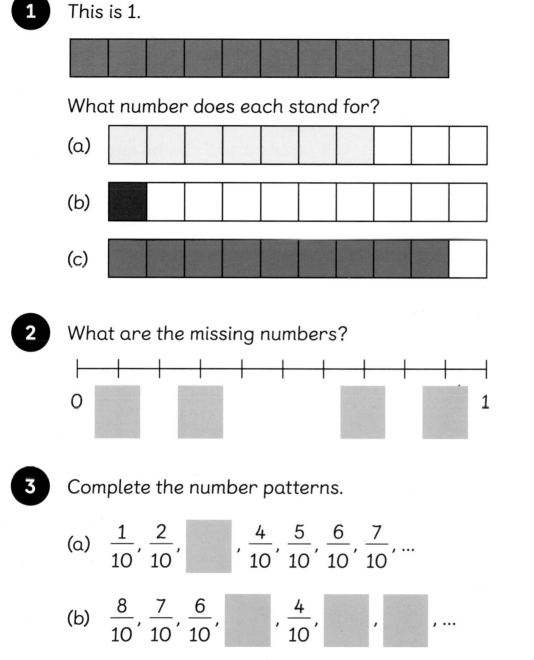

What number does each stand for?

(a)

(b)

(c)

2 What are the missing numbers?

0   1

3 Complete the number patterns.

(a) $\dfrac{1}{10}$, $\dfrac{2}{10}$, ⬜, $\dfrac{4}{10}$, $\dfrac{5}{10}$, $\dfrac{6}{10}$, $\dfrac{7}{10}$, ...

(b) $\dfrac{8}{10}$, $\dfrac{7}{10}$, $\dfrac{6}{10}$, ⬜, $\dfrac{4}{10}$, ⬜, ⬜, ...

(c) $\dfrac{3}{10}$, $\dfrac{5}{10}$, ⬜, $\dfrac{9}{10}$, ...

(d) $\dfrac{9}{10}$, $\dfrac{6}{10}$, ⬜, 0, ...

Complete Worksheet 1 – Page 91

Making Number Pairs

In Focus

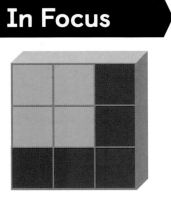

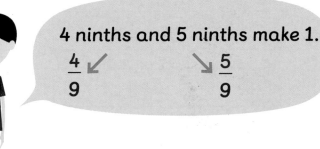

4 ninths and 5 ninths make 1.

$\dfrac{4}{9}$ ↙   ↘ $\dfrac{5}{9}$

What other fractions make 1?

Let's Learn

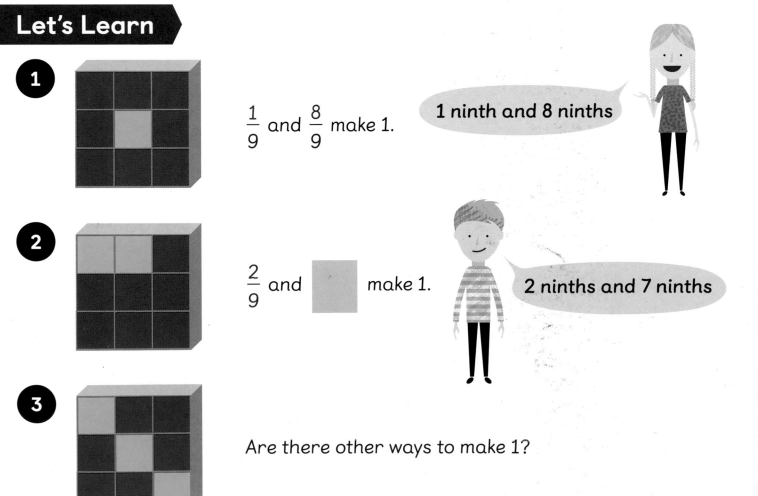

1 $\dfrac{1}{9}$ and $\dfrac{8}{9}$ make 1.

1 ninth and 8 ninths

2 $\dfrac{2}{9}$ and ☐ make 1.

2 ninths and 7 ninths

3 Are there other ways to make 1?

Guided Practice

1 (a) $\frac{1}{3}$ and [ ] make 1.

(b) [ ] and [ ] make 1.

(c) [ ] and [ ] make 1.

(d) [ ] and [ ] make 1.

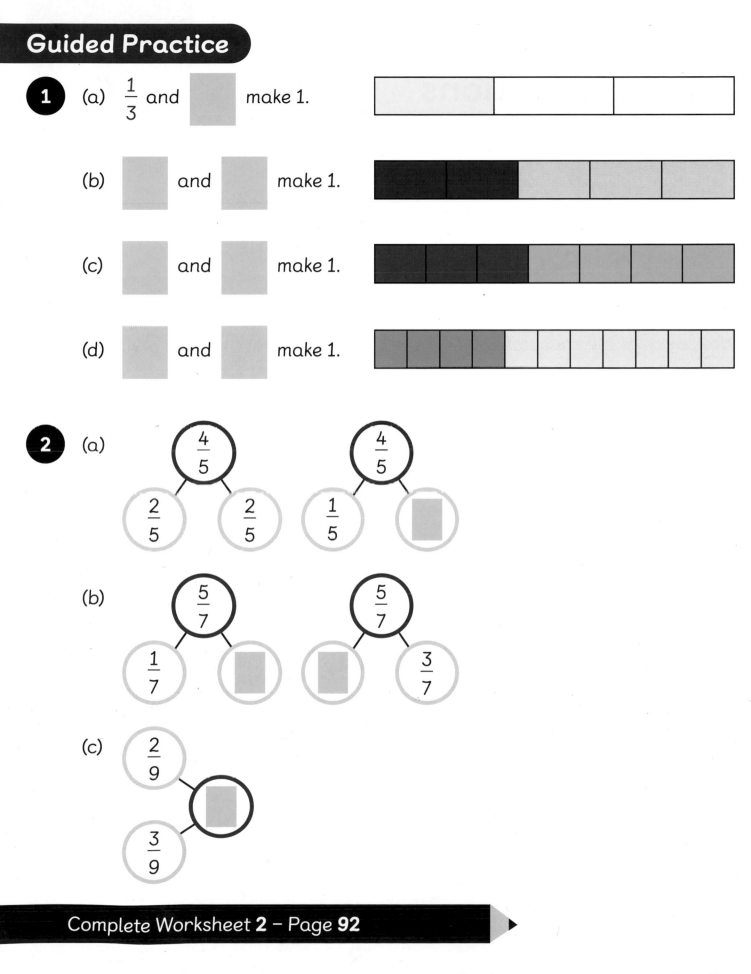

2 (a) $\frac{4}{5}$ → $\frac{2}{5}$, $\frac{2}{5}$ $\frac{4}{5}$ → $\frac{1}{5}$, [ ]

(b) $\frac{5}{7}$ → $\frac{1}{7}$, [ ] $\frac{5}{7}$ → [ ] , $\frac{3}{7}$

(c) $\frac{2}{9}$, $\frac{3}{9}$ → [ ]

Complete Worksheet **2** – Page **92**

Adding Fractions

Let's share this chocolate bar. I will have a piece.

I will have 2 pieces.

How much of the chocolate bar did the two children eat?

Let's Learn

$\frac{1}{5}$

1 Each piece is 1 fifth of the bar.

$\frac{1}{5}$

eats 1 fifth of the bar.

$\frac{2}{5}$

eats 2 fifths of the bar.

Together, eat 3 fifths of the chocolate bar.

1 fifth + 2 fifths = 3 fifths

$$\frac{1}{5} + \frac{2}{5} = \frac{3}{5}$$

2 Add $\frac{2}{5}$ and $\frac{2}{5}$.

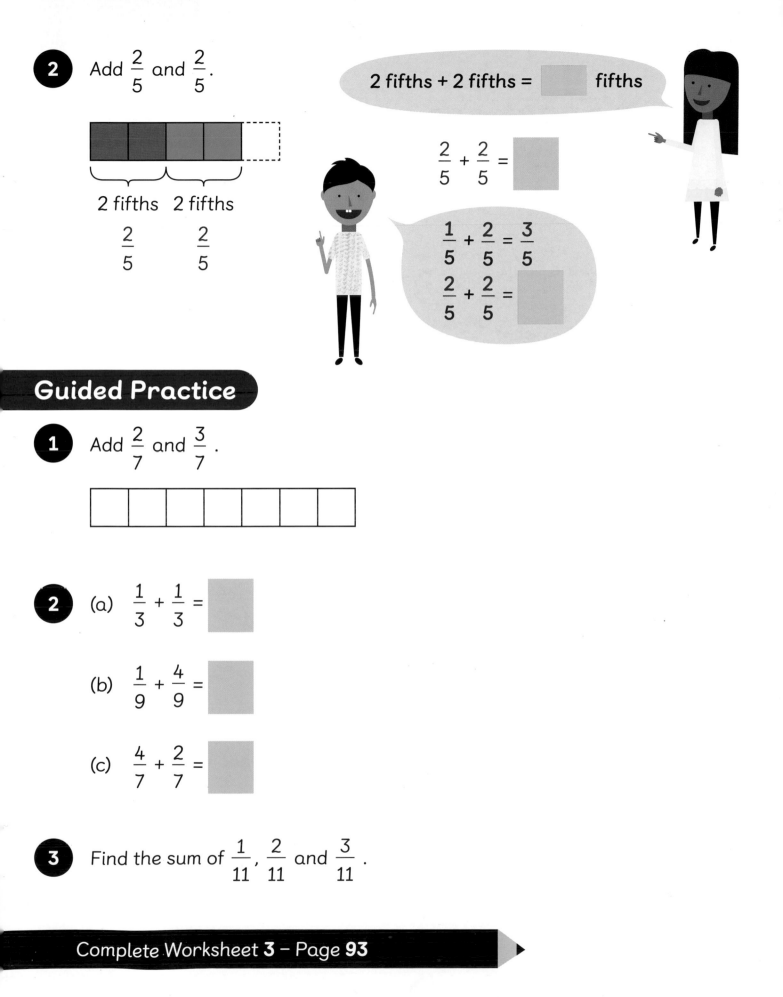

2 fifths + 2 fifths = ▢ fifths

2 fifths   2 fifths

$\frac{2}{5}$ $\frac{2}{5}$

$\frac{2}{5} + \frac{2}{5} = $ ▢

$\frac{1}{5} + \frac{2}{5} = \frac{3}{5}$

$\frac{2}{5} + \frac{2}{5} = $ ▢

Guided Practice

1 Add $\frac{2}{7}$ and $\frac{3}{7}$.

2 (a) $\frac{1}{3} + \frac{1}{3} = $ ▢

(b) $\frac{1}{9} + \frac{4}{9} = $ ▢

(c) $\frac{4}{7} + \frac{2}{7} = $ ▢

3 Find the sum of $\frac{1}{11}$, $\frac{2}{11}$ and $\frac{3}{11}$.

Complete Worksheet **3** – Page **93**

Adding Fractions

In Focus

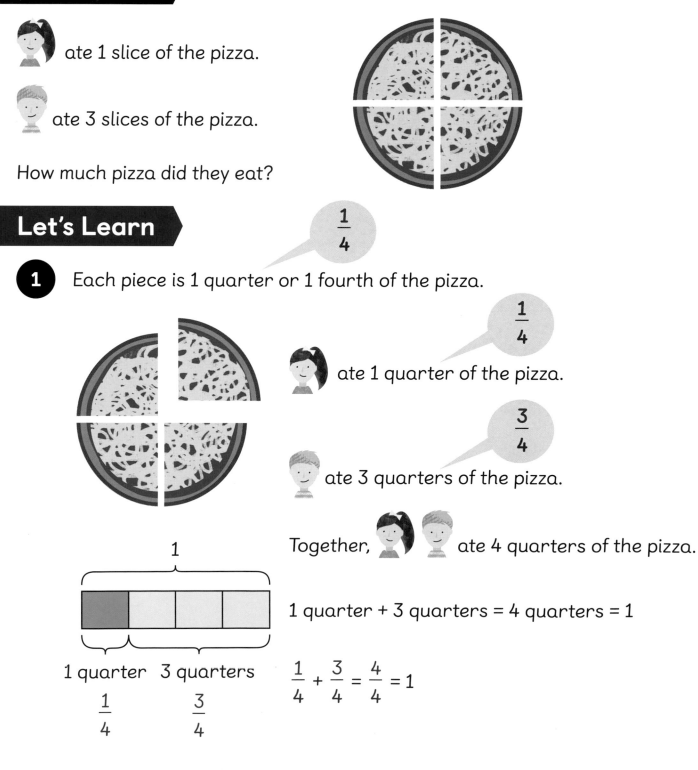

ate 1 slice of the pizza.

ate 3 slices of the pizza.

How much pizza did they eat?

Let's Learn

$\frac{1}{4}$

1 Each piece is 1 quarter or 1 fourth of the pizza.

$\frac{1}{4}$

ate 1 quarter of the pizza.

$\frac{3}{4}$

ate 3 quarters of the pizza.

Together, ate 4 quarters of the pizza.

1 quarter + 3 quarters = 4 quarters = 1

1

1 quarter   3 quarters

$\frac{1}{4}$ $\frac{3}{4}$

$\frac{1}{4} + \frac{3}{4} = \frac{4}{4} = 1$

2 Add $\frac{1}{6}$ and $\frac{3}{6}$.

$\frac{1}{6}$ $\frac{3}{6}$

?

$\frac{1}{6} + \frac{3}{6} = \frac{4}{6}$

1 sixth + 3 sixths = 4 sixths

3 Add $\frac{1}{7}$ and $\frac{3}{7}$.

1 seventh   3 sevenths

$\frac{1}{7} + \frac{3}{7} = $

1 seventh + 3 sevenths = seventh

1 = 7 sevenths

$\frac{1}{7}$? $\frac{3}{7}$

4 $\frac{1}{7} + \boxed{} + \frac{3}{7} = 1$

Guided Practice

1 Add.

(a) $\frac{1}{5} + \frac{3}{5} = $

(b) $\frac{2}{5} + \frac{3}{5} = $

(c) $\frac{4}{7} + \frac{3}{7} = $

2 Name 2 fractions that add up to 1.

$\boxed{} + \boxed{} = 1$

$\frac{1}{4}$ and $\frac{3}{4}$ make 1.

Complete Worksheet 4 – Page **94**

Subtracting Fractions

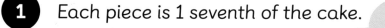

How much of the cake is left?

Two pieces have already been eaten. I am taking another piece.

Let's Learn

1 Each piece is 1 seventh of the cake.

$\dfrac{5}{7}$

There are 5 sevenths of the cake.

$\dfrac{1}{7}$

is taking 1 seventh of the cake.

5 sevenths − 1 seventh = 4 sevenths

$$\dfrac{5}{7} - \dfrac{1}{7} = \dfrac{4}{7}$$

4 sevenths of the cake is left.

2 Subtract $\dfrac{1}{9}$ from $\dfrac{5}{9}$.

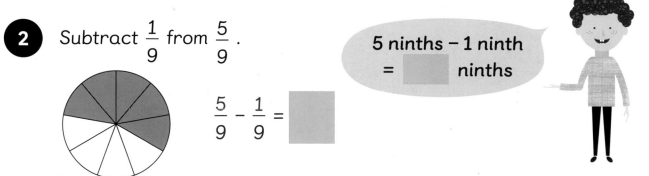

$$\dfrac{5}{9} - \dfrac{1}{9} = \boxed{}$$

5 ninths − 1 ninth = ☐ ninths

Guided Practice

1 Subtract.

(a)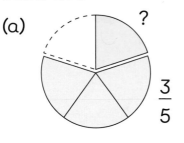

$$\frac{3}{5}$$

$$\frac{4}{5} - \frac{3}{5} = \boxed{}$$

(b)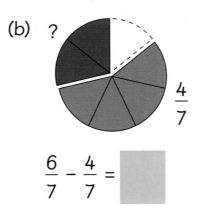

$$\frac{4}{7}$$

$$\frac{6}{7} - \frac{4}{7} = \boxed{}$$

2 Subtract.

(a)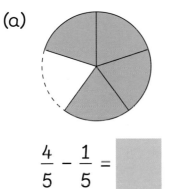

$$\frac{4}{5} - \frac{1}{5} = \boxed{}$$

(b)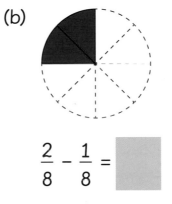

$$\frac{2}{8} - \frac{1}{8} = \boxed{}$$

(c)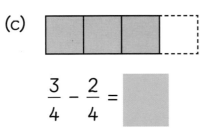

$$\frac{3}{4} - \frac{2}{4} = \boxed{}$$

(d)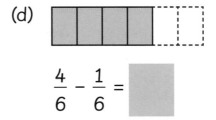

$$\frac{4}{6} - \frac{1}{6} = \boxed{}$$

3 Subtract.

(a) $\dfrac{6}{7} - \dfrac{3}{7} = \boxed{}$

(b) $\dfrac{6}{9} - \dfrac{2}{9} = \boxed{}$

(c) $\dfrac{7}{8} - \dfrac{1}{8} = \boxed{}$

Complete Worksheet **5** – Page **95**

Finding Equivalent Fractions

In Focus

This is my share.
I get 1 part out of 4 parts.

Is it possible to get more parts but still the same amount?

Let's Learn

1

I get 1 part.
Four of these make 1.

This is 1 fourth or 1 quarter.

$$\frac{1}{4}$$

2

This one part can be
cut into 2 equal parts.

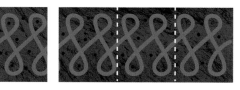

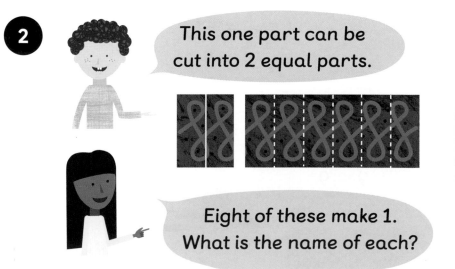

Eight of these make 1.
What is the name of each?

3 This one part can be cut into 4 equal parts.

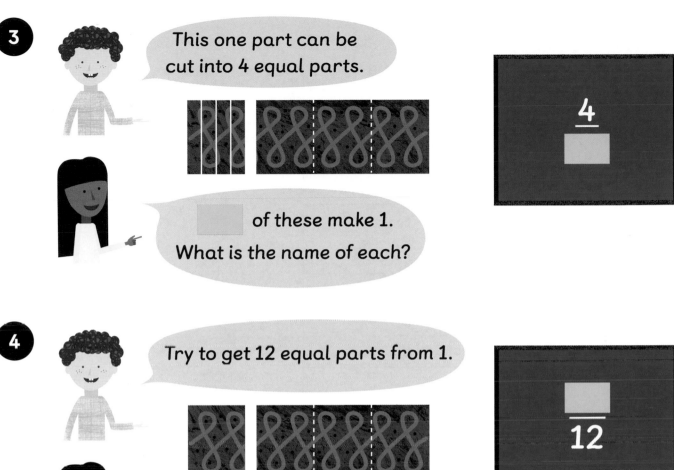

$$\frac{4}{\boxed{}}$$

[ ] of these make 1.
What is the name of each?

4 Try to get 12 equal parts from 1.

$$\frac{\boxed{}}{12}$$

This one piece is cut into [ ] equal parts to get twelfths.

5 What can you say about $\frac{1}{4}$, $\frac{2}{8}$ and $\frac{3}{12}$?

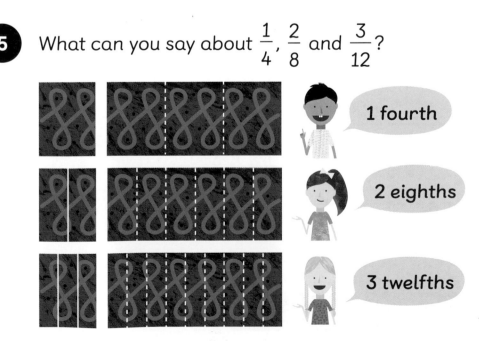

1 fourth

2 eighths

3 twelfths

Find the missing numbers.

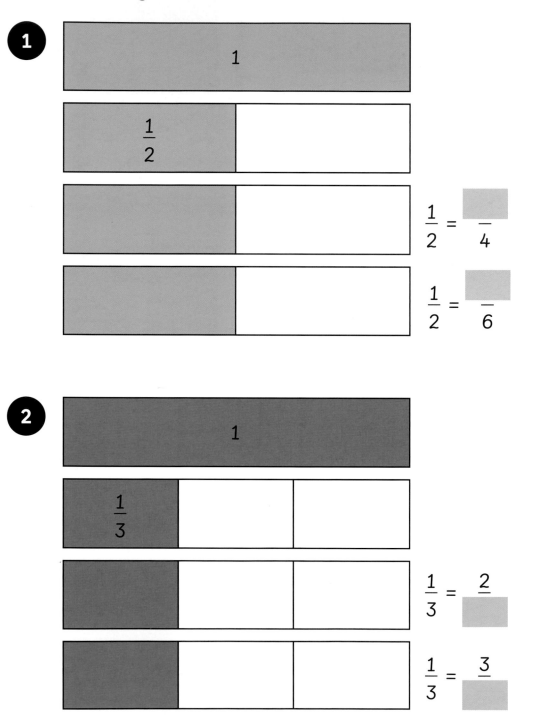

1

$$\frac{1}{2} = \frac{}{4}$$

$$\frac{1}{2} = \frac{}{6}$$

2

$$\frac{1}{3} = \frac{2}{}$$

$$\frac{1}{3} = \frac{3}{}$$

Complete Worksheet **6** – Page **96**

Finding Equivalent Fractions

In Focus

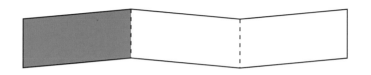

Sam thinks that $\frac{1}{3}$ can be written in other ways.

Is Sam correct?

Let's Learn

Fold a piece of paper into 3 equal parts. Shade 1 part.

How many parts are shaded? What is the name of each part?

1 part out of 3 equal parts is shaded.

$\frac{1}{3}$ of the paper is shaded.

$\frac{1}{3}$ ← numerator
← denominator

In $\frac{1}{3}$, 1 is the numerator and 3 is the denominator.

Are there other ways to write $\frac{1}{3}$?

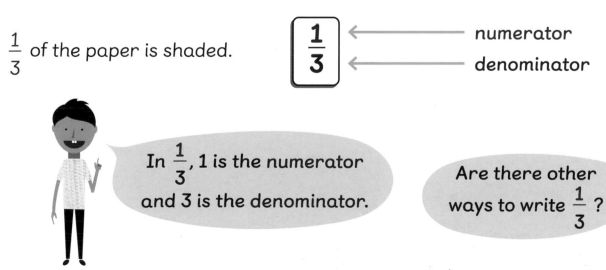

Fold the paper again to get 6 equal parts.

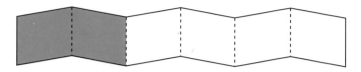

2 parts out of 6 equal parts are shaded now.

$\frac{2}{6}$ of the paper is shaded.

Fold the paper to get 12 equal parts.

How many parts are shaded?
What is the name of each part?

The fractions $\frac{1}{3}$, $\frac{2}{6}$ and $\frac{4}{12}$ have different numerators and denominators.
But they are equal.

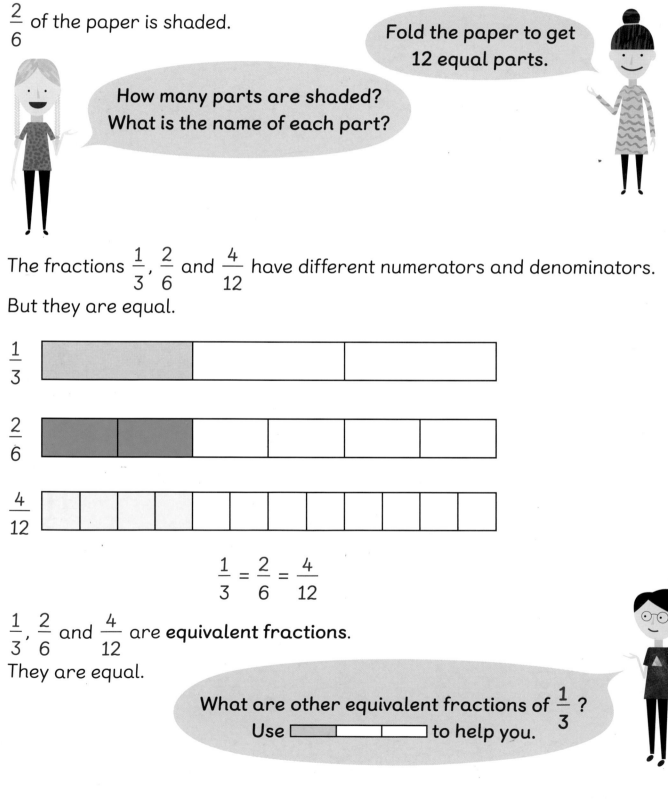

$$\frac{1}{3} = \frac{2}{6} = \frac{4}{12}$$

$\frac{1}{3}$, $\frac{2}{6}$ and $\frac{4}{12}$ are **equivalent fractions**.
They are equal.

What are other equivalent fractions of $\frac{1}{3}$?
Use ▭ to help you.

1

1			
$\frac{1}{2}$		$\frac{1}{2}$	
$\frac{1}{4}$	$\frac{1}{4}$	$\frac{1}{4}$	$\frac{1}{4}$
$\frac{1}{8}$ $\frac{1}{8}$	$\frac{1}{8}$ $\frac{1}{8}$	$\frac{1}{8}$ $\frac{1}{8}$	$\frac{1}{8}$ $\frac{1}{8}$

Look at the diagram.
Find the missing numerators.

(a) $1 = \dfrac{}{4}$

(b) $\dfrac{1}{2} = \dfrac{}{8}$

(c) $\dfrac{3}{4} = \dfrac{}{8}$

2   The 3 figures are cut into equal parts.
What fraction of each figure is shaded?

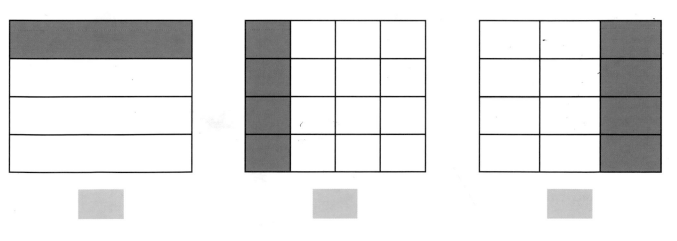

Are the fractions equivalent?
Why or why not?

Complete Worksheet 7 – Page 97

Finding Equivalent Fractions

In Focus

Fold the paper strips to show halves, quarters and eighths.

Can you also show sixths?

Let's Learn

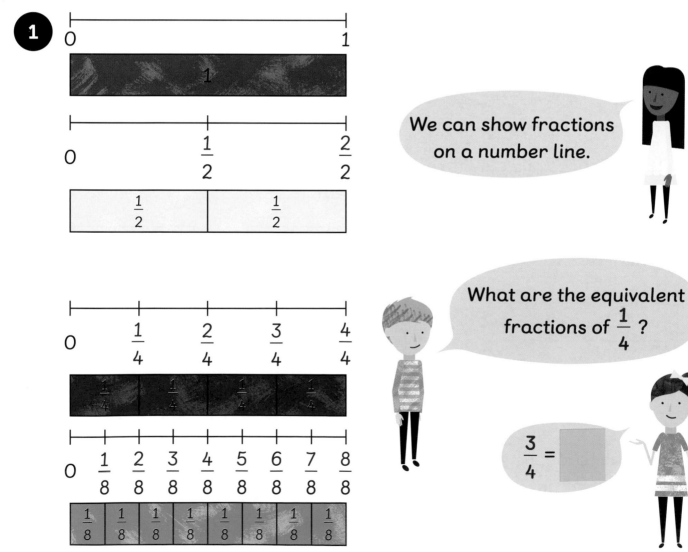

1

0 ——————————————— 1

1

0 ———— $\frac{1}{2}$ ———— $\frac{2}{2}$

| $\frac{1}{2}$ | $\frac{1}{2}$ |

We can show fractions on a number line.

0 — $\frac{1}{4}$ — $\frac{2}{4}$ — $\frac{3}{4}$ — $\frac{4}{4}$

| $\frac{1}{4}$ | $\frac{1}{4}$ | $\frac{1}{4}$ | $\frac{1}{4}$ |

0 — $\frac{1}{8}$ — $\frac{2}{8}$ — $\frac{3}{8}$ — $\frac{4}{8}$ — $\frac{5}{8}$ — $\frac{6}{8}$ — $\frac{7}{8}$ — $\frac{8}{8}$

| $\frac{1}{8}$ | $\frac{1}{8}$ | $\frac{1}{8}$ | $\frac{1}{8}$ | $\frac{1}{8}$ | $\frac{1}{8}$ | $\frac{1}{8}$ | $\frac{1}{8}$ |

What are the equivalent fractions of $\frac{1}{4}$?

$\frac{3}{4} =$

$$\frac{1}{2} = \frac{2}{4} = \frac{4}{8}$$

$\frac{1}{2}$, $\frac{2}{4}$ and $\frac{4}{8}$ are equivalent fractions.

They are equal.

2

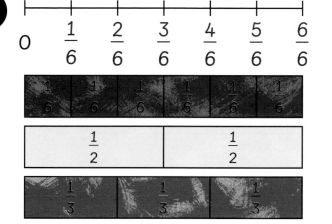

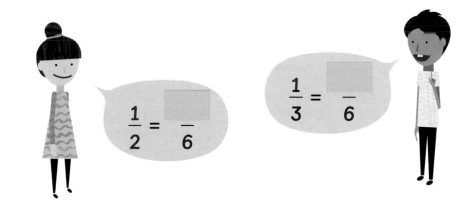

$\frac{1}{2} = \frac{\square}{6}$

$\frac{1}{3} = \frac{\square}{6}$

Can you name more pairs of equivalent fractions?

Guided Practice

1 Complete each of the following number lines.

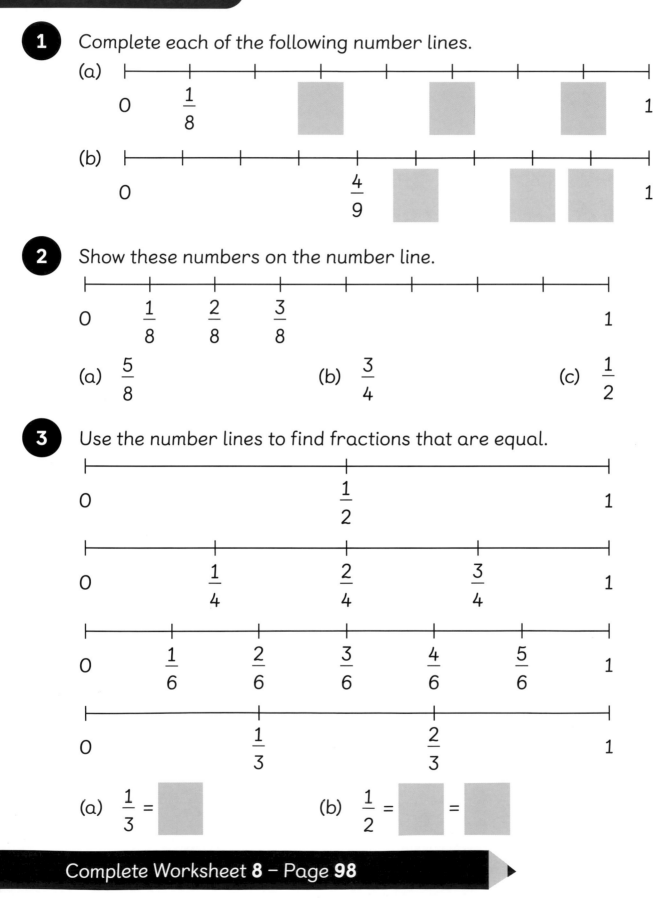

(a) 0 $\dfrac{1}{8}$ 1

(b) 0 $\dfrac{4}{9}$ 1

2 Show these numbers on the number line.

0    $\dfrac{1}{8}$ $\dfrac{2}{8}$ $\dfrac{3}{8}$ 1

(a) $\dfrac{5}{8}$ (b) $\dfrac{3}{4}$ (c) $\dfrac{1}{2}$

3 Use the number lines to find fractions that are equal.

0                  $\dfrac{1}{2}$ 1

0      $\dfrac{1}{4}$ $\dfrac{2}{4}$ $\dfrac{3}{4}$ 1

0    $\dfrac{1}{6}$ $\dfrac{2}{6}$ $\dfrac{3}{6}$ $\dfrac{4}{6}$ $\dfrac{5}{6}$ 1

0         $\dfrac{1}{3}$ $\dfrac{2}{3}$ 1

(a) $\dfrac{1}{3} = \quad\Box$ (b) $\dfrac{1}{2} = \quad\Box\ = \quad\Box$

Complete Worksheet 8 – Page 98

Finding Equivalent Fractions

In Focus

What are the equivalent fractions of $\frac{1}{2}$?
Help Charles see a pattern.

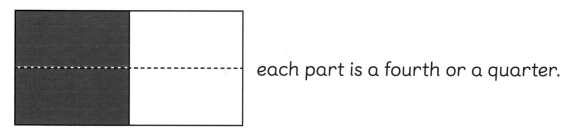

$$\frac{1}{2} = ?$$

Let's Learn

 1

This is $\frac{1}{2}$.

When the shaded part becomes 2 equal parts,

each part is a fourth or a quarter.

$$\frac{1}{2} = \frac{2}{4}$$

 2 When the shaded part becomes 4 equal parts,

each part is an eighth.

$$\frac{1}{2} = \frac{4}{8}$$

3 When the shaded part becomes 3 equal parts,

each part is a sixth. $\dfrac{1}{2} = \dfrac{3}{6}$

4 $\dfrac{1}{2} = \dfrac{2}{4}$

$\dfrac{1}{2} = \dfrac{3}{6}$

$\dfrac{1}{2} = \dfrac{4}{8}$

What do you notice?

What do you notice about numerators and denominators of equivalent fractions?

$$\dfrac{1}{2} = \dfrac{2}{4} \qquad \dfrac{1}{2} = \dfrac{3}{6} \qquad \dfrac{1}{2} = \dfrac{4}{8}$$

$$\times 2 \qquad \times 3 \qquad \times 4$$

$$\dfrac{1}{2} = \dfrac{2}{4} \qquad \dfrac{1}{2} = \dfrac{3}{6} \qquad \dfrac{1}{2} = \dfrac{4}{8}$$

$$\times 2 \qquad \times 3 \qquad \times 4$$

5

$\times 5$

$$\dfrac{1}{2} = \dfrac{\square}{\square}$$

$\times 5$

$$\dfrac{1}{2} = \dfrac{5}{10}$$

Is this correct?

Guided Practice

1 Find the missing numerators and denominators.

(a)

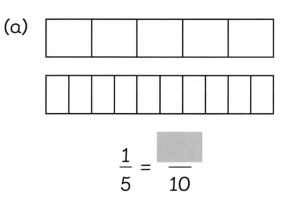

$$\frac{1}{5} = \frac{\boxed{}}{10}$$

(b)

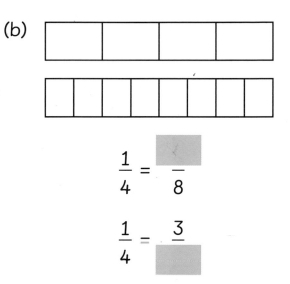

$$\frac{1}{4} = \frac{\boxed{}}{8}$$

$$\frac{1}{4} = \frac{3}{\boxed{}}$$

2 Amira finds equal fractions this way.

Use Amira's method to find the missing numerators and denominators.

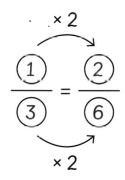

$$\overset{\times 2}{\underset{\times 2}{\frac{①}{③} = \frac{②}{⑥}}}$$

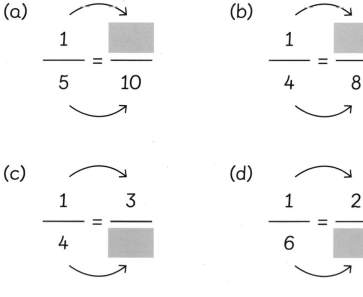

(a)

$$\frac{1}{5} = \frac{\boxed{}}{10}$$

(b)

$$\frac{1}{4} = \frac{\boxed{}}{8}$$

(c)

$$\frac{1}{4} = \frac{3}{\boxed{}}$$

(d)

$$\frac{1}{6} = \frac{2}{\boxed{}}$$

Complete Worksheet 9 – Page 99

Finding Equivalent Fractions

In Focus

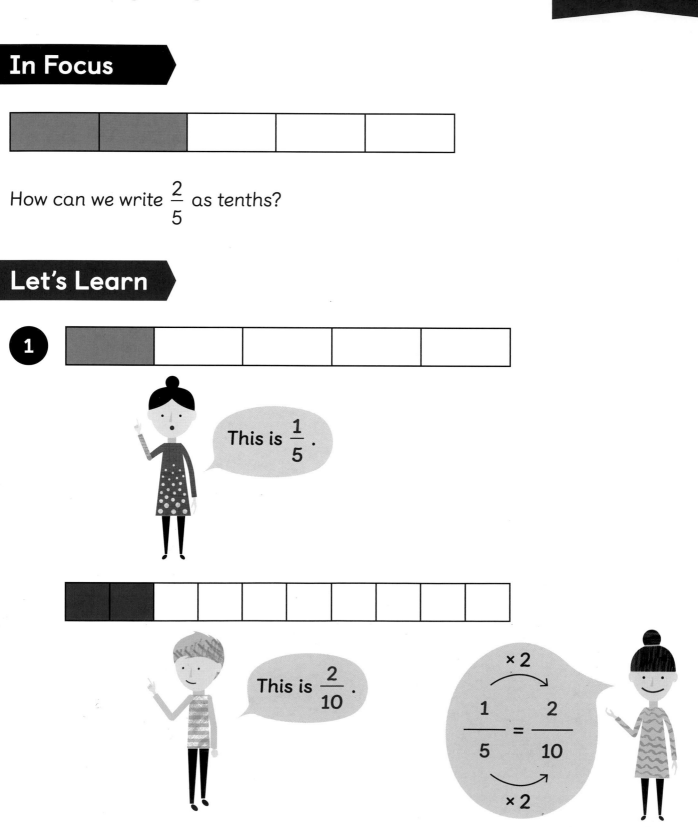

How can we write $\frac{2}{5}$ as tenths?

Let's Learn

1

This is $\frac{1}{5}$.

This is $\frac{2}{10}$.

$$\frac{1}{5} = \frac{2}{10}$$
×2
×2

2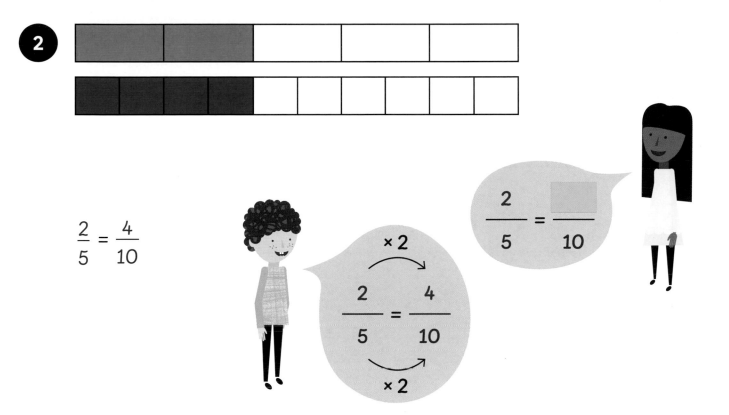

$$\frac{2}{5} = \frac{4}{10}$$

$$\frac{2}{5} \overset{\times 2}{\underset{\times 2}{=}} \frac{4}{10}$$

$$\frac{2}{5} = \frac{\boxed{}}{10}$$

3 Find the missing numerator.

$$\frac{2}{3} = \frac{\boxed{}}{9}$$

$$\frac{2}{3} = \frac{\boxed{}}{9}$$

Guided Practice

1 Find the missing numerators.

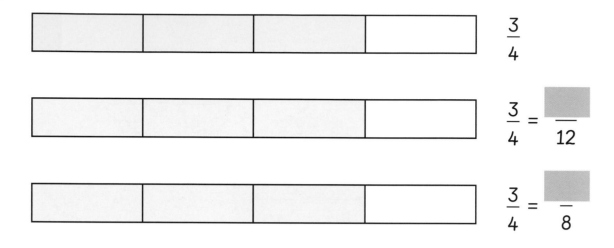

$\dfrac{3}{4}$

$\dfrac{3}{4} = \dfrac{\boxed{}}{12}$

$\dfrac{3}{4} = \dfrac{\boxed{}}{8}$

2 Find the missing numerators and denominators.

(a) $\dfrac{2}{5} = \dfrac{\boxed{}}{10}$

(b) $\dfrac{5}{6} = \dfrac{\boxed{}}{12}$

(c) $\dfrac{2}{3} = \dfrac{\boxed{}}{\boxed{}}$

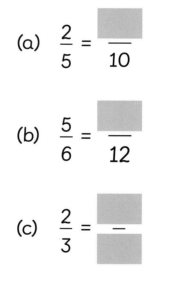

The denominator is more than 10 but less than 15.

Complete Worksheet 10 – Page 100

Finding Equivalent Fractions

In Focus

Is it possible to write $\dfrac{2}{3}$ as $\dfrac{8}{\boxed{}}$?

Let's Learn

Let's put these 2 parts into 8 equal parts.

The 2 parts become 8 equal parts.
Each part is a twelfth.

$$\dfrac{2}{3} = \dfrac{8}{\boxed{12}}$$

$$\dfrac{2}{3} = \dfrac{8}{\boxed{12}}$$

Guided Practice

1 Find the missing denominator.

$$\dfrac{3}{5}$$

$$\dfrac{3}{5} = \dfrac{6}{\boxed{}}$$

2 Find the missing denominator.

(a) $\dfrac{1}{2} = \dfrac{6}{\boxed{}}$

(b) $\dfrac{2}{3} = \dfrac{6}{\boxed{}}$

(c) $\dfrac{3}{4} = \dfrac{6}{\boxed{}}$

Complete Worksheet **11** – Page **101**

Finding the Simplest Fraction

In Focus

A cake is cut into 12 pieces.

Ruby: I take 3 pieces.

Ravi: I take 4 pieces.

Lulu: I take 2 pieces.

Can we figure out what fraction of the cake each person takes?

Let's Learn

1

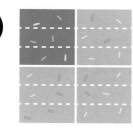

$$3 \text{ pieces} = \frac{3}{12}$$

$$3 \text{ pieces} = \frac{1}{4}$$

$$\frac{3}{12} = \frac{1}{4}$$

Ruby takes $\frac{1}{4}$ of the cake.

When 3 pieces become 1 part, 12 pieces become 4 parts.

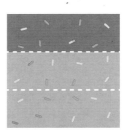

4 pieces = $\dfrac{4}{12}$

1 piece = $\dfrac{1}{3}$

When 4 pieces become 1 part, 12 pieces become 3 parts.

$\dfrac{4}{12} = \dfrac{1}{3}$

Ravi takes $\dfrac{1}{3}$ of the cake.

2 pieces = $\dfrac{2}{12}$

1 piece = $\dfrac{1}{\boxed{}}$

$\dfrac{2}{12} = \dfrac{1}{\boxed{}}$

When 2 pieces become 1 part, 12 pieces become 6 parts.

Lulu takes $\dfrac{1}{\boxed{}}$ of the cake.

Guided Practice

Write each fraction in its simplest form.

1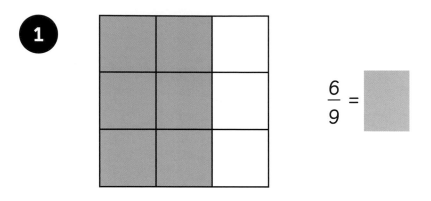

$$\frac{6}{9} = \boxed{}$$

2 (a) $\dfrac{4}{12} = \boxed{}$

(b) $\dfrac{4}{10} = \boxed{}$

(c) $\dfrac{4}{6} = \boxed{}$

Complete Worksheet **12** – Page **102**

Finding the Simplest Fraction

In Focus

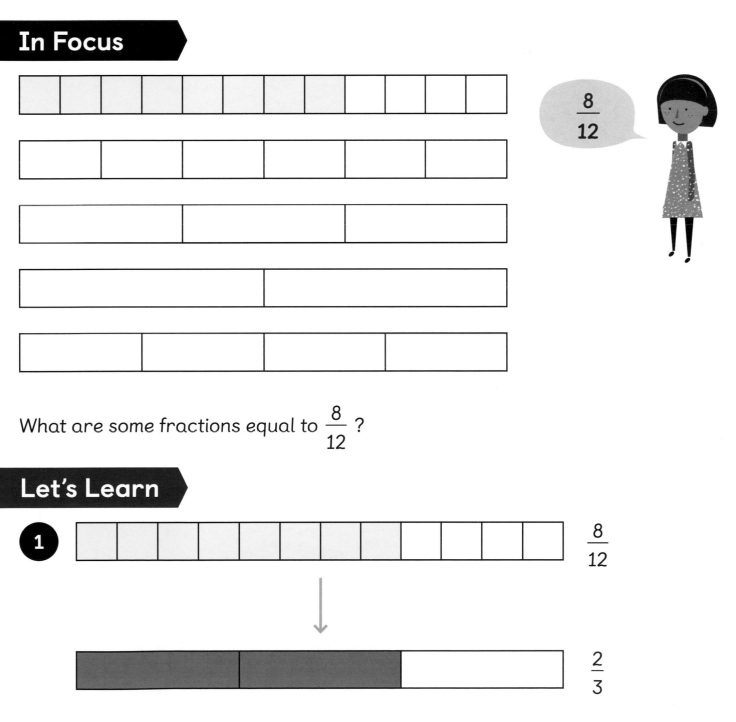

$\dfrac{8}{12}$

What are some fractions equal to $\dfrac{8}{12}$?

Let's Learn

1

$\dfrac{8}{12}$

$\dfrac{2}{3}$

$\dfrac{8}{12} = \dfrac{2}{3}$

What do you notice?

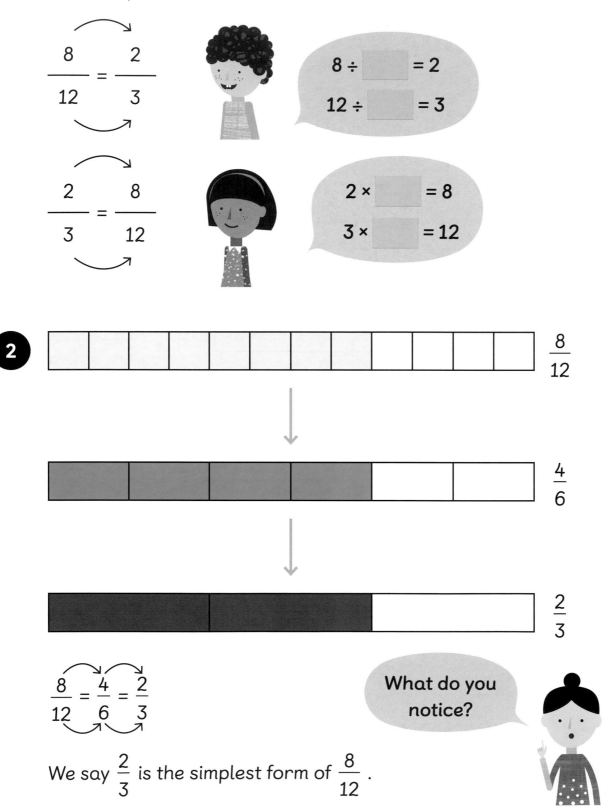

$$\frac{8}{12} = \frac{2}{3}$$

$8 \div \boxed{} = 2$

$12 \div \boxed{} = 3$

$$\frac{2}{3} = \frac{8}{12}$$

$2 \times \boxed{} = 8$

$3 \times \boxed{} = 12$

2

$\frac{8}{12}$

$\frac{4}{6}$

$\frac{2}{3}$

$$\frac{8}{12} = \frac{4}{6} = \frac{2}{3}$$

What do you notice?

We say $\frac{2}{3}$ is the simplest form of $\frac{8}{12}$.

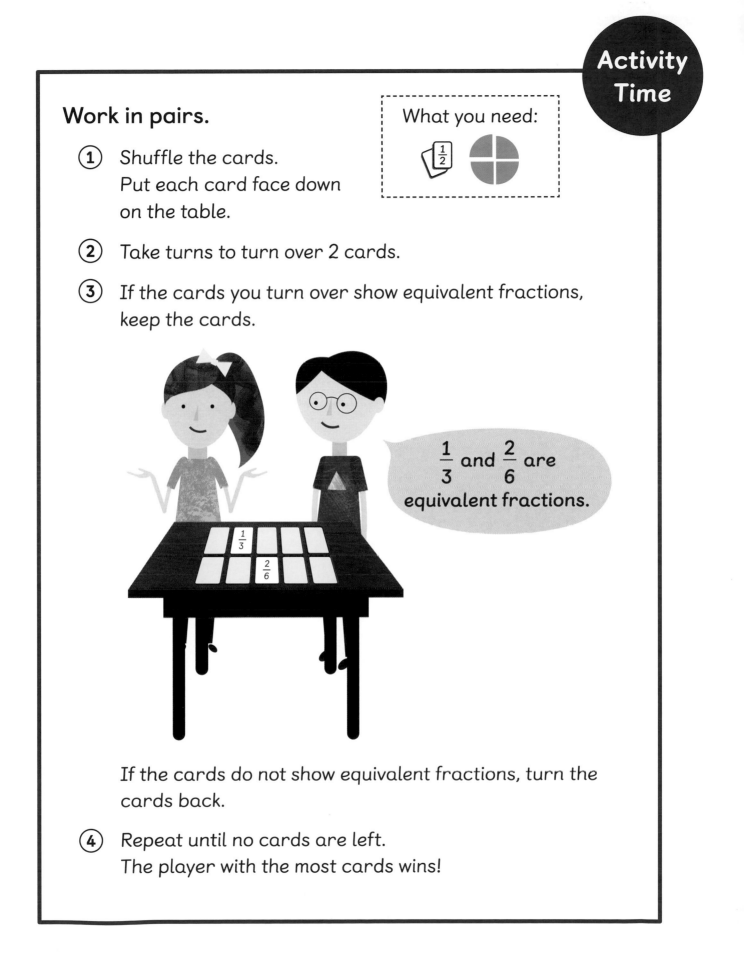

Activity Time

Work in pairs.

What you need:

① Shuffle the cards.
Put each card face down on the table.

② Take turns to turn over 2 cards.

③ If the cards you turn over show equivalent fractions, keep the cards.

$\frac{1}{3}$ and $\frac{2}{6}$ are equivalent fractions.

If the cards do not show equivalent fractions, turn the cards back.

④ Repeat until no cards are left.
The player with the most cards wins!

Guided Practice

1 Give three fractions that are equal to $\dfrac{6}{12}$.

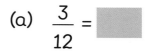

2 Write each fraction in its simplest form.

(a) $\dfrac{3}{12} = $ ▢

(b) $\dfrac{9}{12} = $ ▢

(c) $\dfrac{8}{12} = $ ▢

Complete Worksheet 13 – Page 103

Finding Equivalent Fractions

In Focus

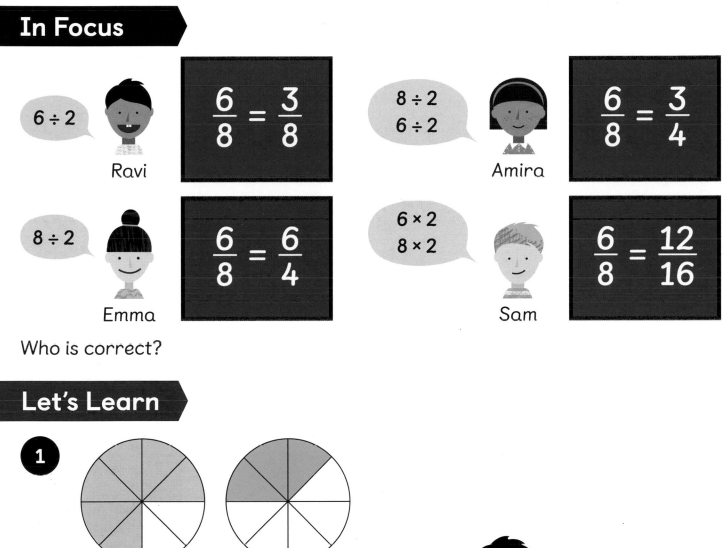

Ravi: $6 \div 2$ — $\dfrac{6}{8} = \dfrac{3}{8}$

Amira: $8 \div 2$, $6 \div 2$ — $\dfrac{6}{8} = \dfrac{3}{4}$

Emma: $8 \div 2$ — $\dfrac{6}{8} = \dfrac{6}{4}$

Sam: 6×2, 8×2 — $\dfrac{6}{8} = \dfrac{12}{16}$

Who is correct?

Let's Learn

1

$\dfrac{6}{8}$ $\qquad$ $\dfrac{3}{8}$

$\dfrac{6}{8} > \dfrac{3}{8}$

$\dfrac{6}{8}$ is more than $\dfrac{3}{8}$.

$\dfrac{6}{8}$ is not equal to $\dfrac{3}{8}$.

Ravi is not correct.

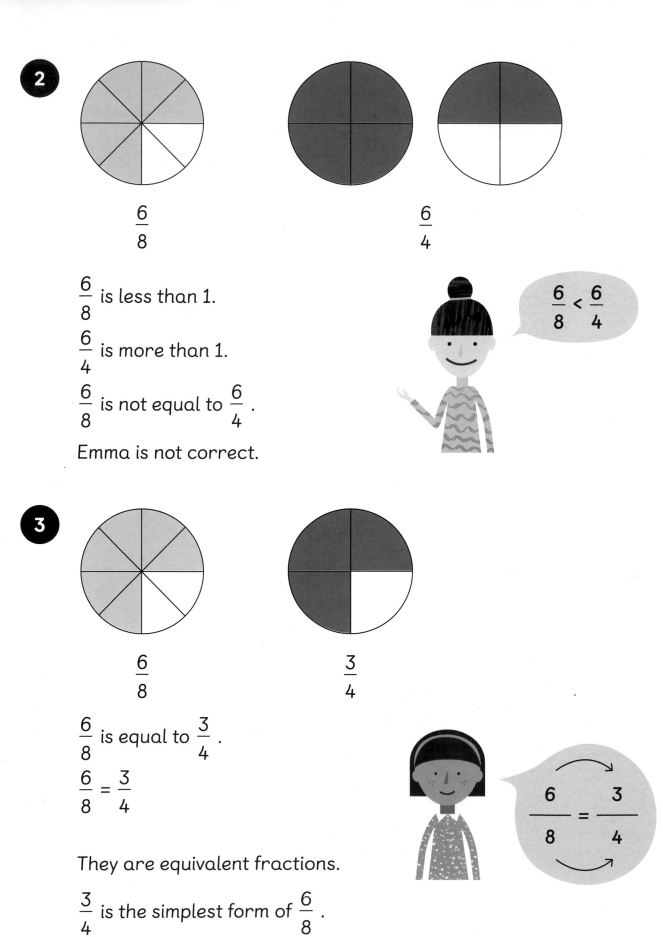

2

$$\frac{6}{8}$$

$$\frac{6}{4}$$

$\frac{6}{8}$ is less than 1.

$\frac{6}{4}$ is more than 1.

$\frac{6}{8}$ is not equal to $\frac{6}{4}$.

Emma is not correct.

$$\frac{6}{8} < \frac{6}{4}$$

3

$$\frac{6}{8}$$

$$\frac{3}{4}$$

$\frac{6}{8}$ is equal to $\frac{3}{4}$.

$$\frac{6}{8} = \frac{3}{4}$$

They are equivalent fractions.

$\frac{3}{4}$ is the simplest form of $\frac{6}{8}$.

Amira is correct.

$$\frac{6}{8} = \frac{3}{4}$$

4

$\dfrac{6}{8}$

$\dfrac{12}{16}$

Is $\dfrac{6}{8}$ the simplest form?

$\dfrac{6}{8}$ is equal to $\dfrac{12}{16}$.

$\dfrac{6}{8} = \dfrac{12}{16}$

$\dfrac{6}{8} = \dfrac{12}{16}$

They are equivalent fractions.
Sam is correct.

Guided Practice

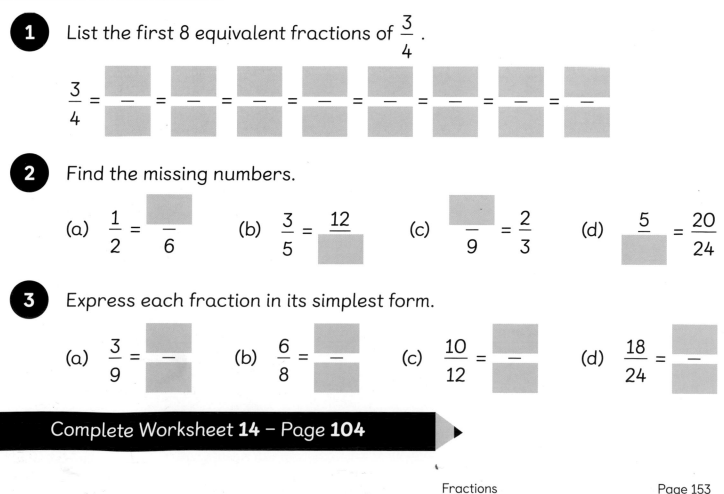

1 List the first 8 equivalent fractions of $\dfrac{3}{4}$.

$\dfrac{3}{4} = \dfrac{\square}{\square} = \dfrac{\square}{\square} = \dfrac{\square}{\square} = \dfrac{\square}{\square} = \dfrac{\square}{\square} = \dfrac{\square}{\square} = \dfrac{\square}{\square} = \dfrac{\square}{\square}$

2 Find the missing numbers.

(a) $\dfrac{1}{2} = \dfrac{\square}{6}$

(b) $\dfrac{3}{5} = \dfrac{12}{\square}$

(c) $\dfrac{\square}{9} = \dfrac{2}{3}$

(d) $\dfrac{5}{\square} = \dfrac{20}{24}$

3 Express each fraction in its simplest form.

(a) $\dfrac{3}{9} = \dfrac{\square}{\square}$

(b) $\dfrac{6}{8} = \dfrac{\square}{\square}$

(c) $\dfrac{10}{12} = \dfrac{\square}{\square}$

(d) $\dfrac{18}{24} = \dfrac{\square}{\square}$

Complete Worksheet **14** – Page **104**

Comparing Fractions

In Focus

Sam and Ruby each have a paper circle of the same size.

Sam cuts the circle into 2 equal parts and keeps 1 part.
Ruby cuts the circle into 4 equal parts and keeps 1 part.
Who keeps a bigger part, Sam or Ruby?

Let's Learn

1 Which is greater, $\frac{1}{2}$ or $\frac{1}{4}$?

Use ⊕ or 🂠 to show each fraction and compare.

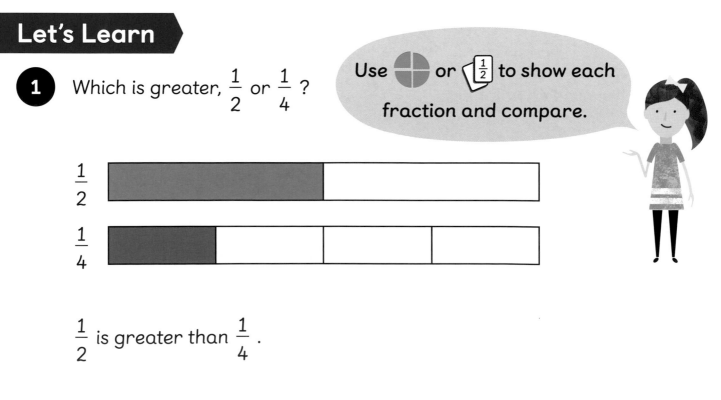

$\frac{1}{2}$ is greater than $\frac{1}{4}$.

2

$\frac{1}{4}$

$\frac{1}{2}$

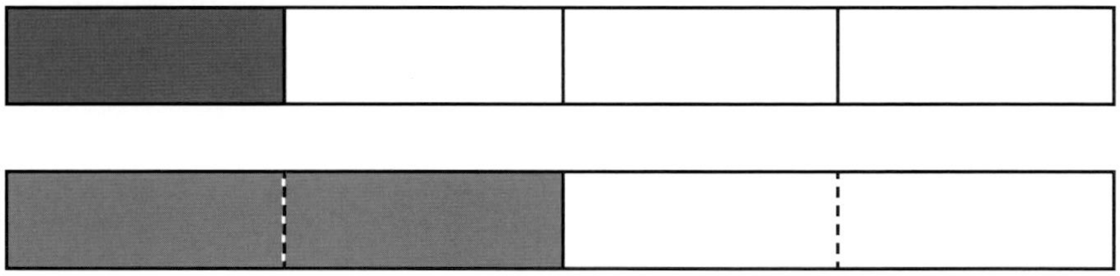

$\frac{1}{2} = \frac{2}{4}$

So, $\frac{1}{2}$ is greater than $\frac{1}{4}$.

2 quarters is greater than 1 quarter.

3 Ruby cuts 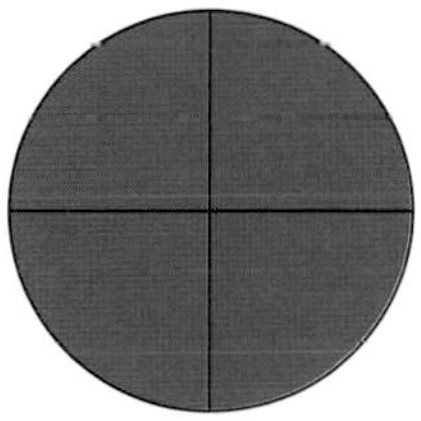 into 4 equal parts.

Sam cuts 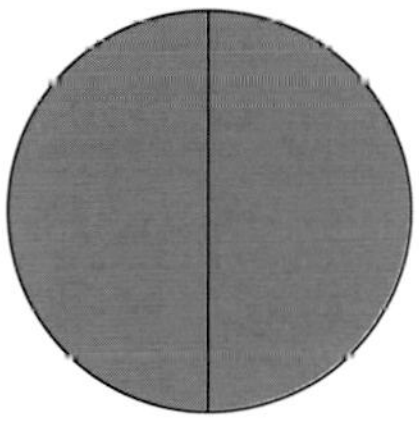 into 2 equal parts.

The parts Ruby gets are smaller.

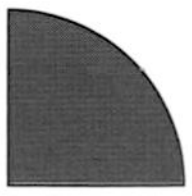

is less than  .

So, $\frac{1}{4}$ is less than $\frac{1}{2}$.

$\frac{1}{2}$ is greater than $\frac{1}{4}$.

Guided Practice

1 Which number is greater?

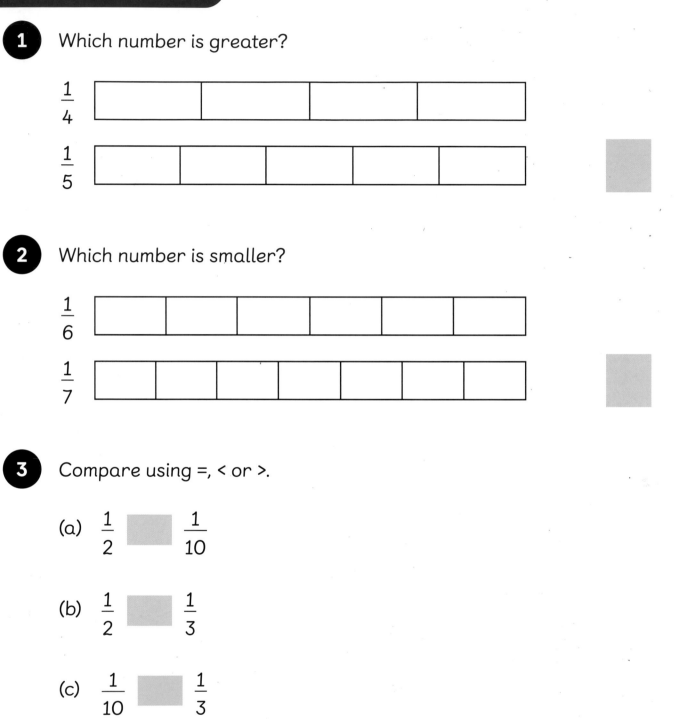

$\frac{1}{4}$

$\frac{1}{5}$

2 Which number is smaller?

$\frac{1}{6}$

$\frac{1}{7}$

3 Compare using =, < or >.

(a) $\frac{1}{2}$ ▢ $\frac{1}{10}$

(b) $\frac{1}{2}$ ▢ $\frac{1}{3}$

(c) $\frac{1}{10}$ ▢ $\frac{1}{3}$

Complete Worksheet **15** – Page **105 - 106**

Comparing Fractions

In Focus

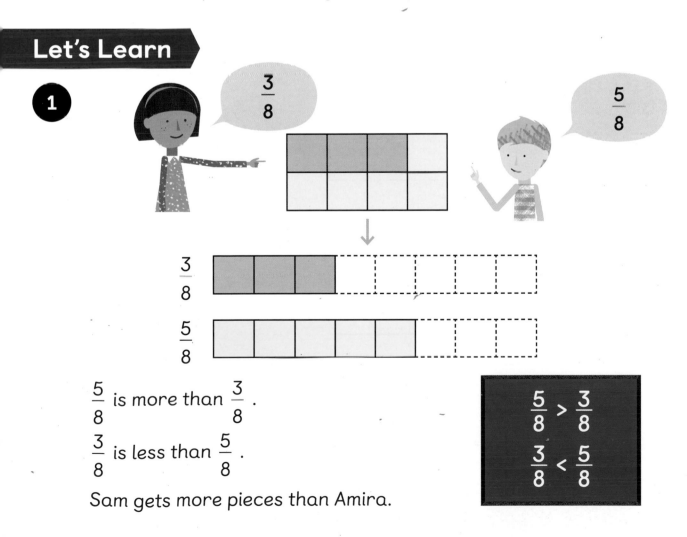

I get 3 pieces.

Amira

I get 5 pieces.

Sam

Who gets more?

Are there other ways for Sam to get more pieces than Amira?

Let's Learn

1

$\frac{3}{8}$

$\frac{5}{8}$

$\frac{3}{8}$

$\frac{5}{8}$

$\frac{5}{8}$ is more than $\frac{3}{8}$.

$\frac{3}{8}$ is less than $\frac{5}{8}$.

Sam gets more pieces than Amira.

$$\frac{5}{8} > \frac{3}{8}$$

$$\frac{3}{8} < \frac{5}{8}$$

2

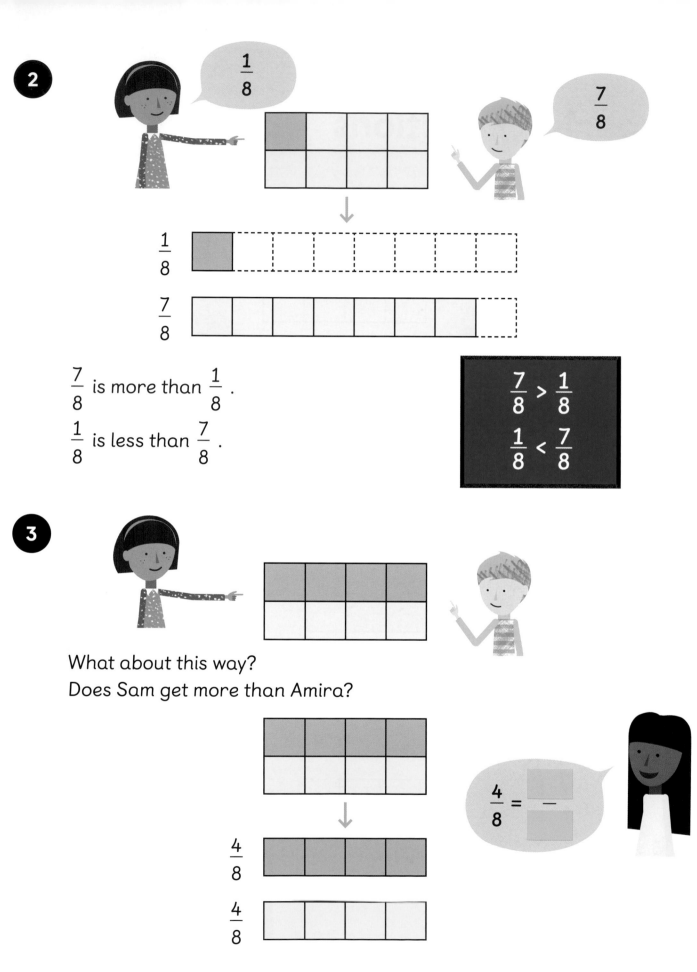

$\dfrac{7}{8}$ is more than $\dfrac{1}{8}$.

$\dfrac{1}{8}$ is less than $\dfrac{7}{8}$.

$$\dfrac{7}{8} > \dfrac{1}{8}$$

$$\dfrac{1}{8} < \dfrac{7}{8}$$

3

What about this way?
Does Sam get more than Amira?

$\dfrac{4}{8} = \dfrac{}{}$

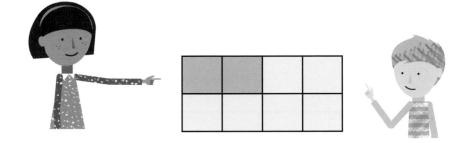

What about this way?

Does Sam get more than Amira?

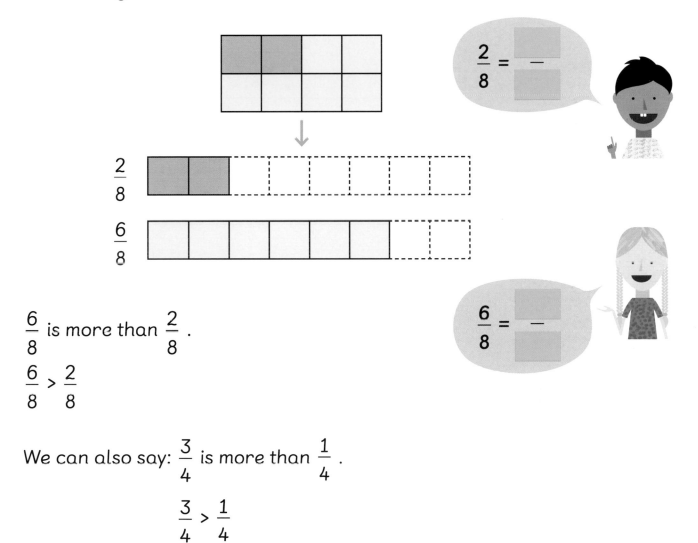

$\frac{2}{8} = \frac{\boxed{}}{\boxed{}}$

$\frac{6}{8} = \frac{\boxed{}}{\boxed{}}$

$\frac{6}{8}$ is more than $\frac{2}{8}$.

$\frac{6}{8} > \frac{2}{8}$

We can also say: $\frac{3}{4}$ is more than $\frac{1}{4}$.

$\frac{3}{4} > \frac{1}{4}$

Guided Practice

1 Which number is greater?

$\dfrac{1}{6}$

$\dfrac{5}{6}$

2 Which number is smaller?

$\dfrac{4}{9}$

$\dfrac{7}{9}$

3 Compare using =, < or >.

(a) $\dfrac{2}{7}$ ☐ $\dfrac{5}{7}$

(b) $\dfrac{4}{5}$ ☐ $\dfrac{3}{5}$

(c) $\dfrac{8}{11}$ ☐ $\dfrac{7}{11}$

(d) $\dfrac{2}{7}$ ☐ $\dfrac{7}{2}$

Complete Worksheet 16 – Page 107 - 108

Comparing Fractions

In Focus

Which number is greater,
$\frac{3}{4}$ or $\frac{3}{5}$?

Let's Learn

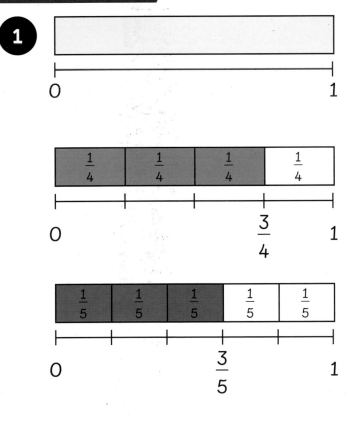

$\frac{3}{4}$ is greater than $\frac{3}{5}$.

This is 1.

This is $\frac{3}{4}$.

This is $\frac{3}{5}$.

$\frac{3}{4} > \frac{3}{5}$

2 Compare $\dfrac{2}{3}$ and $\dfrac{2}{5}$.

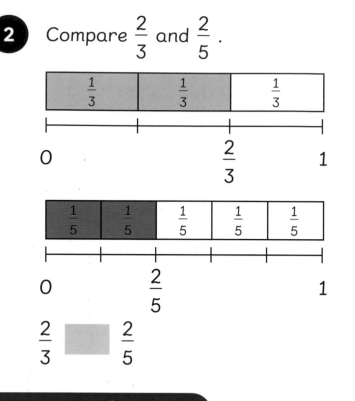

| $\dfrac{1}{3}$ | $\dfrac{1}{3}$ | $\dfrac{1}{3}$ |

0          $\dfrac{2}{3}$ 1

| $\dfrac{1}{5}$ | $\dfrac{1}{5}$ | $\dfrac{1}{5}$ | $\dfrac{1}{5}$ | $\dfrac{1}{5}$ |

0     $\dfrac{2}{5}$ 1

$\dfrac{2}{3}$ ☐ $\dfrac{2}{5}$

=, > or <

Guided Practice

1 Which number is greater?

$\dfrac{2}{5}$

$\dfrac{2}{7}$

2 Which number is smaller?

$\dfrac{3}{4}$

$\dfrac{3}{5}$

3 Compare using =, > or <.

(a) $\dfrac{1}{4}$ ☐ $\dfrac{1}{6}$ (b) $\dfrac{3}{4}$ ☐ $\dfrac{3}{7}$ (c) $\dfrac{7}{8}$ ☐ $\dfrac{5}{9}$

Complete Worksheet 17 – Page 109 - 110

Adding Fractions

In Focus

I took $\frac{1}{6}$ of the sweets in the box.

I took $\frac{3}{6}$ of the sweets in the box.

Charles

Ruby

What fraction of the sweets did Charles and Ruby take altogether?

Let's Learn

1

$\frac{1}{6}$

$\frac{3}{6}$

Isn't $\frac{3}{6} = \frac{1}{2}$?

1 sixth + 3 sixths = 4 sixths

$$\frac{1}{6} + \frac{3}{6} = \frac{4}{6}$$

Charles and Ruby took $\frac{4}{6}$ of the sweets.

2 Add $\frac{1}{6}$ and $\frac{3}{6}$.

$$\frac{1}{6} \qquad \frac{3}{6}$$

1 sixth + 3 sixths = 4 sixths

?

$$\frac{1}{6} + \frac{3}{6} = \frac{4}{6}$$

$$\frac{4}{6} = \frac{\boxed{}}{3}$$

So, $\frac{1}{6} + \frac{3}{6} = \frac{2}{3}$

3 $\frac{1}{6} + \frac{2}{6} = \boxed{}$

$$\frac{1}{6} \qquad \frac{2}{6}$$

add $\frac{2}{6}$

$$0 \qquad \frac{1}{6} \qquad \frac{2}{6} \qquad \frac{3}{6} \qquad \frac{4}{6} \qquad \frac{5}{6} \qquad 1$$

Guided Practice

1 Add.

(a)

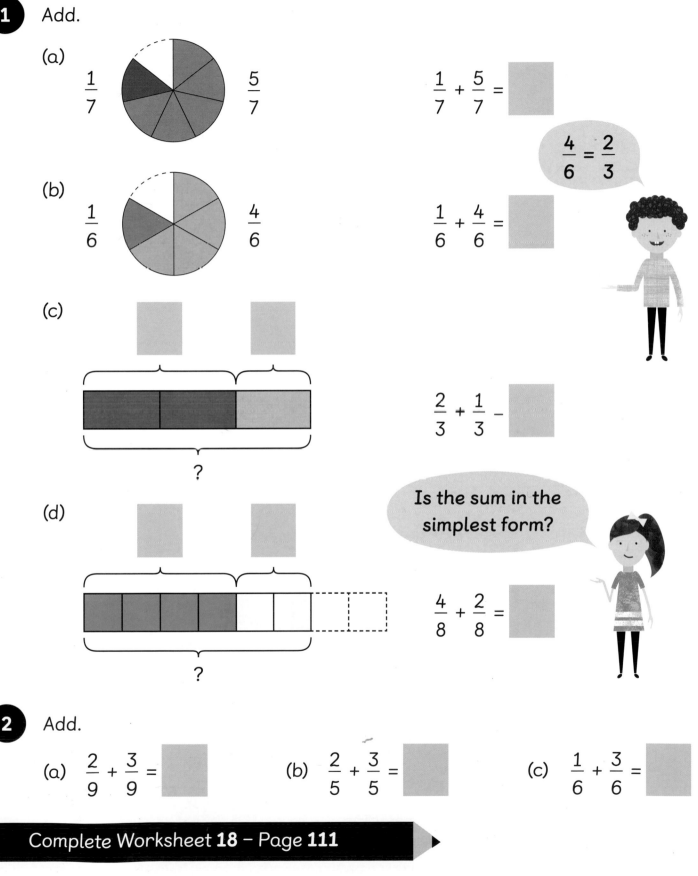

$\dfrac{1}{7}$ $\dfrac{5}{7}$

$\dfrac{1}{7} + \dfrac{5}{7} = $ ☐

$\dfrac{4}{6} = \dfrac{2}{3}$

(b)

$\dfrac{1}{6}$ $\dfrac{4}{6}$

$\dfrac{1}{6} + \dfrac{4}{6} = $ ☐

(c)

☐   ☐

?

$\dfrac{2}{3} + \dfrac{1}{3} = $ ☐

Is the sum in the simplest form?

(d)

☐   ☐

?

$\dfrac{4}{8} + \dfrac{2}{8} = $ ☐

2 Add.

(a) $\dfrac{2}{9} + \dfrac{3}{9} = $ ☐

(b) $\dfrac{2}{5} + \dfrac{3}{5} = $ ☐

(c) $\dfrac{1}{6} + \dfrac{3}{6} = $ ☐

Complete Worksheet **18** – Page **111**

Subtracting Fractions

In Focus

What fraction of the box of cupcakes remains after 5 cupcakes are eaten?

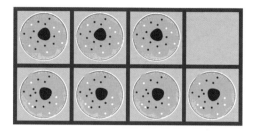

Let's Learn

 Each piece is 1 eighth of the box of cupcakes.

7 eighths

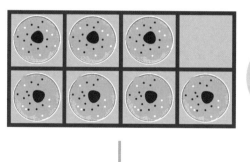

This is $\dfrac{7}{8}$ of a box of cupcakes.

5 eighths are eaten

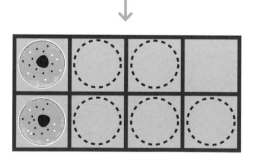

7 eighths − 5 eighths = 2 eighths

$$\frac{7}{8} \quad - \quad \frac{5}{8} \quad = \quad \frac{2}{8}$$

$\dfrac{1}{4}$ of the box of cupcakes remains.

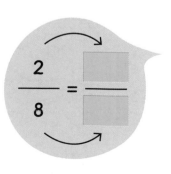

2 Subtract $\frac{3}{8}$ from $\frac{7}{8}$.

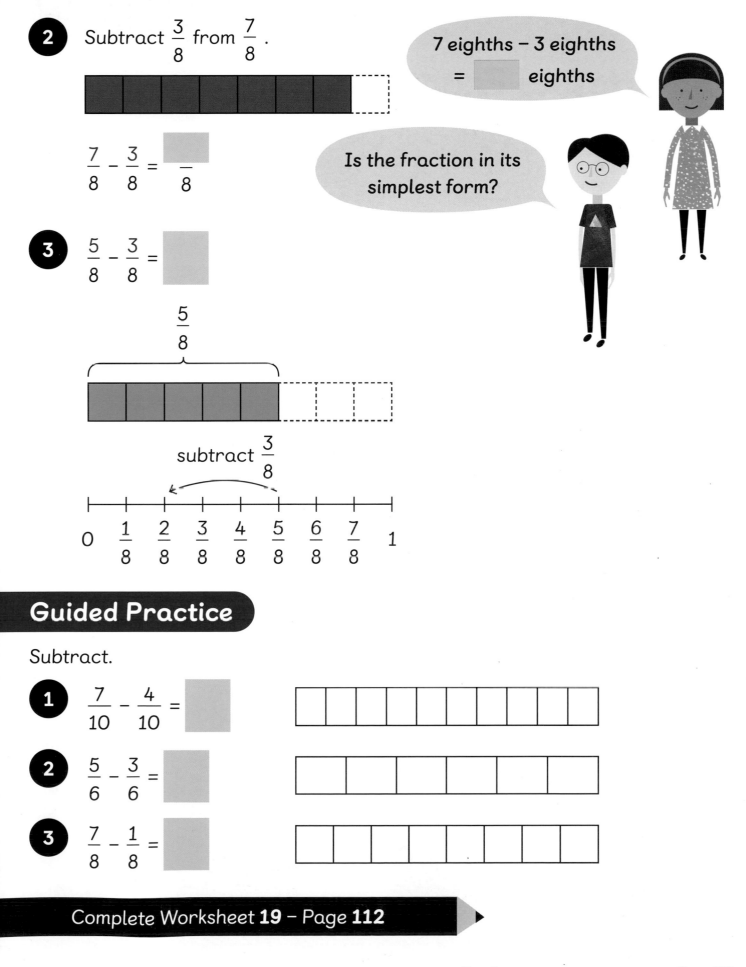

7 eighths – 3 eighths = ▢ eighths

Is the fraction in its simplest form?

$\frac{7}{8} - \frac{3}{8} = \frac{}{8}$

3 $\frac{5}{8} - \frac{3}{8} = $

$\frac{5}{8}$

subtract $\frac{3}{8}$

$$0 \quad \frac{1}{8} \quad \frac{2}{8} \quad \frac{3}{8} \quad \frac{4}{8} \quad \frac{5}{8} \quad \frac{6}{8} \quad \frac{7}{8} \quad 1$$

Guided Practice

Subtract.

1 $\frac{7}{10} - \frac{4}{10} = $

2 $\frac{5}{6} - \frac{3}{6} = $

3 $\frac{7}{8} - \frac{1}{8} = $

Complete Worksheet **19** – Page **112**

Subtracting Fractions

In Focus

What fraction of the pizza was left?

Let's Learn

1 The pizza was cut into 5 equal slices.

Sam ate $\frac{1}{5}$ of the pizza.

Subtract $\frac{1}{5}$ from $\frac{5}{5}$.

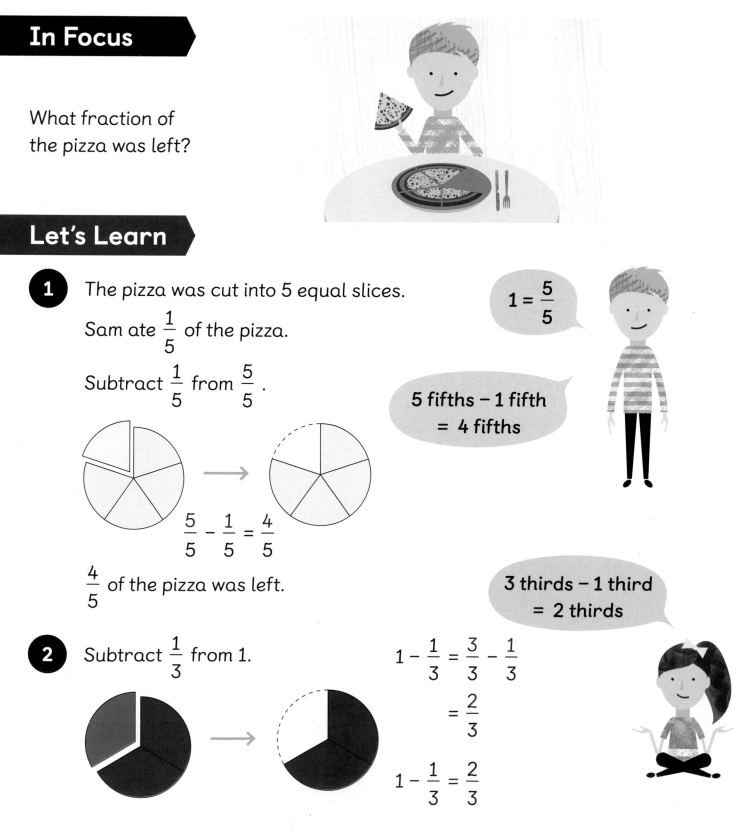

$$\frac{5}{5} - \frac{1}{5} = \frac{4}{5}$$

$\frac{4}{5}$ of the pizza was left.

$1 = \frac{5}{5}$

5 fifths − 1 fifth = 4 fifths

2 Subtract $\frac{1}{3}$ from 1.

$$1 - \frac{1}{3} = \frac{3}{3} - \frac{1}{3}$$
$$= \frac{2}{3}$$

$$1 - \frac{1}{3} = \frac{2}{3}$$

3 thirds − 1 third = 2 thirds

3 $1 - \dfrac{1}{4} = \boxed{}$

$$1 - \dfrac{1}{4} = \dfrac{4}{4} - \dfrac{1}{4}$$

$$= \dfrac{\boxed{}}{4}$$

$$1 - \dfrac{1}{4} = \boxed{}$$

1 = 4 quarters

4 quarters – 1 quarter = $\boxed{}$ quarters

Work in groups of 4.

What you need:

① Use fractions to make an addition story and a subtraction story.

② Write the stories on the 🗒 .

Write the correct addition and subtraction equations.

Example

Sam eats $\dfrac{1}{5}$ of a cake.

Lulu eats $\dfrac{2}{5}$ of a cake.

$\dfrac{1}{5} + \dfrac{2}{5} = \dfrac{3}{5}$

They eat $\dfrac{3}{5}$ of a cake together.

1 fifth + 2 fifths = 3 fifths

③ Show your group's stories to the class.

Use 🔴 to show how you add or subtract.

Guided Practice

Subtract.

1 $1 - \dfrac{1}{5} = \boxed{}$

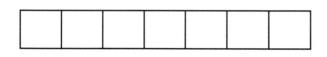

2 $1 - \dfrac{4}{7} = \boxed{}$

3

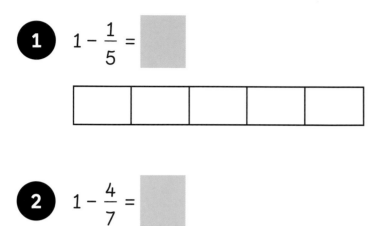

$1 - \dfrac{2}{6} = \boxed{} - \dfrac{2}{6}$

$= \boxed{}$

4   (a) $1 - \dfrac{3}{4} = \boxed{}$

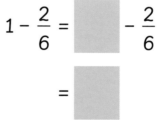

Which is greater, $\dfrac{1}{4}$ or $\dfrac{2}{5}$?

(b) $1 - \dfrac{3}{5} = \boxed{}$

Complete Worksheet **20** – Page **113**

Finding Part of a Set

In Focus

What if 4 children share this box of sweets equally?

Let's Learn

1

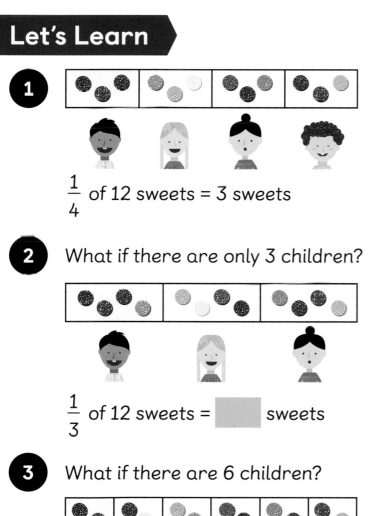

$\frac{1}{4}$ of 12 sweets = 3 sweets

12 ÷ 4 = 3

2 What if there are only 3 children?

$\frac{1}{3}$ of 12 sweets = ☐ sweets

12 ÷ 3 = ☐

3 What if there are 6 children?

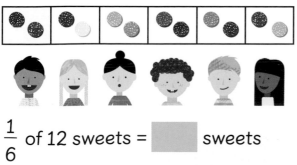

$\frac{1}{6}$ of 12 sweets = ☐ sweets

12 ÷ ☐ = ☐

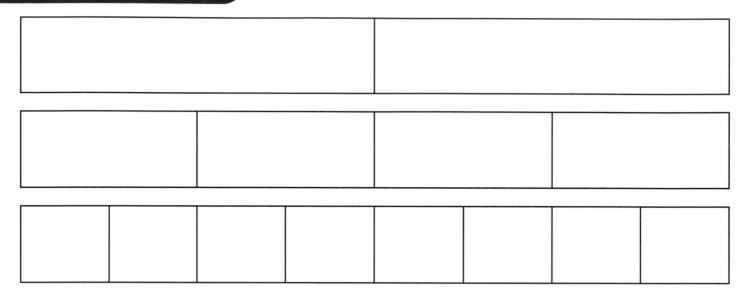

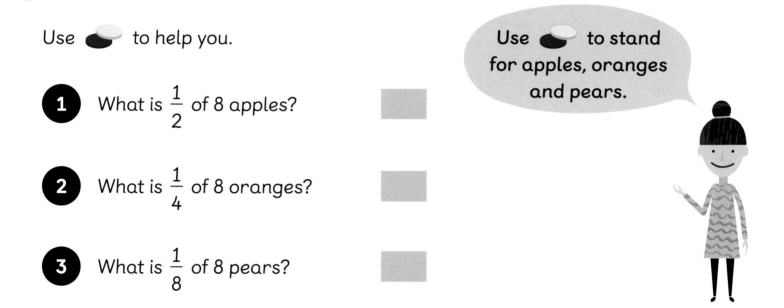

Use ⬤ to help you.

Use ⬤ **to stand for apples, oranges and pears.**

1 What is $\dfrac{1}{2}$ of 8 apples?

2 What is $\dfrac{1}{4}$ of 8 oranges?

3 What is $\dfrac{1}{8}$ of 8 pears?

Complete Worksheet 21 – Page 114 - 116

Finding Part of a Set

In Focus

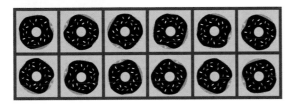

How many doughnuts is $\frac{2}{3}$ of a box of 12 doughnuts?

Let's Learn

1

$\frac{1}{3}$ of 12 doughnuts = 4 doughnuts

$\frac{2}{3}$ of 12 doughnuts = 2 × 4 doughnuts
= 8 doughnuts

2

What is $\frac{5}{6}$ of the box of doughnuts?

What is $\frac{3}{4}$ of the box of doughnuts?

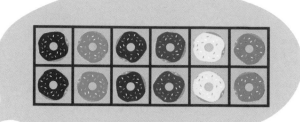

$\dfrac{1}{6}$ of 12 doughnuts = 2 doughnuts

$\dfrac{5}{6}$ of 12 doughnuts = 5 × 2 doughnuts
= 10 doughnuts

$\dfrac{1}{4}$ of 12 doughnuts = 3 doughnuts

$\dfrac{3}{4}$ of 12 doughnuts = 3 × 3 doughnuts
= 9 doughnuts

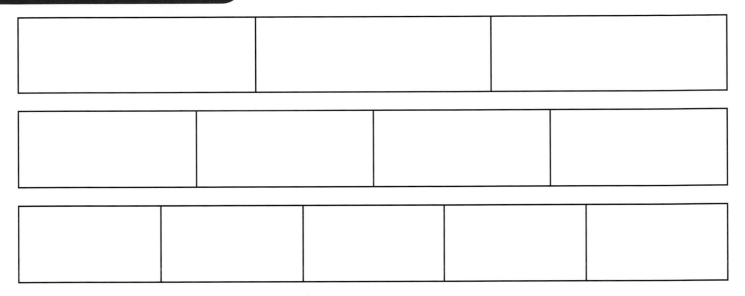

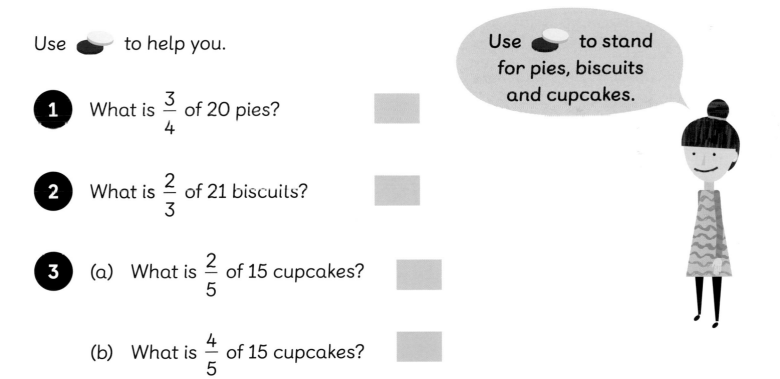

Use ⬤ to help you.

Use ⬤ to stand for pies, biscuits and cupcakes.

1 What is $\frac{3}{4}$ of 20 pies?

2 What is $\frac{2}{3}$ of 21 biscuits?

3 (a) What is $\frac{2}{5}$ of 15 cupcakes?

(b) What is $\frac{4}{5}$ of 15 cupcakes?

Complete Worksheet 22 – Page 117

Finding the Fraction of a Number

In Focus

How can we find $\frac{1}{2}$ of 6?

$$\frac{1}{2} \text{ of } 6$$

Let's Learn

1   Emma shows 6 using 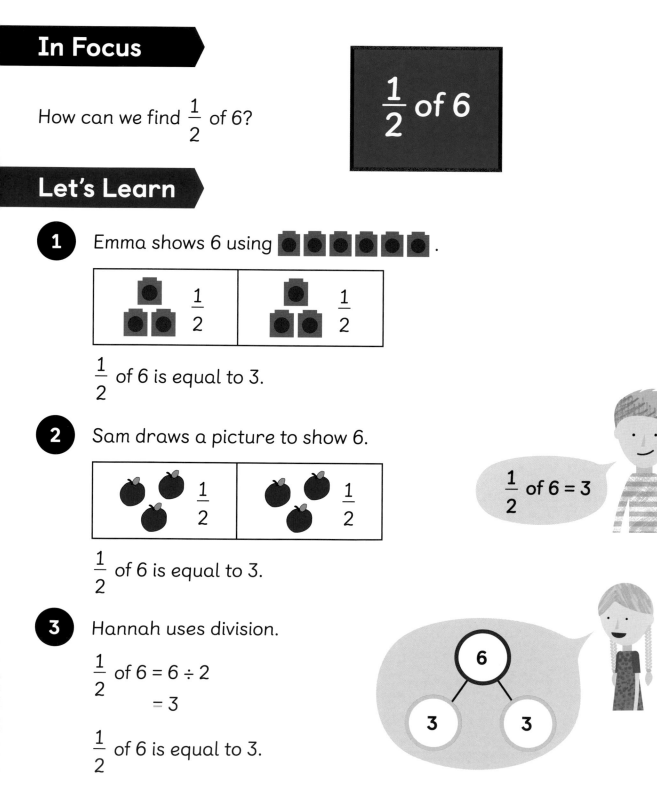 .

$\frac{1}{2}$ of 6 is equal to 3.

2   Sam draws a picture to show 6.

$\frac{1}{2}$ of 6 is equal to 3.

$\frac{1}{2}$ of 6 = 3

3   Hannah uses division.

$\frac{1}{2}$ of 6 = 6 ÷ 2
           = 3

$\frac{1}{2}$ of 6 is equal to 3.

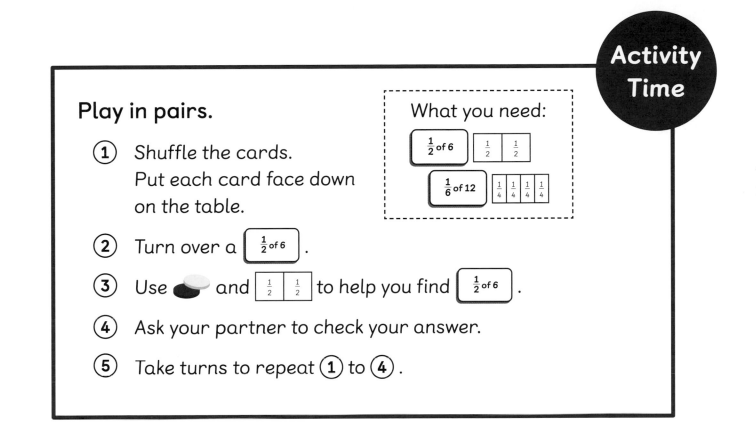

Activity Time

Play in pairs.

What you need:

① Shuffle the cards.
Put each card face down
on the table.

② Turn over a ½ of 6.

③ Use ⬤ and | ½ | ½ | to help you find ½ of 6.

④ Ask your partner to check your answer.

⑤ Take turns to repeat ① to ④.

Guided Practice

1 Calculate.

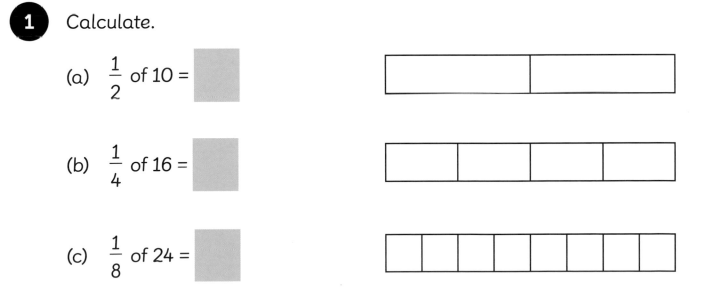

(a) $\frac{1}{2}$ of 10 =

(b) $\frac{1}{4}$ of 16 =

(c) $\frac{1}{8}$ of 24 =

Calculate.

(a) $\frac{3}{5}$ of 10 = [ ]

(b) $\frac{5}{6}$ of 18 = [ ]

Elliott uses this method to calculate.

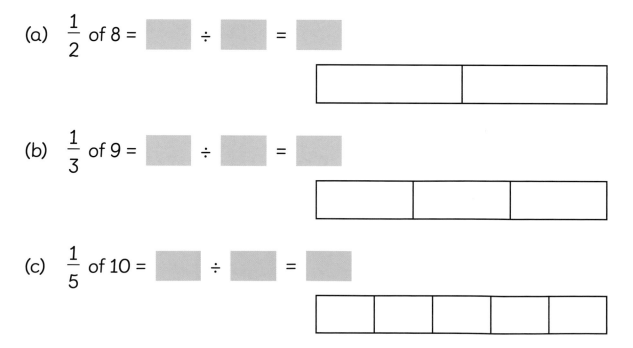

$\frac{1}{2}$ of 4 = 4 ÷ 2 = 2

Use Elliott's method to calculate.

(a) $\frac{1}{2}$ of 8 = [ ] ÷ [ ] = [ ]

(b) $\frac{1}{3}$ of 9 = [ ] ÷ [ ] = [ ]

(c) $\frac{1}{5}$ of 10 = [ ] ÷ [ ] = [ ]

Complete Worksheet 23 – Page 118 - 119

Sharing One

In Focus

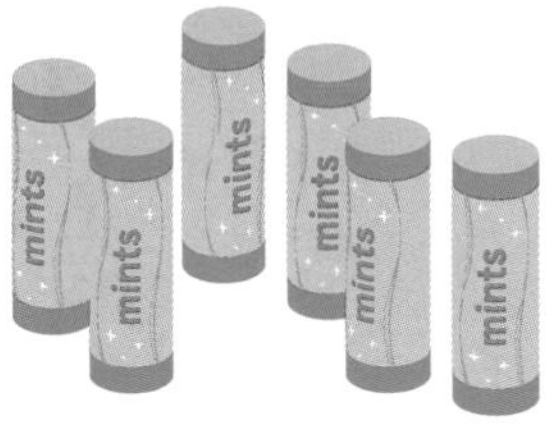

Let 2 of us share the mints.

What if there is only 1 🥫 ?

Let's Learn

1

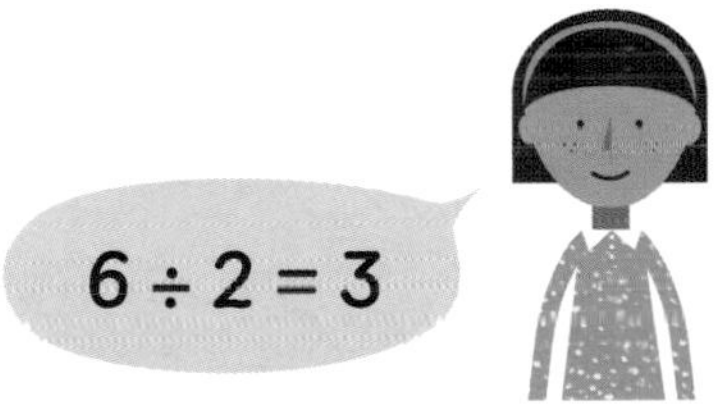

If there is only 1  🥫 , and not 6, then

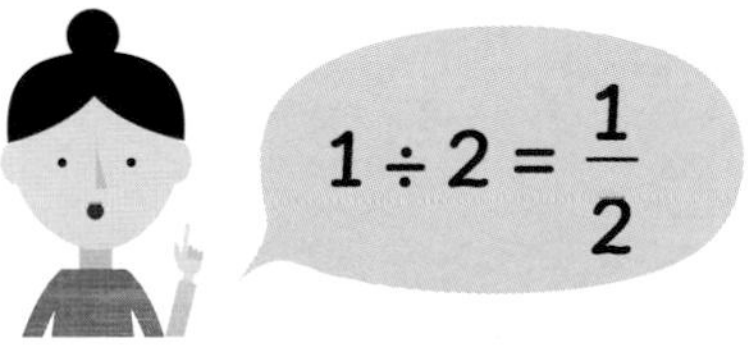

$1 \div 2 = \dfrac{1}{2}$

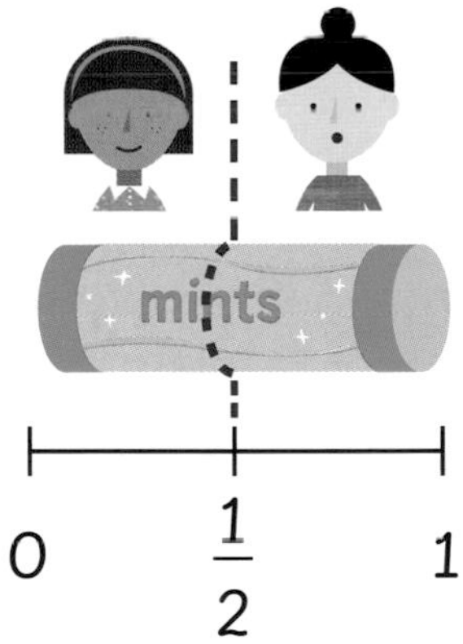

$6 \div 2 = 3$

0      $\dfrac{1}{2}$ 1

2 Share a pizza equally among 🧑🧑🧑 .

$\dfrac{1}{3}$ $\dfrac{1}{3}$

$\dfrac{1}{3}$

$1 \div 3 = \dfrac{1}{3}$

3 Divide 1 by 4.

$1 \div 4 =$ ▢

Guided Practice

Solve.

1 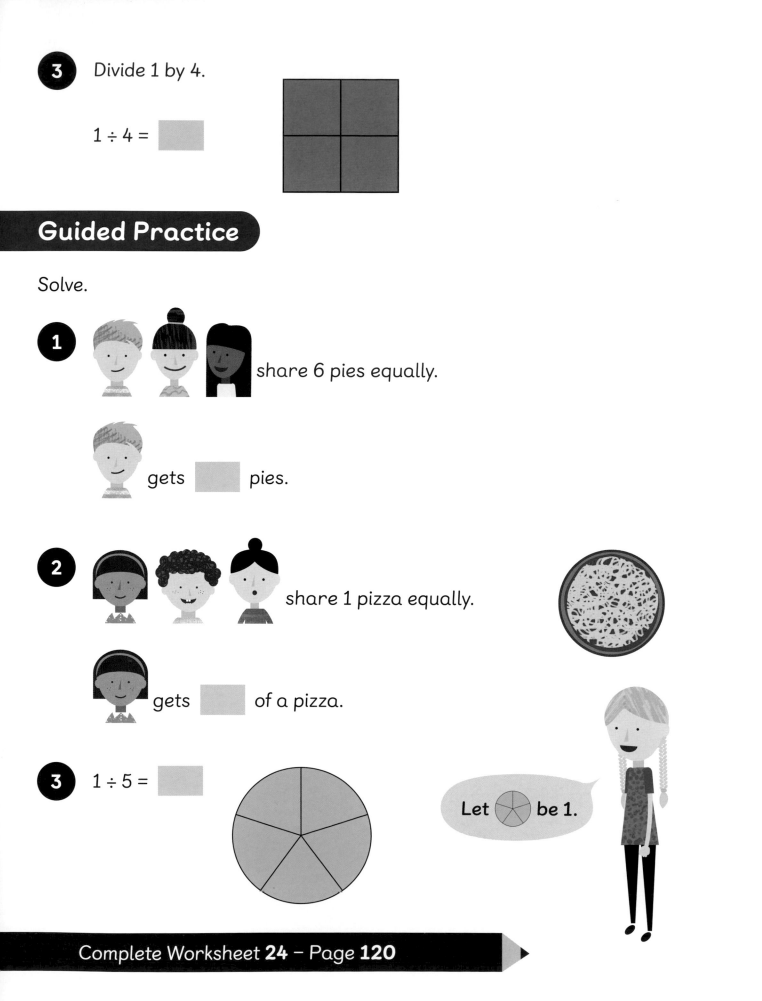 share 6 pies equally.

gets ▢ pies.

2 share 1 pizza equally.

gets ▢ of a pizza.

3 $1 \div 5 =$ ▢

Let ◯ be 1.

Complete Worksheet 24 – Page 120

Sharing More Than 1

In Focus

Sam and Holly drew pictures to show $\frac{2}{3}$ of a circle.

 Sam

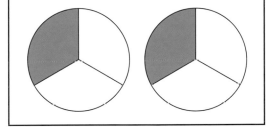 Hannah
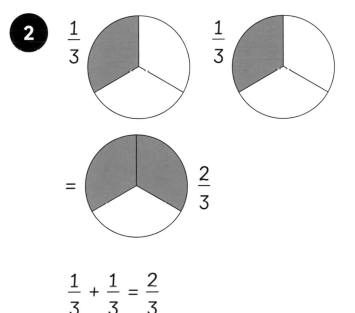

Who is correct?

Let's Learn

1

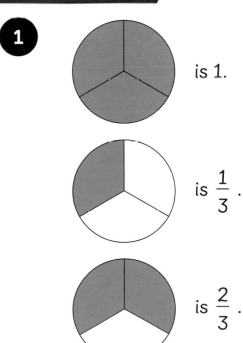

is 1.

is $\frac{1}{3}$.

is $\frac{2}{3}$.

Sam is correct.

2 $\frac{1}{3}$ $\frac{1}{3}$

$=$ $\frac{2}{3}$

$$\frac{1}{3} + \frac{1}{3} = \frac{2}{3}$$

Hannah is also correct.

2

2 pies shared by 3 children
2 ÷ 3

Cut each pie into 3 equal parts.

$2 \div 3 = \dfrac{2}{3}$

Each child gets 2 thirds of a pie.

Guided Practice

Solve.

1 share 12 pies equally.

gets [ ] pies.

2 share 3 pizzas equally.

gets [ ] of a pizza.

3 $4 \div 5 = $ [ ]

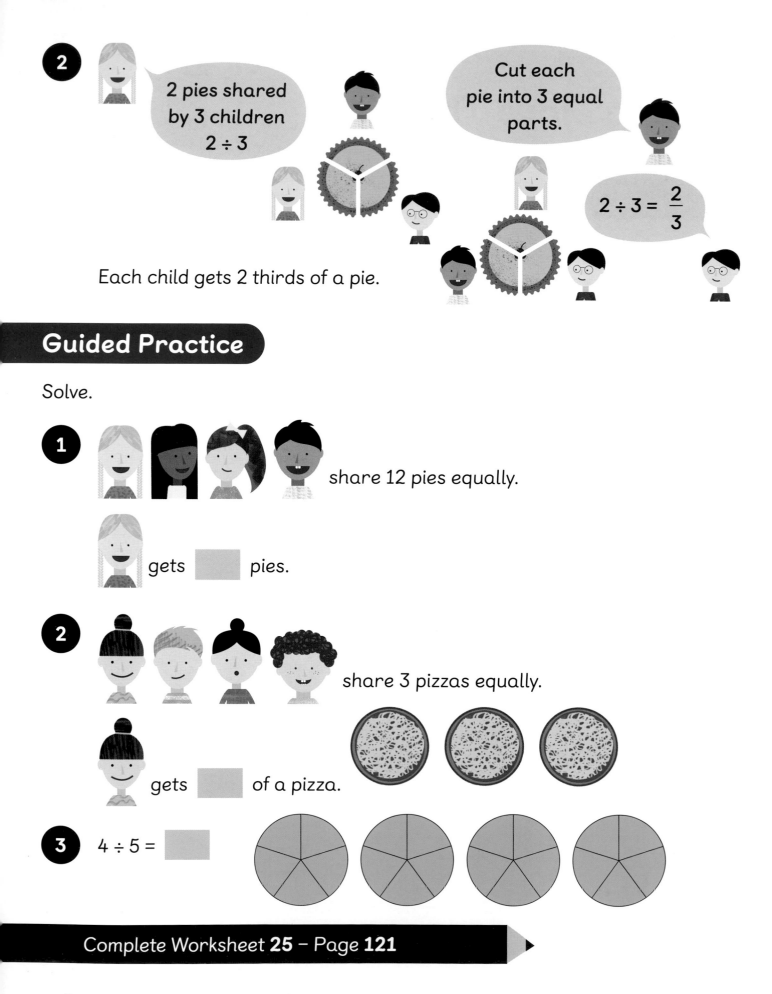

Complete Worksheet **25** – Page **121**

Sharing More Than 1

4 children share 3 pies equally.

How much pie does each child get?

1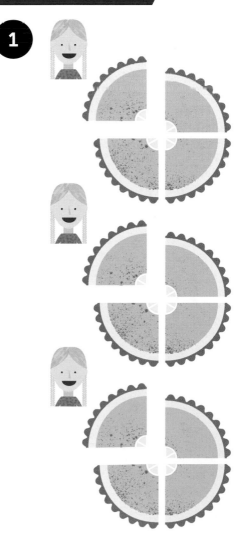

Each piece is 1 quarter of a pie.

 gets 3 pieces.

 gets 3 quarters or $\frac{3}{4}$ of a pie.

2 $3 \div 4 = $ ☐

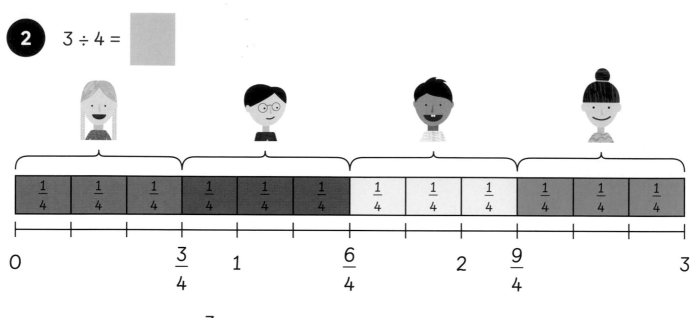

Each child gets $\dfrac{3}{4}$ of a pie.

Guided Practice

Write on the number line.

(a) $\dfrac{1}{3}$

(b) $\dfrac{2}{3}$

(c) $\dfrac{5}{3}$

$2 \div 3 = $ ☐

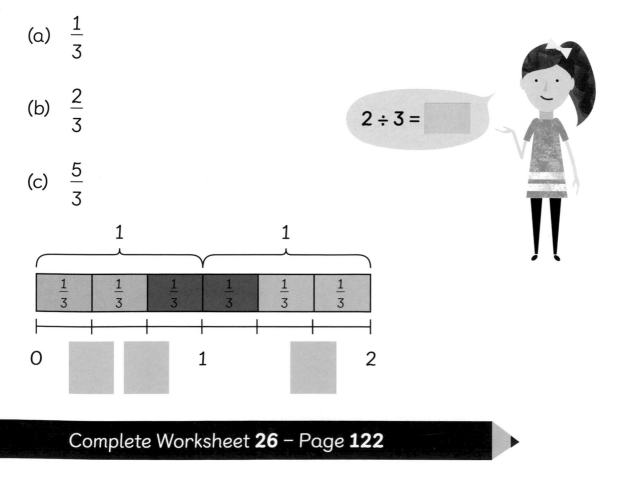

Complete Worksheet **26** – Page **122**

Showing More Than 1

In Focus

3 children share 4 pies equally.

How much pie does each child get?

Let's Learn

1

Each piece is 1 third of a pie.

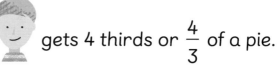 gets 4 pieces.

gets 4 thirds or $\frac{4}{3}$ of a pie.

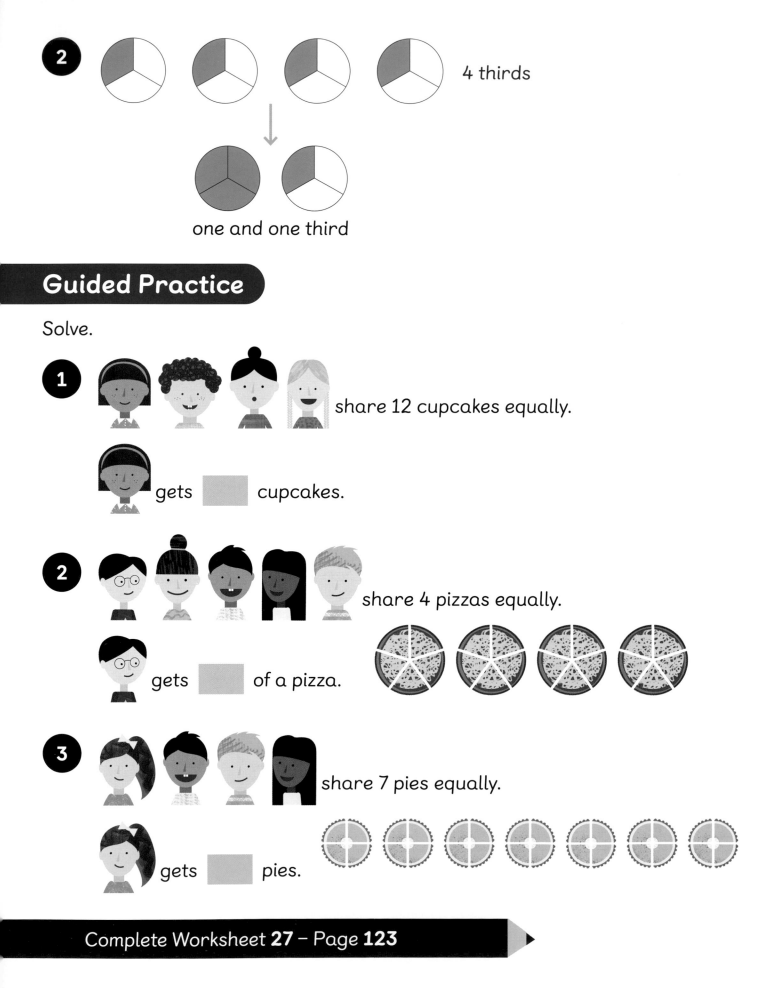

2

4 thirds

one and one third

Guided Practice

Solve.

1 share 12 cupcakes equally.

gets ☐ cupcakes.

2 share 4 pizzas equally.

gets ☐ of a pizza.

3 share 7 pies equally.

gets ☐ pies.

Complete Worksheet **27** – Page **123**

Solving Word Problems

In Focus

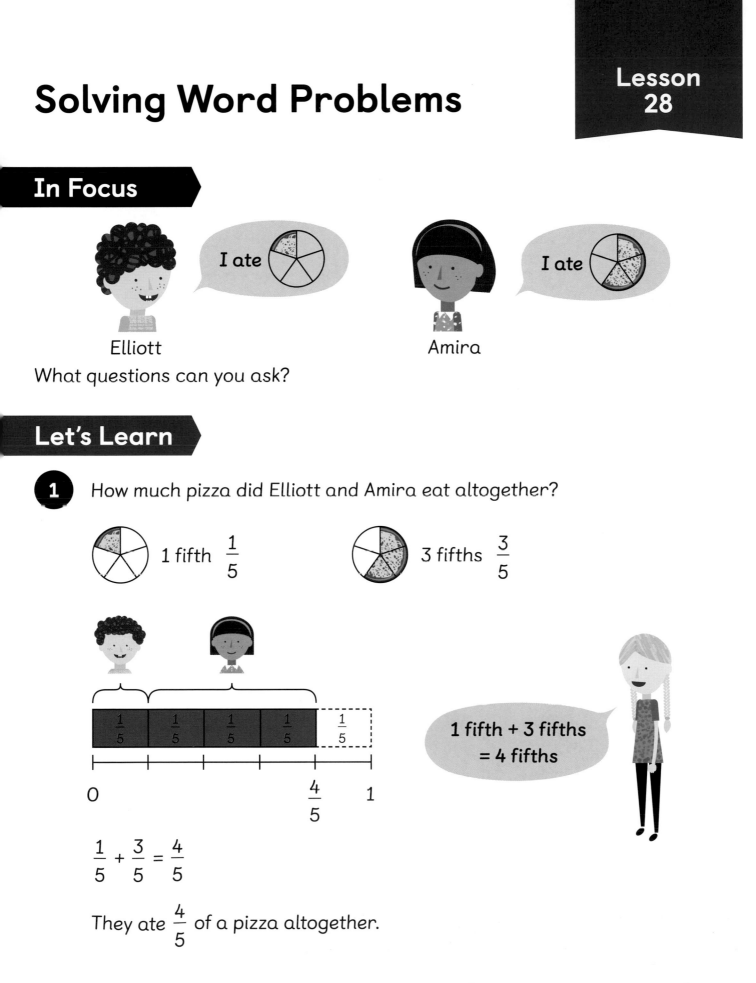

Elliott   I ate

Amira   I ate

What questions can you ask?

Let's Learn

1 How much pizza did Elliott and Amira eat altogether?

1 fifth $\frac{1}{5}$

3 fifths $\frac{3}{5}$

1 fifth + 3 fifths = 4 fifths

$$\frac{1}{5} + \frac{3}{5} = \frac{4}{5}$$

They ate $\frac{4}{5}$ of a pizza altogether.

2 Who ate more?
How much more?

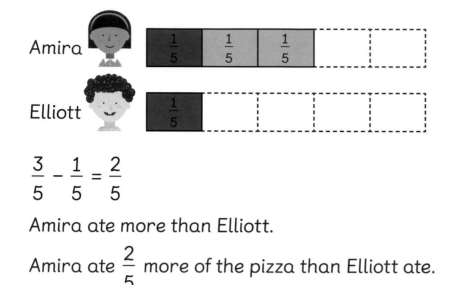

Amira

Elliott

$$\frac{3}{5} - \frac{1}{5} = \frac{2}{5}$$

Amira ate more than Elliott.

Amira ate $\frac{2}{5}$ more of the pizza than Elliott ate.

Guided Practice

Solve.

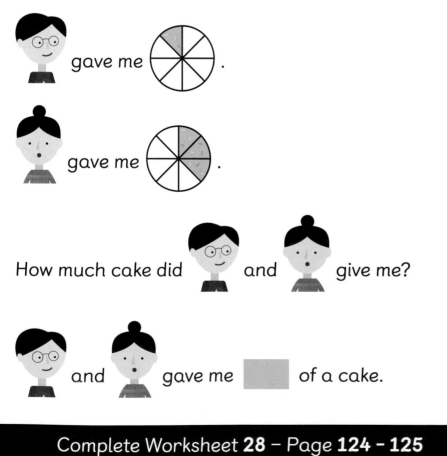

gave me ⬡ .

gave me ⬡ .

How much cake did 🧑 and 👩 give me?

🧑 and 👩 gave me [ ] of a cake.

Complete Worksheet **28** – Page **124 - 125**

Solving Word Problems

In Focus

Emma: I took 6 sweets.

Elliott

Lulu: I took half as many sweets as Emma.

I took twice as many sweets as Emma.

How many sweets did they take altogether?

Let's Learn

1 How many sweets did Elliott take?

Emma | 6

Elliott |

$2 \times 6 = 12$

Elliott took 12 sweets.

2 How many sweets did Lulu take?

Emma | 6

Lulu |

$\frac{1}{2}$ | $\frac{1}{2}$

$6 \div 2 = 3$

Lulu took 3 sweets.

Fractions   Page 189

3

	number of sweets
Emma	6
Elliott	12
Lulu	3

6 + 12 = 18

18 + 3 = 21

6 + 12 + 3 = 21

They took 21 sweets altogether.

Guided Practice

Solve.

1 buys 10 cupcakes. buys $\frac{1}{2}$ as many cupcakes as buys.

How many cupcakes does buy?

2 buys 10 cookies. buys $\frac{1}{2}$ as many cookies as buys.

(a) How many cookies does buy?

(b) How many cookies do and buy altogether?

3 Ravi has $\frac{1}{2}$ as many £2 coins as Hannah has.

Hannah has 8 £2 coins.

(a) How many coins does Ravi have?

(b) How much money does Ravi have?

Complete Worksheet **29** – Page **126 – 127**

Solving Word Problems

In Focus

April						
M	T	W	T	F	S	S
		1	2	3	4	5
6	7	8	9	10	11	12
13	14	15	16	17	18	19
20	21	22	23	24	25	26
27	28	29	30			

Elliott spent $\frac{1}{3}$ of the month drawing.

After that, he spent the rest of the month painting his drawing.

He took 30 days to complete the drawing and painting.

How many days is $\frac{1}{3}$ of 30 days?

April						
M	T	W	T	F	S	S
		1	2	3	4	5
6	7	8	9	10	11	12
13	14	15	16	17	18	19
20	21	22	23	24	25	26
27	28	29	30			

1 How many days is $\frac{1}{3}$ of 30 days?

		1	2	3	4	5
6	7	8	9	10	11	12
13	14	15	16	17	18	19
20	21	22	23	24	25	26
27	28	29	30			

I draw a diagram.

$\frac{1}{3}$ of 30 days = 10 days

2 What is $\frac{1}{2}$ of 30 days?

15 days	15 days

$\frac{1}{2}$ of 30 = 30 ÷ 2

$\frac{1}{2}$ of 30 days = 15 days

3 What is $\frac{1}{5}$ of 30 days?

30

$\frac{1}{5}$ of 30 days = 30 days ÷ 5

= ⬜ days

Guided Practice

Solve.

1 Sam used $\frac{1}{3}$ of the piece of ribbon.

How long is the piece of ribbon that Sam used?

30 cm

2  (a) How heavy is half a bag of nuts?

(b) How heavy is a quarter of a bag of nuts?

3 Ruby drank $\frac{1}{2}$ of the milk in the bottle.

(a) How much milk did she drink?

(b) How much milk was left?

4 Elliott has 10 days to finish a project.

He needs to spend $\frac{1}{5}$ of the time planning it.

How many days does Elliott spend on planning?

Complete Worksheet **30** – Page **128 - 129**

Mind Workout

Name a fraction Lulu could be thinking of.
Explain how you get your answer.

Draw a number line to help you.

I am thinking of
a fraction that is more than $\frac{1}{3}$.
It is also less than $\frac{1}{2}$.

Maths Journal

Add or subtract.

Draw diagrams to help you.

(a) $\dfrac{2}{7} + \dfrac{3}{7} =$ ⬜

(b) $\dfrac{1}{5} + \dfrac{2}{5} =$ ⬜

(c) $\dfrac{6}{9} - \dfrac{2}{9} =$ ⬜

(d) $\dfrac{7}{8} - \dfrac{1}{8} =$ ⬜

How do the numerators and the denominators change when you add or subtract?

Self Check

I know how to...

☐ count in tenths.

☐ make number pairs that form one whole.

☐ add and subtract two fractions.

☐ find and list equivalent fractions.

☐ write a fraction in its simplest form.

☐ compare fractions.

☐ find part of a set and fraction of a number.

☐ share a number equally.

☐ write fractions on the number line.

☐ write fractions that are greater than 1.

☐ solve word problems involving fractions.

What are angles?

Chapter 12
Angles

Making Angles

In Focus

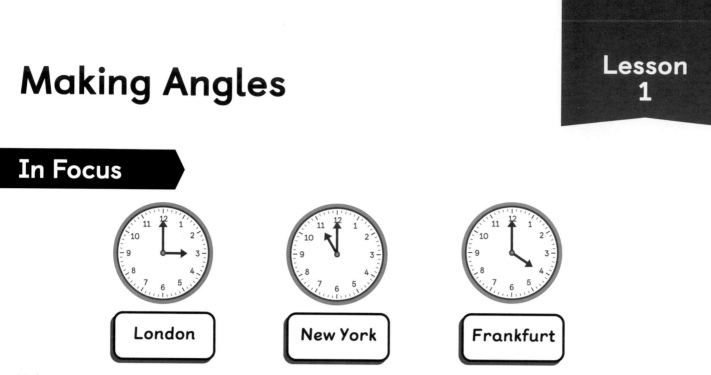

London   New York   Frankfurt

What can you say about the hour and minute hands on the three clocks?

Let's Learn

1 The hour and minute hands make an **angle**.

These are angles.

This is an angle.

2 When two straight lines meet at a point, they make an angle.

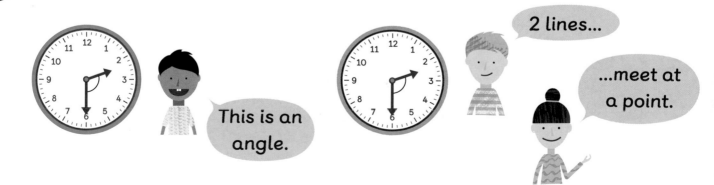

This is an angle.

2 lines...

...meet at a point.

Angles   Page 196

The hour and minute hands make different angles at different times.

Guided Practice

1 Use 2 pencils to make different angles.
Example

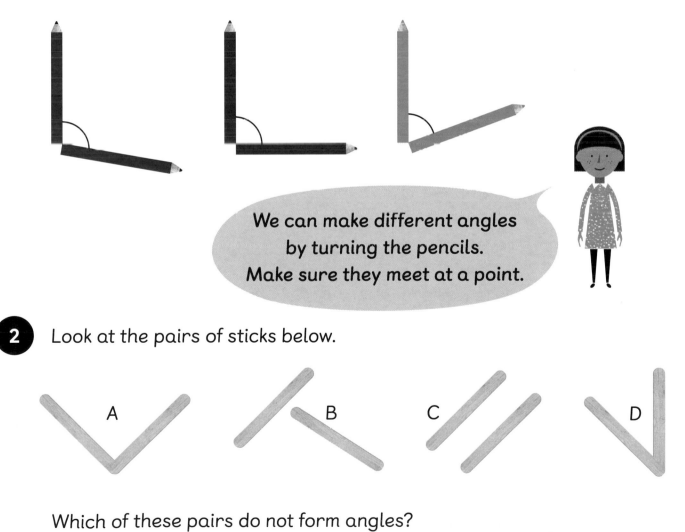

We can make different angles
by turning the pencils.
Make sure they meet at a point.

2 Look at the pairs of sticks below.

A

B

C

D

Which of these pairs do not form angles?

3 Where is an angle made by parts of a pair of scissors?

What happens to the angle when you open and close the scissors?

4 Holly drew 2 lines to make an angle.

(a) Draw 2 lines to make an angle smaller than the one Holly drew.

(b) Draw 2 lines to make an angle larger than the one Holly drew.

Complete Worksheet **1** · Page **135 – 138**

Making Angles

In Focus

At 7 o'clock, the hands make an angle.

Actually, they make 2 angles.

Who is correct? Why?

Let's Learn

1   When 2 lines meet at a point, they make an angle.

Here is one angle.

Here is another angle.

2   Find all the angles in this letter.

Y   Y   Y   Y

Guided Practice

Find as many angles as you can in each of these letters.

(a) V   (b) X   (c) T

Complete Worksheet 2 • Page **139 – 141**

Finding Angles in Shapes

In Focus

A stop sign is a shape.
How many angles does this shape have?

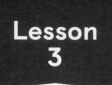

Let's Learn

1 Find all the angles inside the shape. How many angles can you find?

Here is one angle.

Here is another angle.

2 Find the number of sides and angles in Figure A.

Figure A has ▢ sides.

Figure A has ▢ angles.

Figure A

How many angles does a triangle have?

3 Describe this shape.

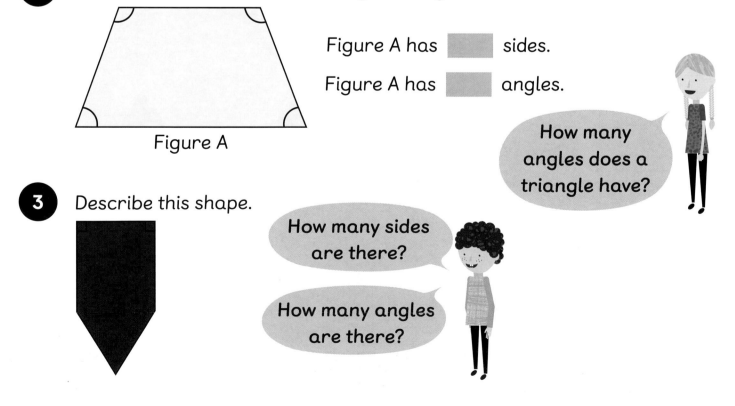

How many sides are there?

How many angles are there?

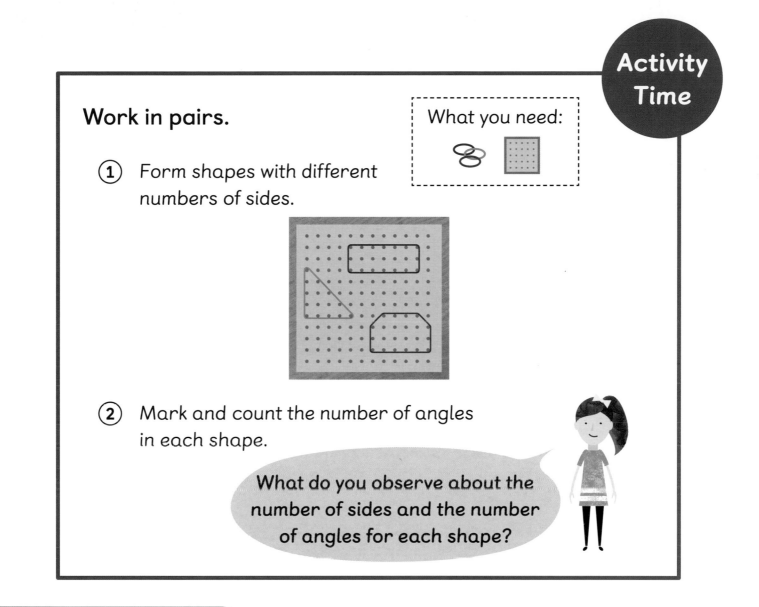

Activity Time

Work in pairs.

What you need:

① Form shapes with different numbers of sides.

② Mark and count the number of angles in each shape.

What do you observe about the number of sides and the number of angles for each shape?

Guided Practice

How many sides and angles does each shape have?
Mark the angles in each shape.

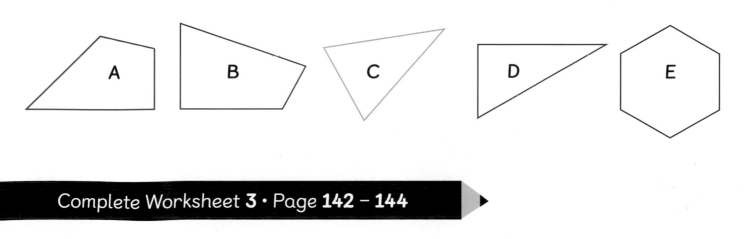

A   B   C   D   E

Complete Worksheet 3 · Page 142 – 144

Finding Right Angles

In Focus

Let's make a "right-angle tester" and use it to find right angles.
Fold a piece of paper in two.
Then fold it in two again to make a right angle.

You have made a right-angle tester.

Look around the room and the school for places with right angles.

Let's Learn

 When 2 lines meet at a point, they make an **angle**.
These lines make **right angles**.

We mark right angles like this.

 There is a right angle at each corner of the board.

The corner of my ruler is a right angle. What other right angles can you find?

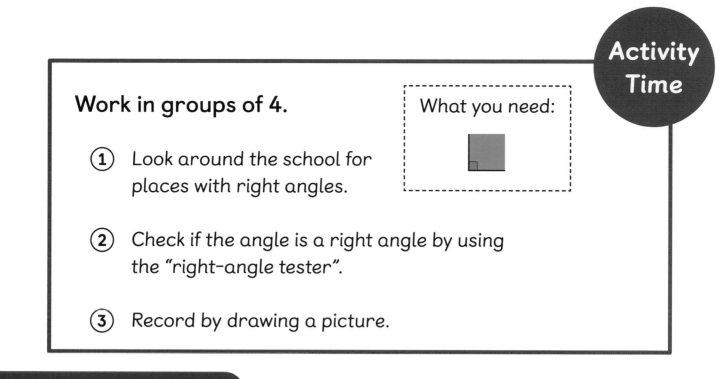

Work in groups of 4.

What you need:

① Look around the school for places with right angles.

② Check if the angle is a right angle by using the "right-angle tester".

③ Record by drawing a picture.

Activity Time

Guided Practice

1 Which pairs of lines meet to make a right angle?

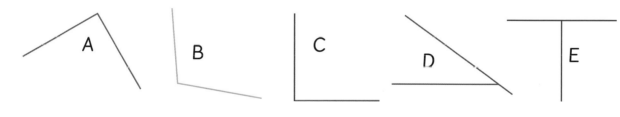

A B C D E

2 Which shapes have at least one right angle?

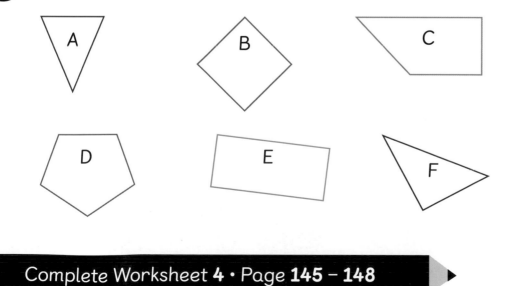

A B C

D E F

Complete Worksheet **4** • Page **145 – 148**

Comparing Angles

In Focus

MATHS

In which letters are there right angles?

> Check using your right-angle tester.

Let's Learn

1 Are there right angles in T ?

T There are 2 right angles in T .

> Which other letters have several right angles?

2 Are there right angles in H ?

There are 4 right angles in H .

> Can you rewrite M so that it has a right angle?

> Use a ruler and pencil.

3 Are there right angles in M ?

Angles a, b and c are less than a right angle.

We call these **acute angles**.

> An acute angle is smaller than a right angle.

4 Are there acute angles in 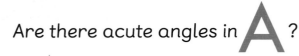 ?

 These angles are smaller than a right angle.
These are acute angles.

5 Are there acute angles in S ?

No, angles are made when straight lines meet.

Guided Practice

1 Draw an acute angle.

2 Which of these are right angles?
Use your right-angle tester or the corner of a ruler to find out.

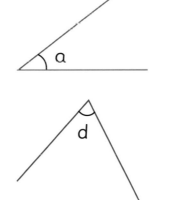
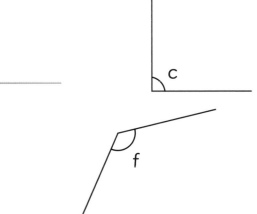

3 Which angles in the shapes are right angles and which are acute angles?

(a) (b)

(c) (d)

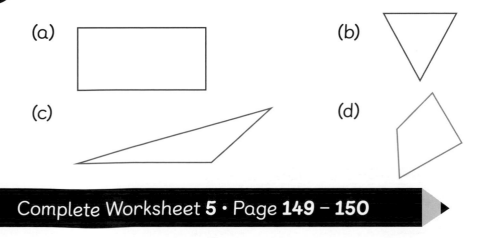

Complete Worksheet **5** • Page **149 – 150**

Comparing Angles

In Focus

ENGLAND

Are there angles that are larger than a right angle in the letters?

Let's Learn

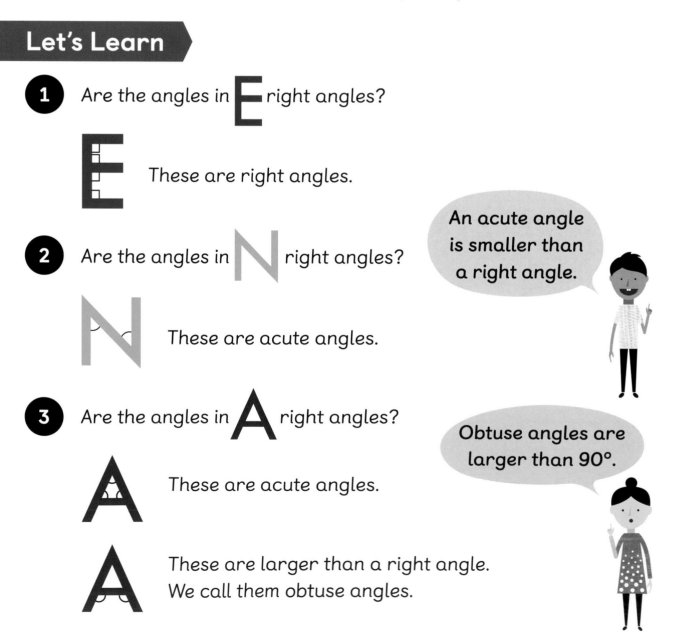

1 Are the angles in **E** right angles?

These are right angles.

2 Are the angles in **N** right angles?

These are acute angles.

An acute angle is smaller than a right angle.

3 Are the angles in **A** right angles?

These are acute angles.

These are larger than a right angle. We call them obtuse angles.

Obtuse angles are larger than 90°.

Work in pairs.

① Take two strips of cardboard of the same length.

② Join the two strips at one end with a fastener to make your own angle strips.

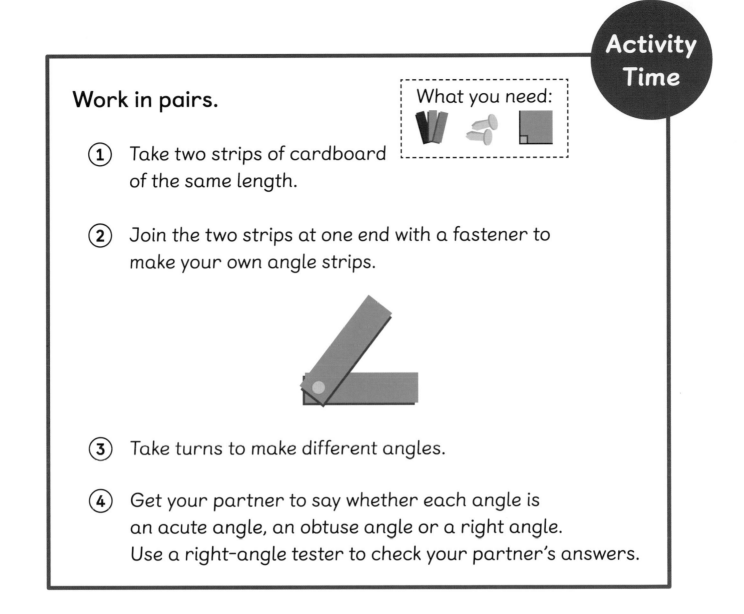

③ Take turns to make different angles.

④ Get your partner to say whether each angle is an acute angle, an obtuse angle or a right angle.
    Use a right-angle tester to check your partner's answers.

Guided Practice

1 Draw an obtuse angle.

2 Is each angle smaller than or larger than a right angle?

(a) a

(b) b

3 Name the acute angles, the obtuse angles and the right angles.

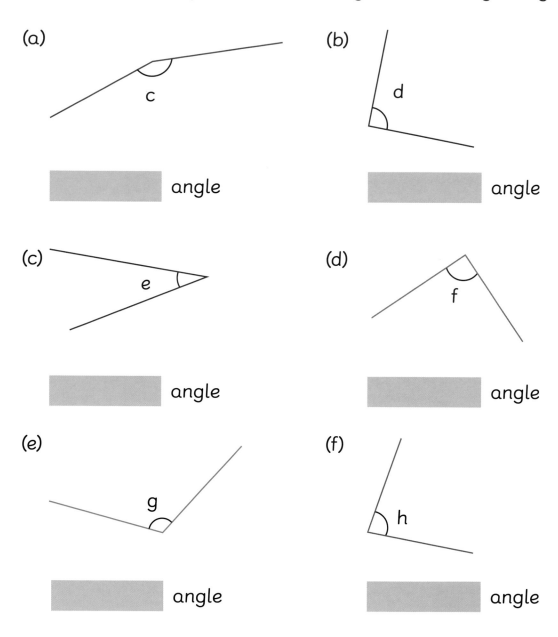

(a)

[   ] angle

(b)

[   ] angle

(c)

[   ] angle

(d)

[   ] angle

(e)

[   ] angle

(f)

[   ] angle

4 Find a right angle, an acute angle and an obtuse angle.

5 Are there obtuse angles in any of these letters?

6 Look at the angles in the shape.

Use your right-angle tester to help you.

Which angles are right angles, acute angles and obtuse angles? Explain your answers.

Complete Worksheet **6** · Page **151 – 154**

Making Turns

In Focus

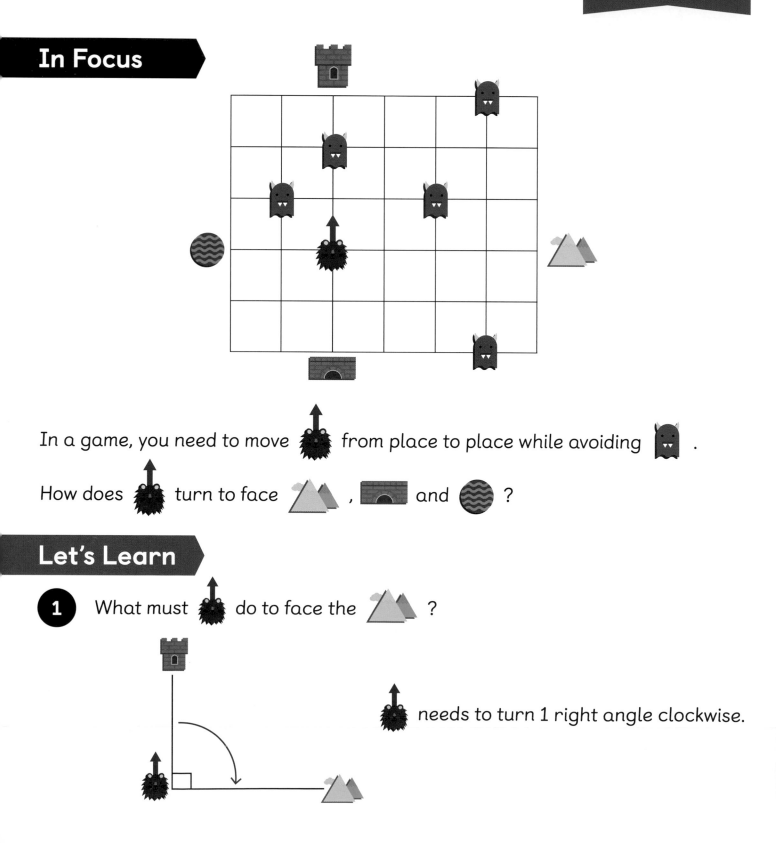

In a game, you need to move 🧔 from place to place while avoiding 👾 .

How does 🧔 turn to face 🏔 , 🚇 and 🌊 ?

Let's Learn

1   What must 🧔 do to face the 🏔 ?

🧔 needs to turn 1 right angle clockwise.

2 What if 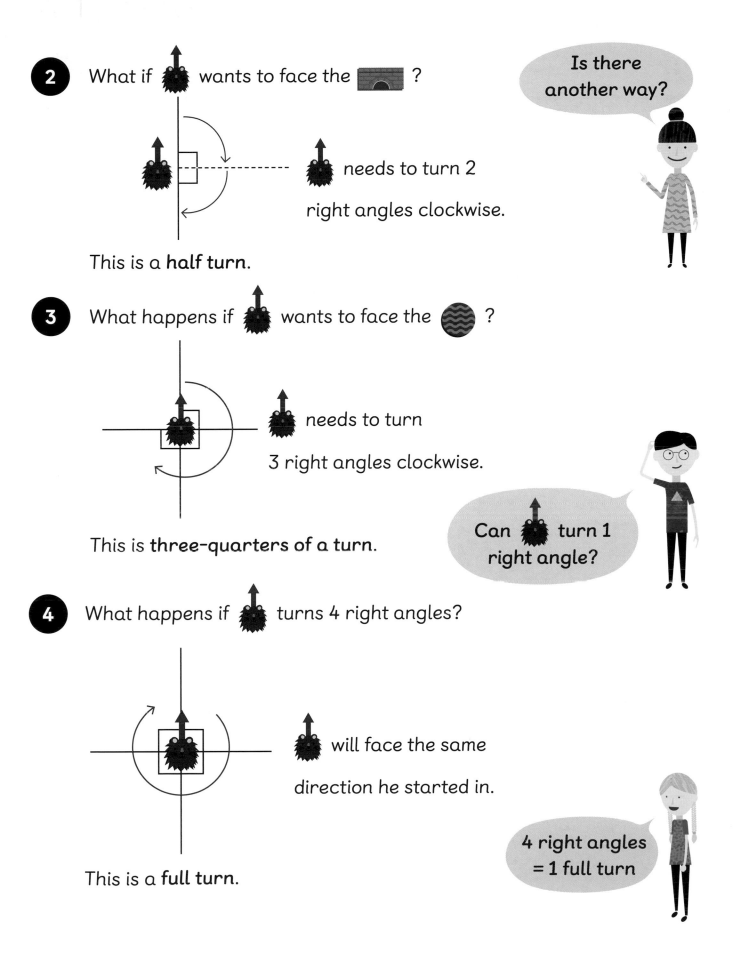 wants to face the 🟫 ?

needs to turn 2 right angles clockwise.

This is a **half turn**.

Is there another way?

3 What happens if wants to face the ⬤ ?

needs to turn 3 right angles clockwise.

This is **three-quarters of a turn**.

Can turn 1 right angle?

4 What happens if turns 4 right angles?

will face the same direction he started in.

This is a **full turn**.

4 right angles = 1 full turn

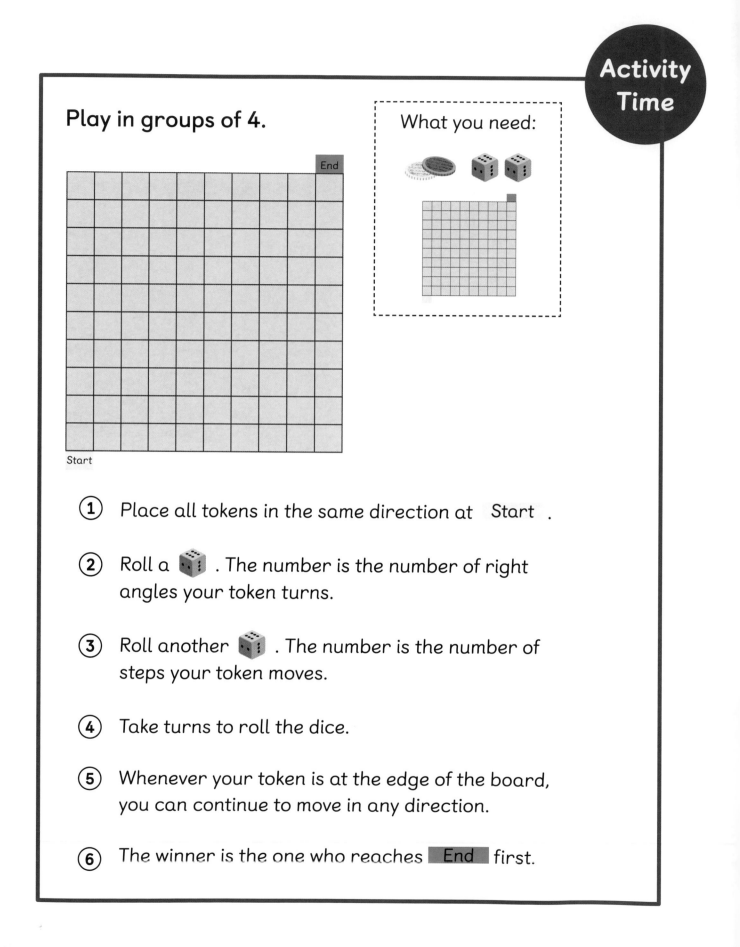

Play in groups of 4.

End

What you need:

Start

1. Place all tokens in the same direction at Start .

2. Roll a [die]. The number is the number of right angles your token turns.

3. Roll another [die]. The number is the number of steps your token moves.

4. Take turns to roll the dice.

5. Whenever your token is at the edge of the board, you can continue to move in any direction.

6. The winner is the one who reaches End first.

Guided Practice

Describe each turn.
How many right angle turns are there and in what direction?

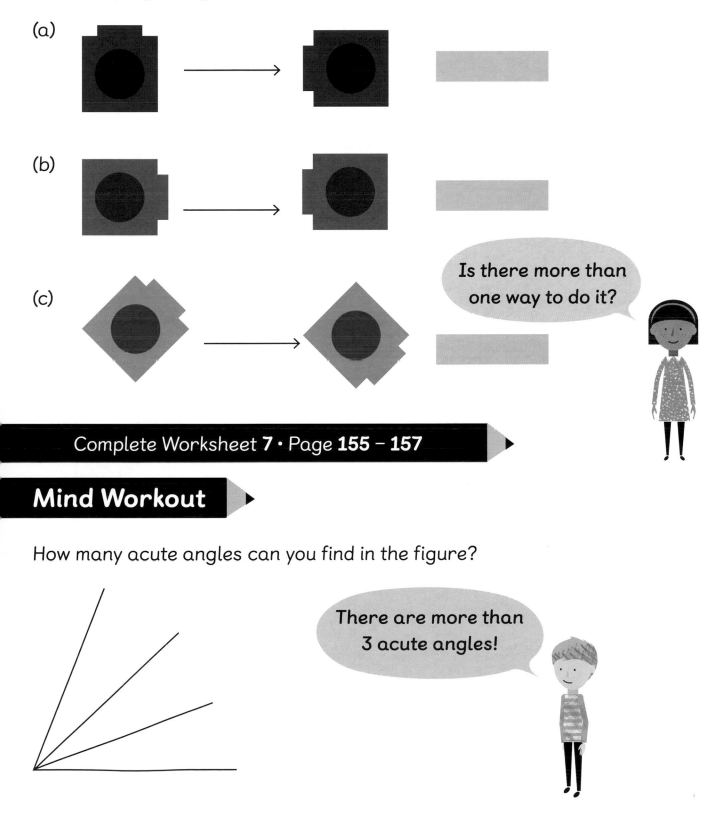

(a)

(b)

(c)

Is there more than one way to do it?

Complete Worksheet 7 • Page 155 – 157

Mind Workout

How many acute angles can you find in the figure?

There are more than 3 acute angles!

Maths Journal

Some athletes need to understand angles to do well in their sport.

Can you think of any sports where athletes need to do this?
Search for pictures of these sports and mark the angles used.

Example

sport	How are angles used?
javelin throw	The athlete uses angles to help him throw the javelin as far as possible.

Self Check

I know how to...

☐ recognise an angle.

☐ find angles in shapes.

☐ find a right angle, an acute angle and an obtuse angle.

☐ compare the sizes of angles.

☐ make a half turn, a three-quarters turn and a full turn.

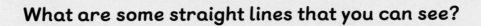

Chapter 13
Lines and Shapes

Identifying Perpendicular Lines

In Focus

Look for two straight lines that meet to make a right angle.

Let's Learn

 1 Find two lines that meet at right angles.

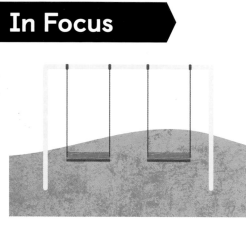

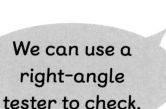 We can use a right-angle tester to check.

 2 Find two lines that meet at right angles.

These lines are called perpendicular lines.

Two straight lines that meet at a right angle are called **perpendicular lines**.

3 Some lines are drawn on a square grid as shown.

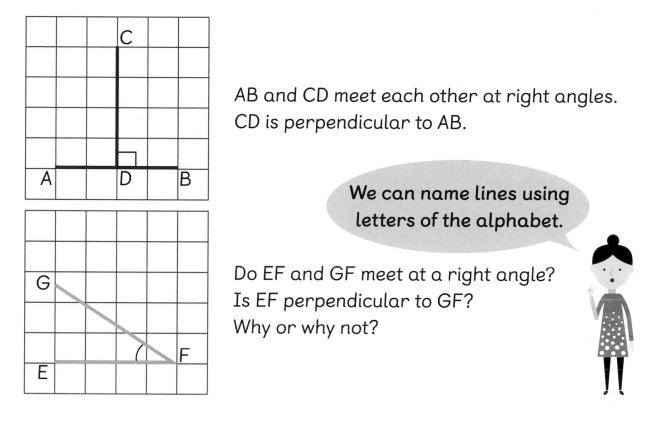

AB and CD meet each other at right angles.
CD is perpendicular to AB.

We can name lines using letters of the alphabet.

Do EF and GF meet at a right angle?
Is EF perpendicular to GF?
Why or why not?

4 Which pairs of lines are perpendicular?

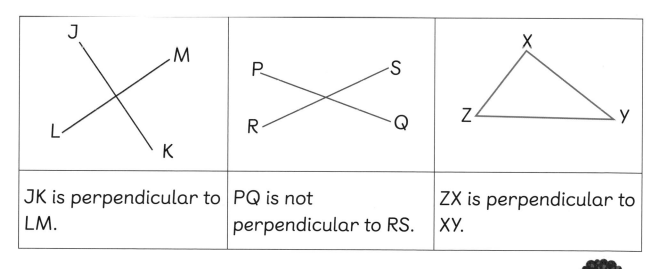

JK is perpendicular to LM.	PQ is not perpendicular to RS.	ZX is perpendicular to XY.

Use a right-angle tester to check for right angles.

Guided Practice

1 List the pairs of perpendicular lines you can find in a table.

2 Which pairs of lines are perpendicular?

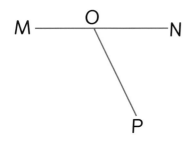

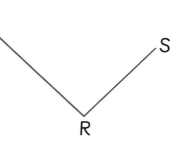

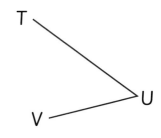

3 Which sides of the shapes are perpendicular?

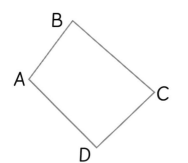

4 Which letters have perpendicular lines?

L I N E S

Complete Worksheet 1 – Page 161 – 164

Identifying Parallel Lines

In Focus

What do you notice about the railway track?

Let's Learn

1

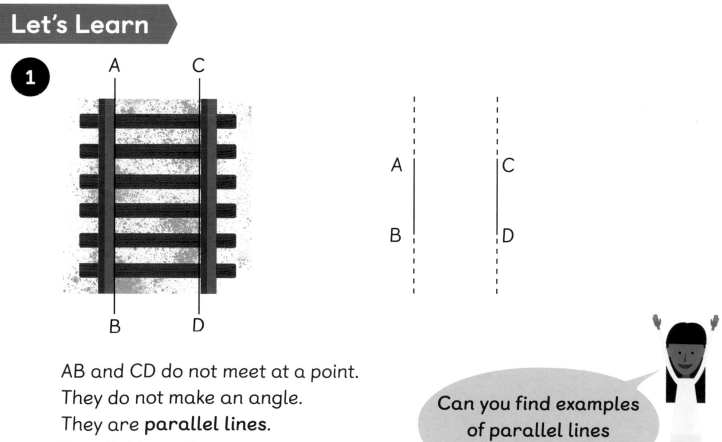

AB and CD do not meet at a point.
They do not make an angle.
They are **parallel lines**.
Parallel lines do not meet, no matter
how long they are drawn.

Can you find examples
of parallel lines
around you?

2 A pair of lines is drawn on a square grid.
Are the lines parallel to each other?

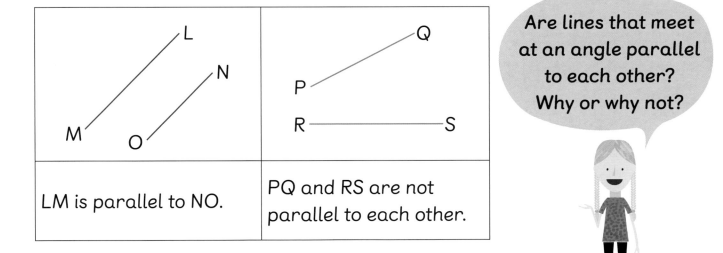

We use arrowheads to show that the lines are parallel.

EF and GH are parallel.

3 Which pairs of lines are parallel?

L N M O	Q P R S
LM is parallel to NO.	PQ and RS are not parallel to each other.

Are lines that meet at an angle parallel to each other? Why or why not?

4 Which sides are parallel?
How can you tell?

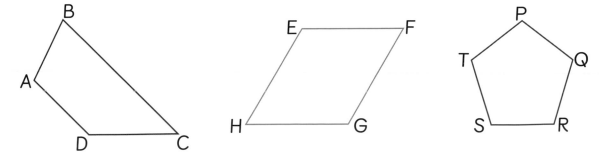

Guided Practice

1 List the pairs of parallel lines you can find in a table.

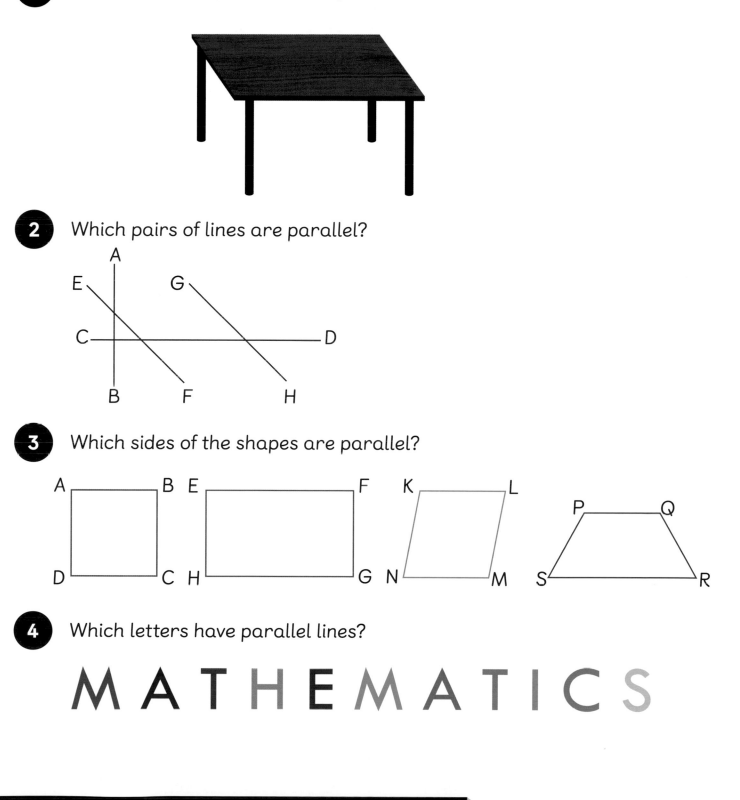

2 Which pairs of lines are parallel?

3 Which sides of the shapes are parallel?

4 Which letters have parallel lines?

MATHEMATICS

Complete Worksheet 2 – Page 165 - 168

Finding Vertical and Horizontal Lines

In Focus

The pictures are rectangular in shape and are hanging upright on the wall.
What can you say about the sides of the rectangles?

Let's Learn

1 What can you say about line AD and line BC?

> They are **vertical lines.**

Vertical lines are perpendicular to the floor.
Vertical lines are parallel to each other.

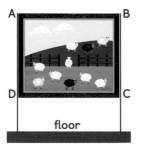

2 What can you say about line AB and line DC?

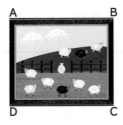

> They are **horizontal lines.**

Horizontal lines are parallel to the floor.

3 The picture shows a table on a level floor.

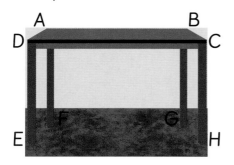

List all the horizontal and vertical lines in the picture.

List all the pairs of perpendicular and parallel lines in the picture.

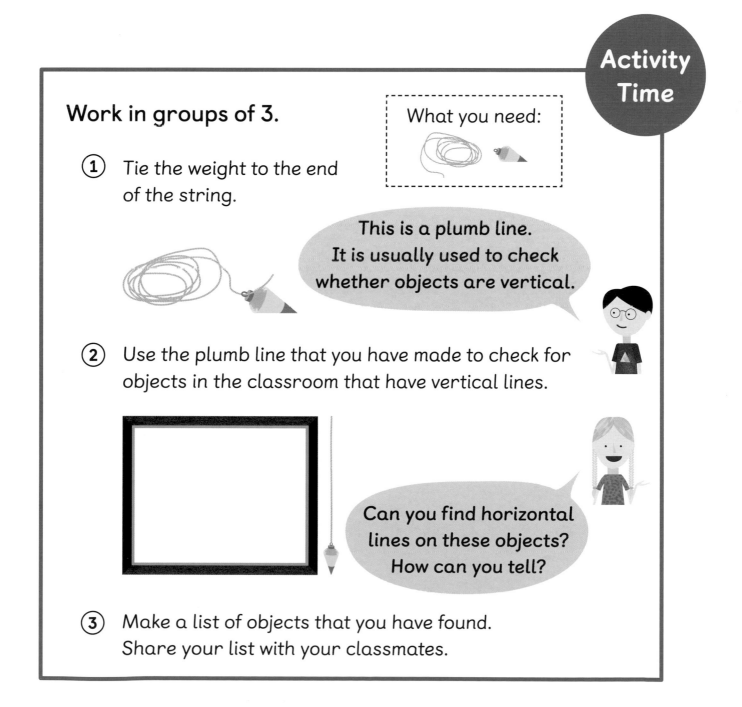

Activity Time

Work in groups of 3.

What you need:

① Tie the weight to the end of the string.

This is a plumb line. It is usually used to check whether objects are vertical.

② Use the plumb line that you have made to check for objects in the classroom that have vertical lines.

Can you find horizontal lines on these objects? How can you tell?

③ Make a list of objects that you have found. Share your list with your classmates.

Guided Practice

1 Find vertical lines in your room.
Find horizontal lines in your room.

vertical lines	horizontal lines

2 Look at the shelf.

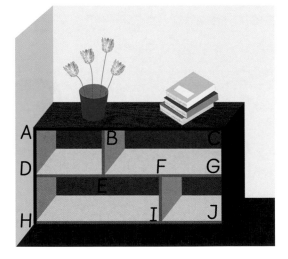

(a) List 5 horizontal lines.

 , ▢ , ▢ , ▢ , ▢

(b) List 3 vertical lines that have the same length.

▢ , ▢ , ▢

Complete Worksheet 3 – Page 169 – 170

Describing Two-Dimensional Shapes

In Focus

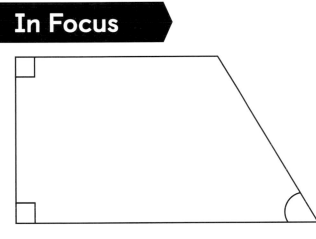

How can we describe the shape?

Let's Learn

1   Describe the angles of the shape.

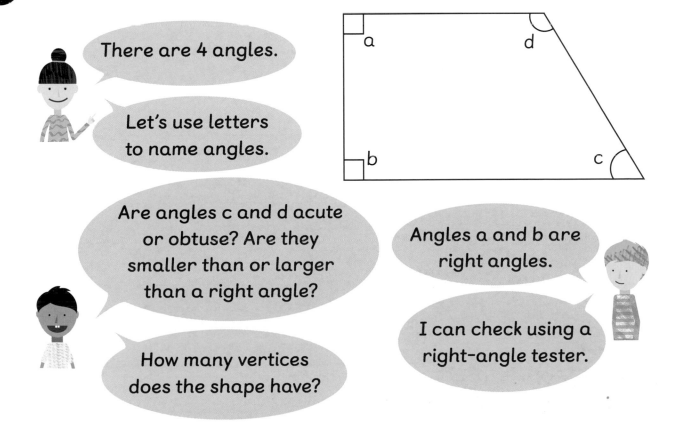

There are 4 angles.

Let's use letters to name angles.

Are angles c and d acute or obtuse? Are they smaller than or larger than a right angle?

How many vertices does the shape have?

Angles a and b are right angles.

I can check using a right-angle tester.

2 Describe the sides of the shape.

Let's use letters to name sides.

There are 4 sides. It is a quadrilateral.

FR is perpendicular to FO.

FR is also perpendicular to RU.

FO is parallel to RU.

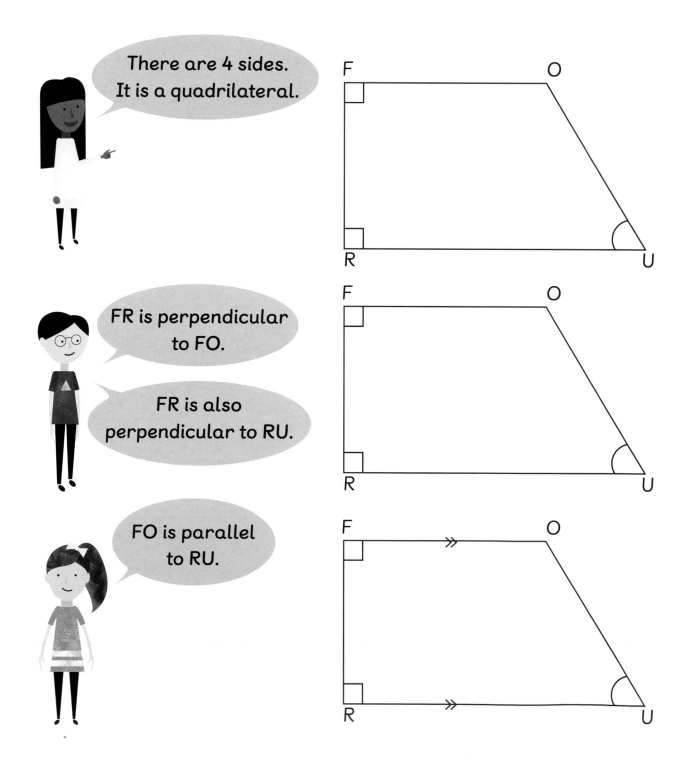

3 What are the lengths of the sides?

This side is 5 cm.

This side is also 5 cm.

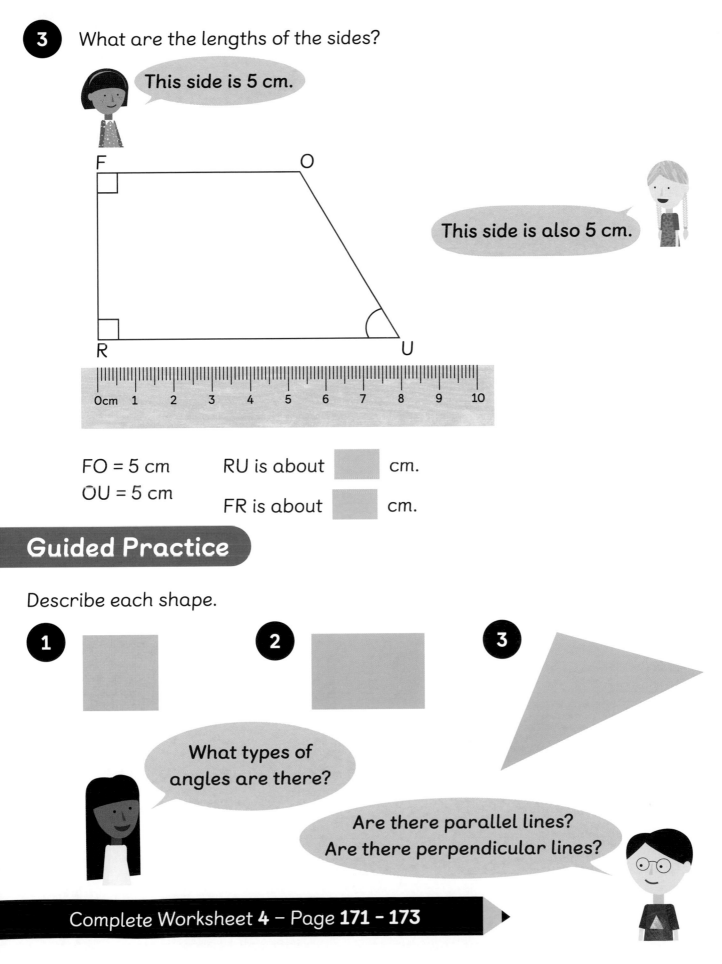

FO = 5 cm

OU = 5 cm

RU is about ⬜ cm.

FR is about ⬜ cm.

Guided Practice

Describe each shape.

1

2

3

What types of angles are there?

Are there parallel lines?
Are there perpendicular lines?

Complete Worksheet 4 – Page **171 – 173**

Drawing Two-Dimensional Shapes

In Focus

These figures show the lengths of the sides.
The drawings are illustrations: they are not exact.

This is a square.

5 cm   5 cm

This is a rectangle.

2 cm

5 cm

The square looks smaller than the rectangle.
Is this true?

Let's Learn

1 Draw the square.

2 Draw the rectangle.

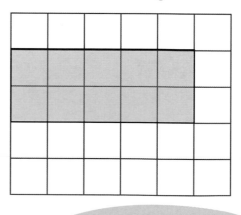

Is the square smaller than the rectangle?

Work in groups of 3 or 4.

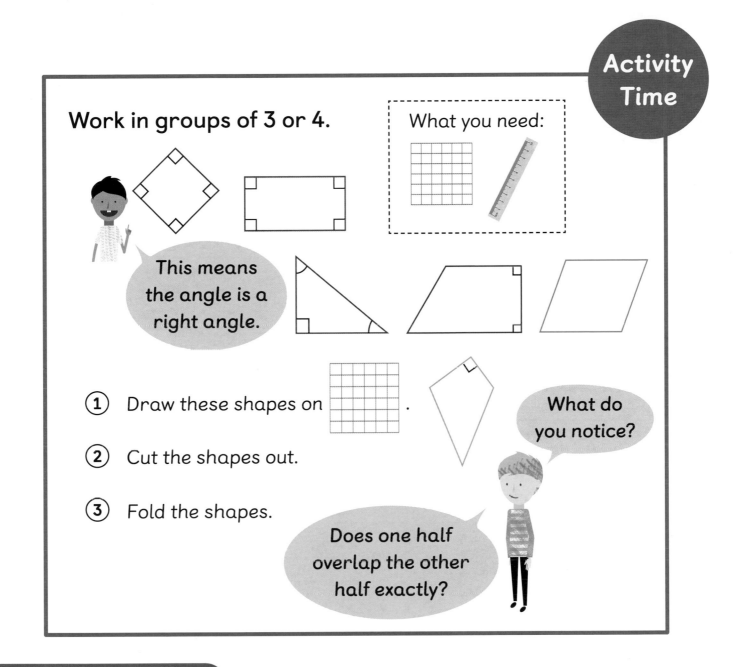

What you need:

This means the angle is a right angle.

(1) Draw these shapes on [grid].

(2) Cut the shapes out.

(3) Fold the shapes.

What do you notice?

Does one half overlap the other half exactly?

Guided Practice

1 Draw a square with 4 cm sides.

2 Draw a rectangle.
The sides are 3 cm and 5 cm.

Complete Worksheet 5 – Page **174 - 175**

Making Three-Dimensional Shapes

In Focus

What do we get when we fold these into three dimensional shapes?

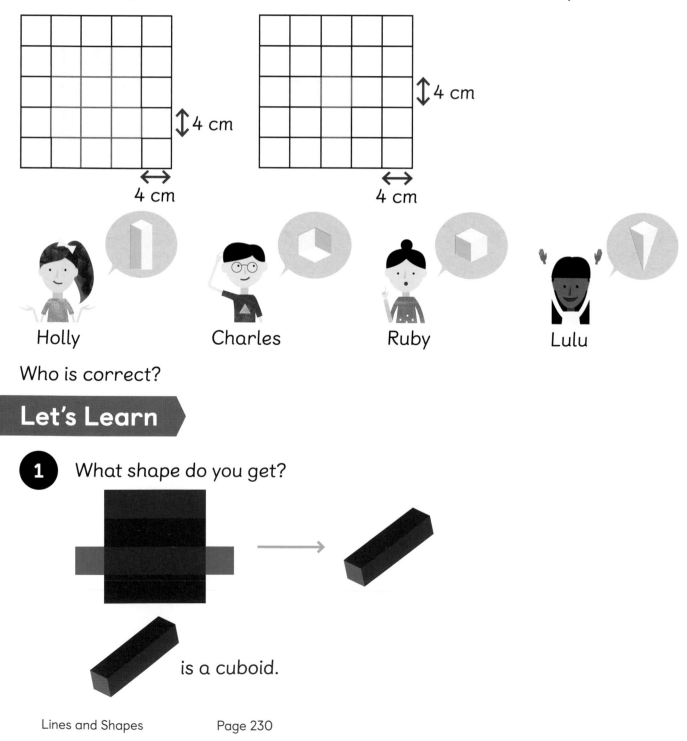

4 cm

4 cm

4 cm

4 cm

Holly   Charles   Ruby   Lulu

Who is correct?

Let's Learn

1   What shape do you get?

is a cuboid.

2 What shape do you get?

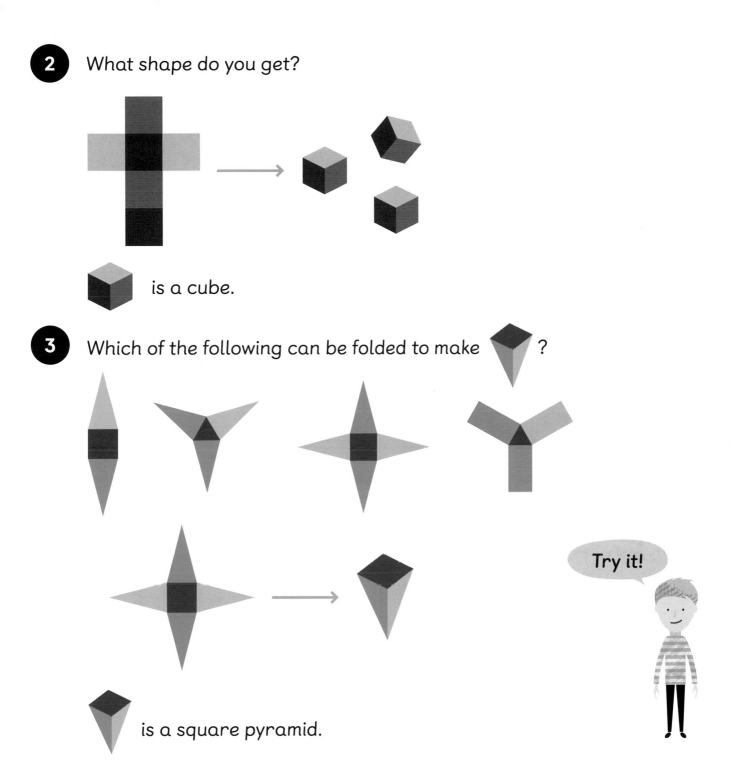

is a cube.

3 Which of the following can be folded to make ?

is a square pyramid.

Try it!

4 How many faces, vertices and sides does the shape have?

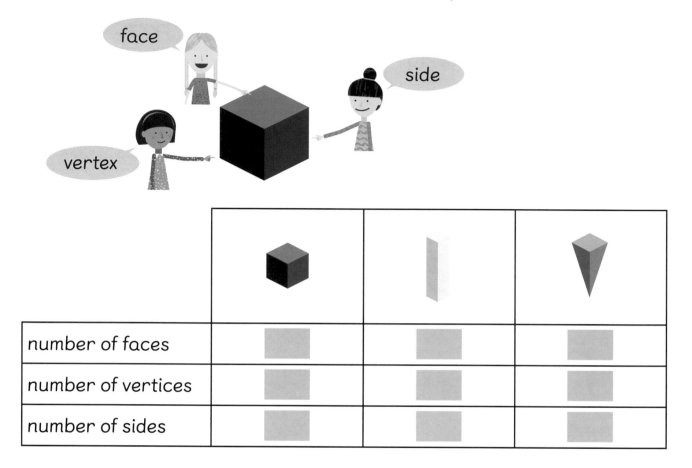

number of faces			
number of vertices			
number of sides			

Guided Practice

1 All these shapes have squares in them.
Name these shapes.

2 Match shapes that are the same.

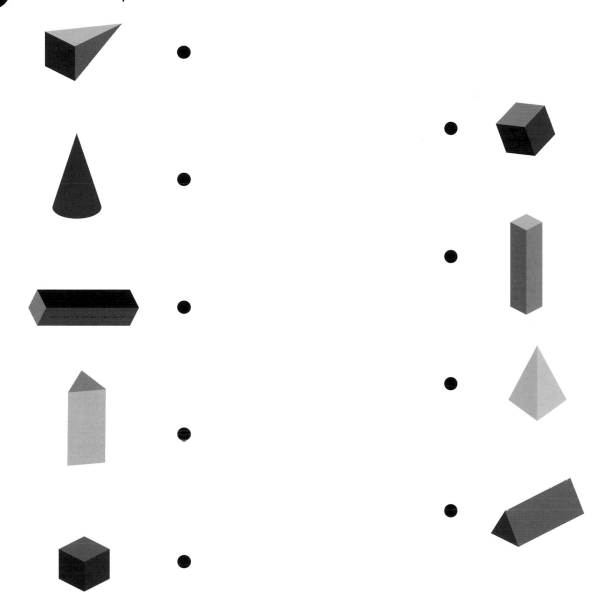

Making Three-Dimensional Shapes

In Focus

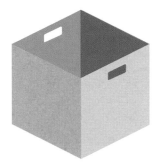

Let's make a model of this shape using some clay.

 It is a cube.

Using the same amount of clay, what other shapes can you make?

Let's Learn

They are identical, like one side is looking into the mirror.

1 Cut the shape into 2 parts.

2 Change the cube into a sphere.

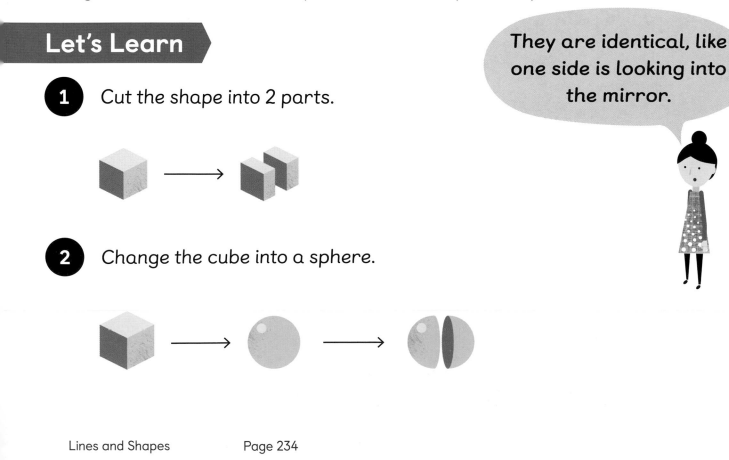

Work in groups of 3 or 4.

What you need:

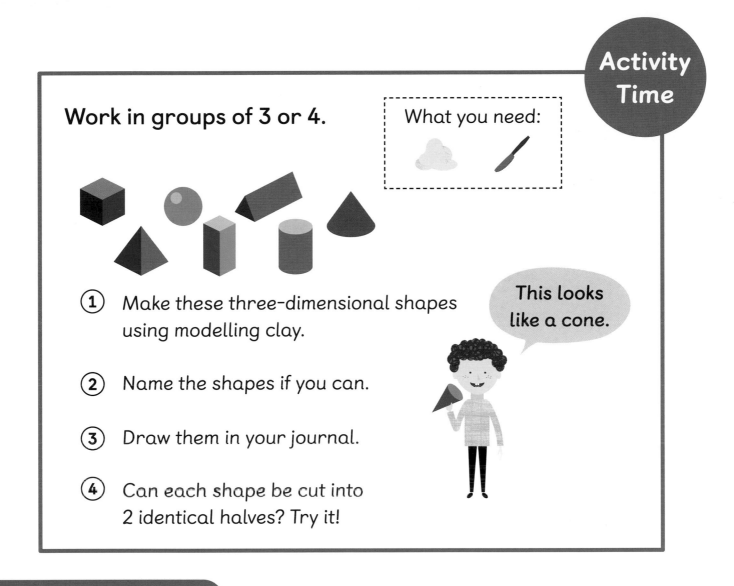

① Make these three-dimensional shapes using modelling clay.

② Name the shapes if you can.

③ Draw them in your journal.

④ Can each shape be cut into 2 identical halves? Try it!

This looks like a cone.

Guided Practice

1 Draw a prism and a pyramid.

2 Name these shapes.

Describing Three-Dimensional Shapes

The edges of the box are lines.
Describe the edges.

Let's Learn

1 How many edges does a cuboid have?

A cuboid has 12 edges.

2 Look for perpendicular lines.

These two lines are perpendicular.

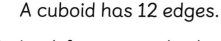

AB is perpendicular to BC.

Are there more pairs of perpendicular lines?

3 Look for parallel lines.

These lines are parallel.

Look for other pairs of parallel lines.

AB and DC are parallel.

D   C

A   B

4 The box sits on a table.
Are there vertical lines?

These are vertical lines.
Are there only three
vertical lines?

5 The box sits on a table.
Are there horizontal lines?

This is a
horizontal line.

How many horizontal lines does the box have?

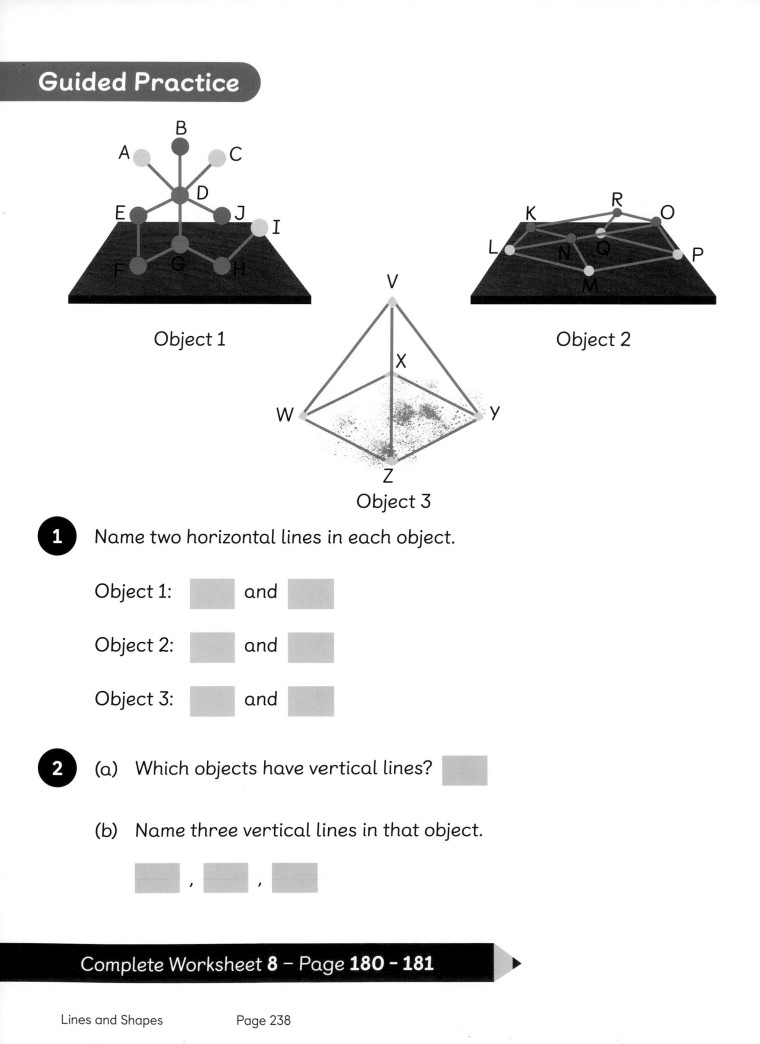

Object 1

Object 2

Object 3

1   Name two horizontal lines in each object.

Object 1: ▢ and ▢

Object 2: ▢ and ▢

Object 3: ▢ and ▢

2   (a)   Which objects have vertical lines? ▢

     (b)   Name three vertical lines in that object.

▢ , ▢ , ▢

Complete Worksheet 8 – Page 180 – 181

A B C D E F G H I
J K L M N O P Q R
S T U V W X Y Z

Can you find perpendicular lines in the letter T?

Can you find parallel lines in the letter W?

In TEN, T has only perpendicular lines. N has only parallel lines and E has both.

What other words in the English language are like TEN?

Maths Journal

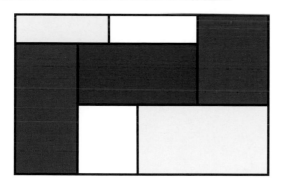

This piece of art is attached to the wall.
It is done in the style of Mondrian.

Mondrian drew vertical and horizontal black lines and coloured some of the spaces with the three primary colours: blue, red and yellow.

Make a piece of art in the style of Mondrian and say what you would use it for.

I use mine to design a mug.

I know how to...

☐ identify and name perpendicular and parallel lines.

☐ find vertical and horizontal lines.

☐ draw and describe two-dimensional shapes.

☐ make and describe three-dimensional shapes.

What does Ruby need to find to get the correct length of yarn for the shapes on the table?

Chapter 14
Perimeter of Figures

Measuring Total Length Around a Shape

In Focus

Ruby uses yarn to outline each shape.
How can she find the length of yarn she needs?

Let's Learn

1 Ruby needs to find the total length around each shape.

She uses yarn and a ruler to find out.

2 The rectangle and the square are on a grid.
What is the total length around each shape?

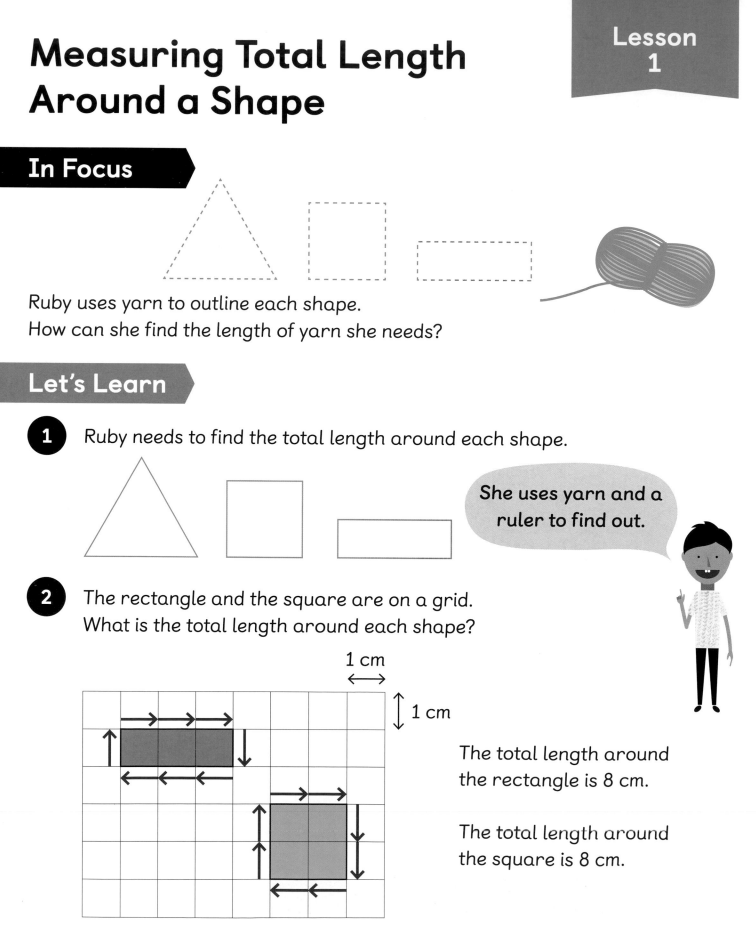

1 cm

1 cm

The total length around the rectangle is 8 cm.

The total length around the square is 8 cm.

Find the total length around each shape.

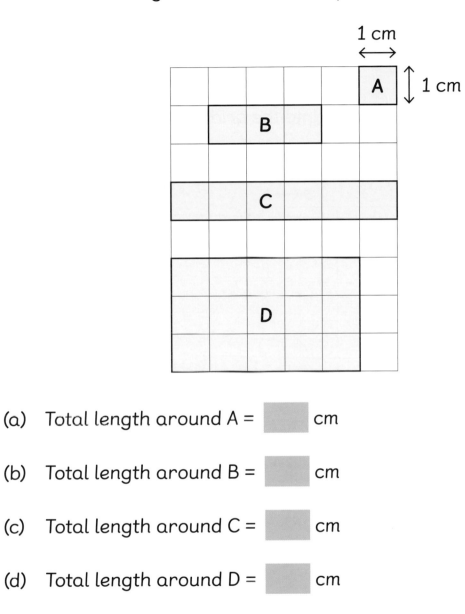

(a) Total length around A = [   ] cm

(b) Total length around B = [   ] cm

(c) Total length around C = [   ] cm

(d) Total length around D = [   ] cm

Complete Worksheet **1** – Page **185 – 186**

Measuring Perimeter

Use  to make a figure that fits into the grid.

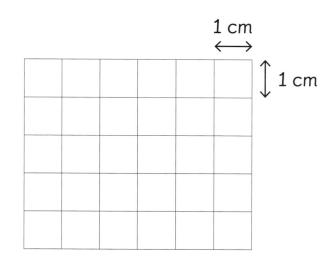

1 cm

1 cm

Find the total length around each figure.

Let's Learn

1

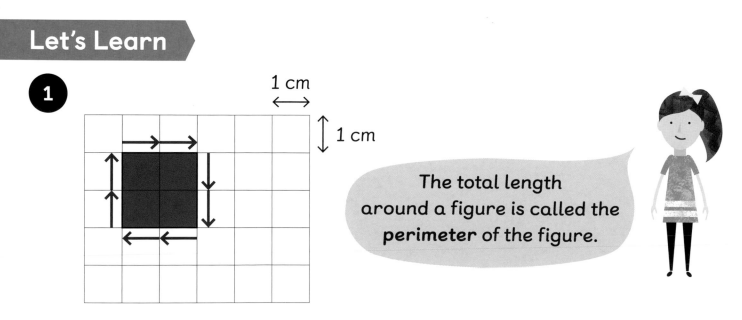

1 cm

1 cm

The total length around a figure is called the **perimeter** of the figure.

The perimeter of the square is 8 cm.

Perimeter of Figures   Page 244

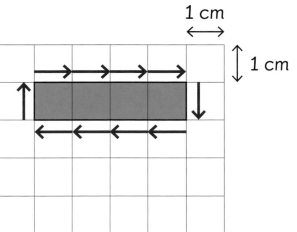 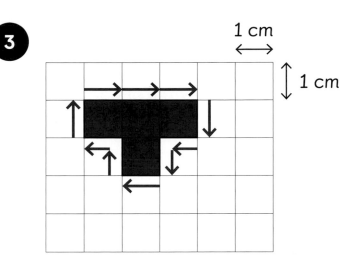

The total length around the rectangle is 10 cm.
The perimeter of the rectangle is 10 cm.

3

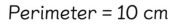

Perimeter = 10 cm

4

Perimeter = ☐ cm

5

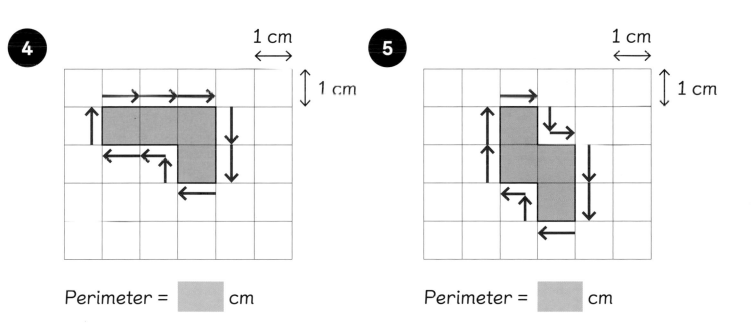

Perimeter = ☐ cm

What is the perimeter of each figure?

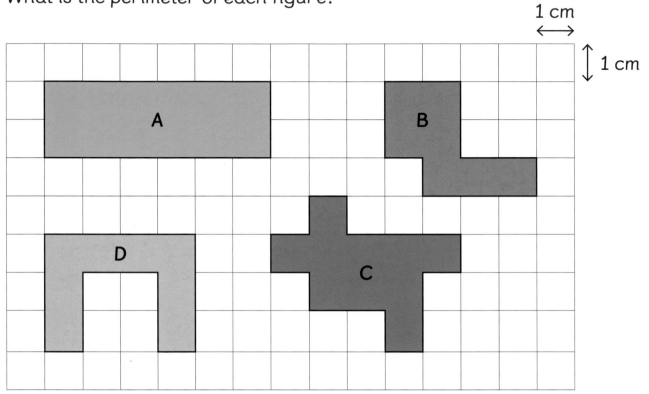

1 cm

1 cm

(a) The perimeter of figure A is ▢ cm.

(b) The perimeter of figure B is ▢ cm.

(c) The perimeter of figure C is ▢ cm.

(d) The perimeter of figure D is ▢ cm.

Complete Worksheet 2 – Page 187 – 188

Measuring Perimeter

In Focus

Four pupils use 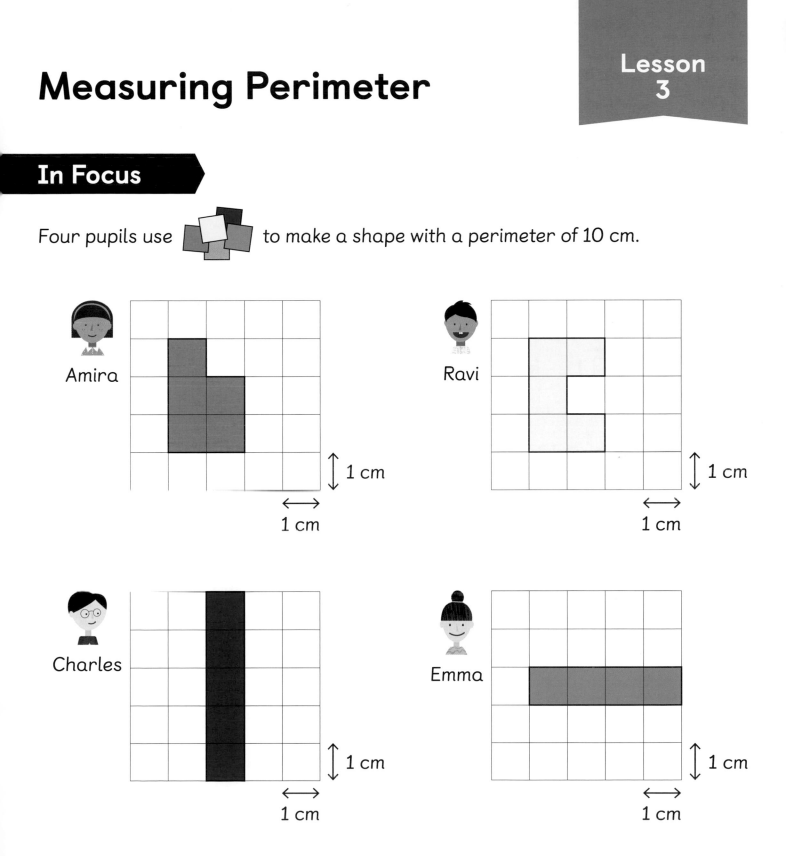 to make a shape with a perimeter of 10 cm.

Amira

1 cm

1 cm

Ravi

1 cm

1 cm

Charles

1 cm

1 cm

Emma

1 cm

1 cm

Who is correct?

1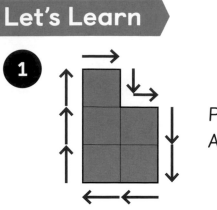

Perimeter = 10 cm
Amira is correct.

2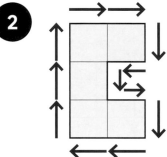

Perimeter = 12 cm
The perimeter is not 10 cm.
Ravi is not correct.

6 cm × 2 = 12 cm

3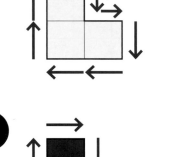

Perimeter = 12 cm
The perimeter is not 10 cm.
Charles is not correct.

4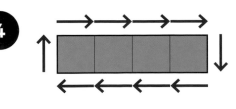

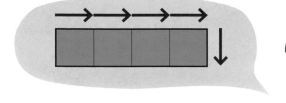

The perimeter is 10 cm.
Emma is correct.
However, she uses only 4 ▢ .

5 cm × 2 = 10 cm

1 Draw another figure with the same perimeter.

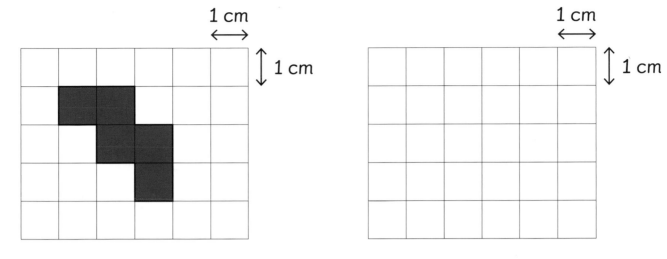

Perimeter = 12 cm

Perimeter = 12 cm

2 Draw 2 different figures, each with a perimeter of 8 cm.

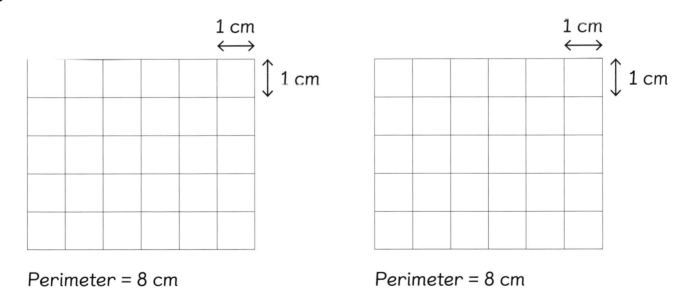

Perimeter = 8 cm

Perimeter = 8 cm

Complete Worksheet 3 – Page 189 – 190

Measuring Perimeter

In Focus

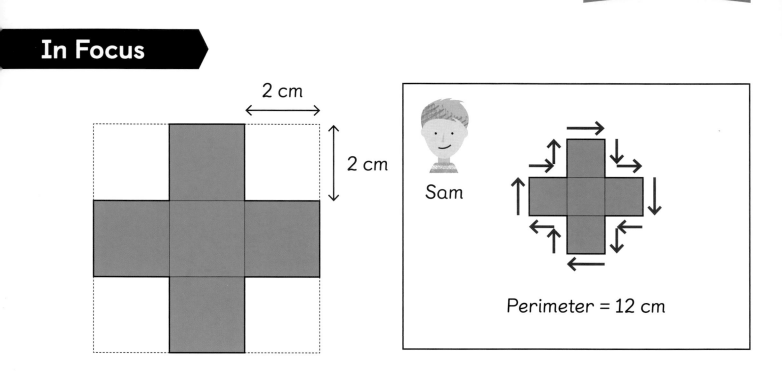

2 cm

2 cm

Sam

Perimeter = 12 cm

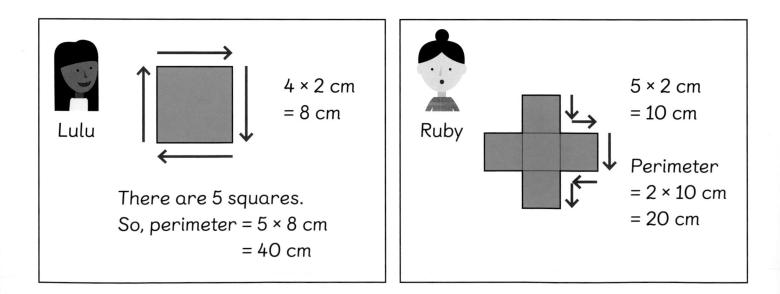

Lulu

4 × 2 cm
= 8 cm

There are 5 squares.
So, perimeter = 5 × 8 cm
                       = 40 cm

Ruby

5 × 2 cm
= 10 cm

Perimeter
= 2 × 10 cm
= 20 cm

What is wrong with their methods?

1 Find the perimeter.

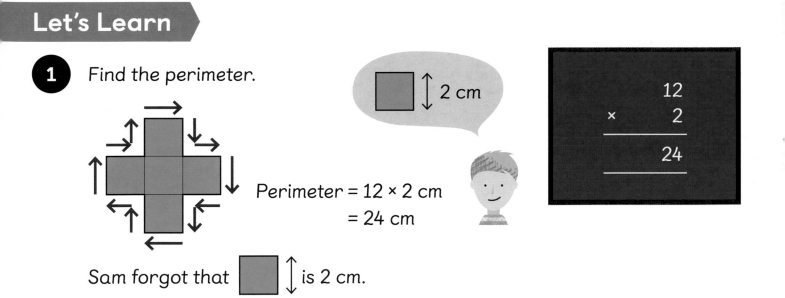

Perimeter = 12 × 2 cm
= 24 cm

$$\begin{array}{r} 12 \\ \times 2 \\ \hline 24 \\ \hline \end{array}$$

Sam forgot that ⬜ ↕ is 2 cm.

2 Find the perimeter.

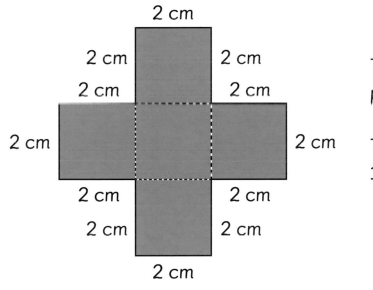

2 cm
2 cm   2 cm
2 cm   2 cm
2 cm   2 cm
2 cm   2 cm
2 cm   2 cm
2 cm

The dotted lines are not part of the perimeter.

The perimeter is
12 × 2 cm = 24 cm.

3 Find the perimeter.

—— 5 × 2 cm = 10 cm
—— 5 × 2 cm = 10 cm

2 × 10 cm = 20 cm
This is not yet the perimeter.

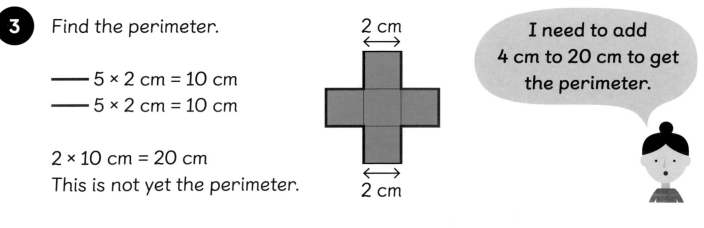

2 cm

2 cm

I need to add 4 cm to 20 cm to get the perimeter.

The perimeter is 20 cm + 4 cm = 24 cm.

Guided Practice

1 Find the perimeter of each figure.

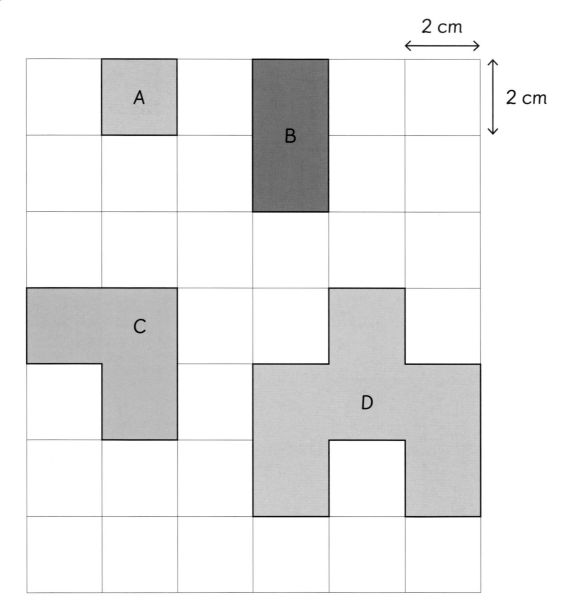

2 cm

2 cm

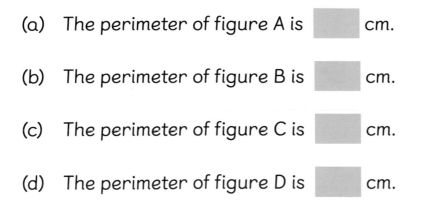

(a)   The perimeter of figure A is ☐ cm.

(b)   The perimeter of figure B is ☐ cm.

(c)   The perimeter of figure C is ☐ cm.

(d)   The perimeter of figure D is ☐ cm.

2 Draw a figure with a perimeter of 18 cm on the grid.

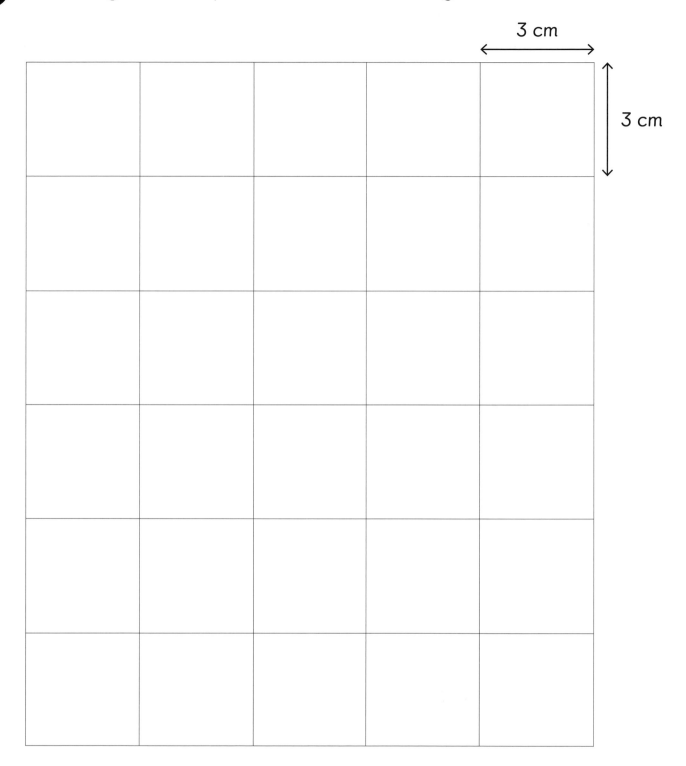

3 cm

3 cm

Complete Worksheet 4 – Page **191 – 192**

Measuring Perimeter

In Focus

How do we find the perimeter of this figure?

Let's Learn

1 Recall that perimeter is the length around the figure.

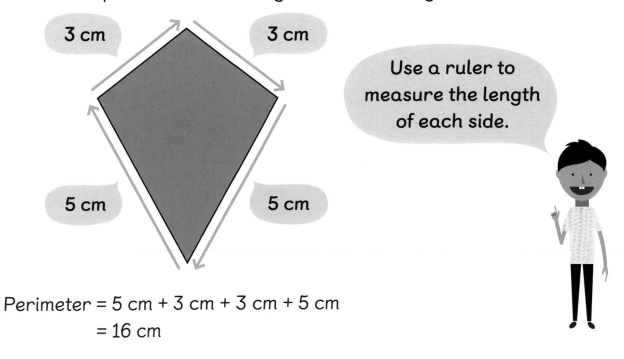

3 cm   3 cm

5 cm   5 cm

Use a ruler to measure the length of each side.

Perimeter = 5 cm + 3 cm + 3 cm + 5 cm
= 16 cm

2 Find the perimeter of this figure.

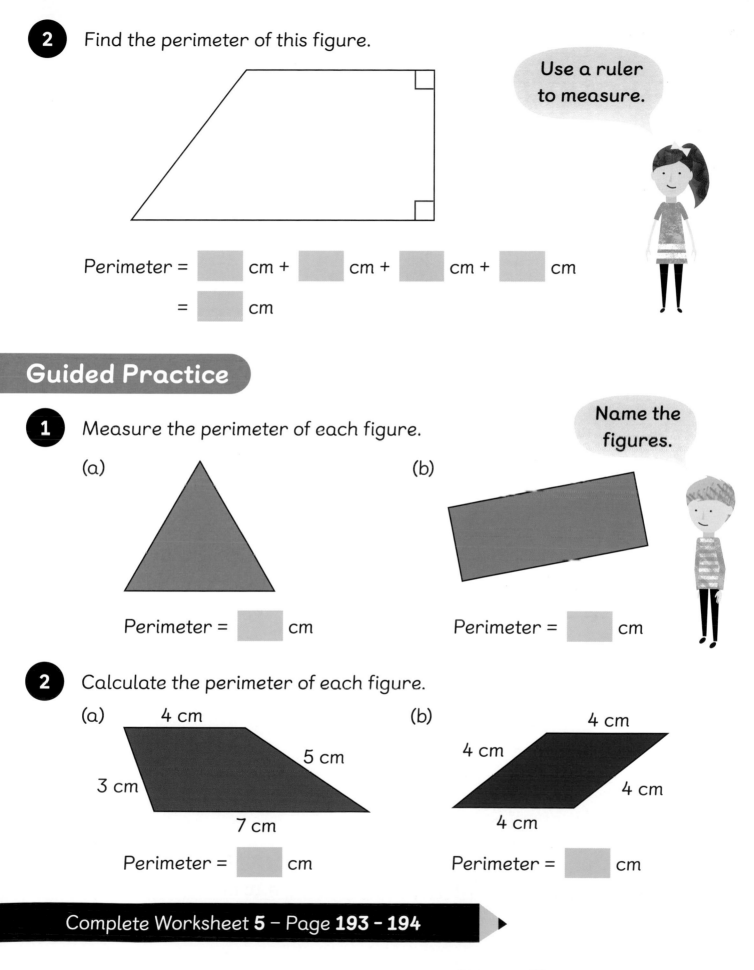

Use a ruler to measure.

Perimeter = ▢ cm + ▢ cm + ▢ cm + ▢ cm

= ▢ cm

Guided Practice

1 Measure the perimeter of each figure.

Name the figures.

(a)

Perimeter = ▢ cm

(b)

Perimeter = ▢ cm

2 Calculate the perimeter of each figure.

(a) 4 cm

3 cm

5 cm

7 cm

Perimeter = ▢ cm

(b)

4 cm

4 cm

4 cm

4 cm

Perimeter = ▢ cm

Complete Worksheet **5** – Page **193 – 194**

Calculating Perimeter

In Focus

Large tiles are used to form a rectangle.

How far is the distance around the rectangle?
Compare it to the perimeter of a tile.

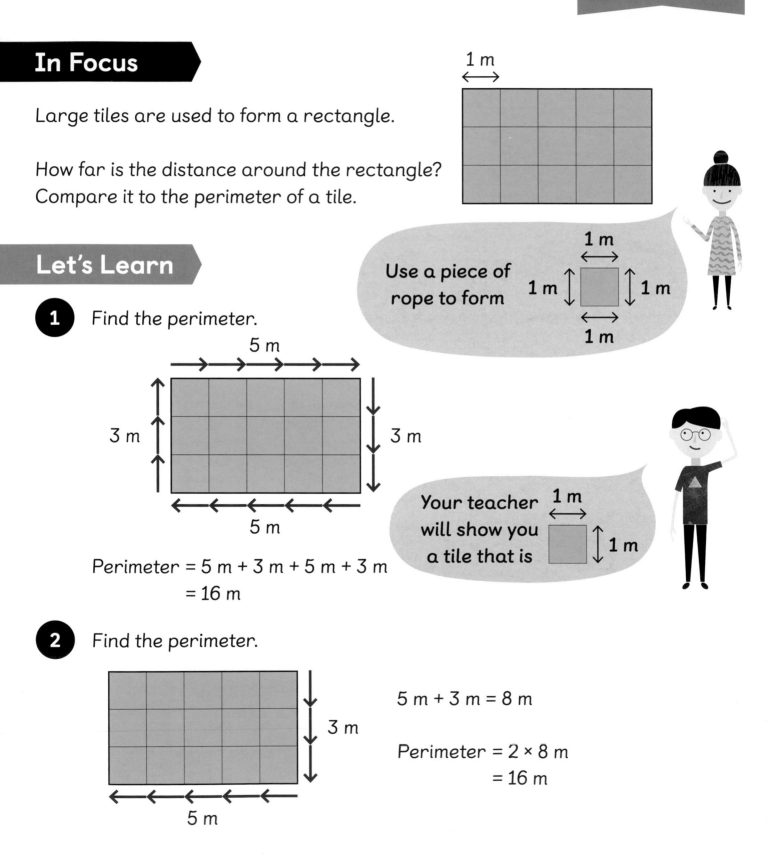

Let's Learn

1 Find the perimeter.

Use a piece of rope to form

Perimeter = 5 m + 3 m + 5 m + 3 m
= 16 m

Your teacher will show you a tile that is

2 Find the perimeter.

5 m + 3 m = 8 m

Perimeter = 2 × 8 m
= 16 m

Figures A, B, C and D are drawn on a 1-m square grid.

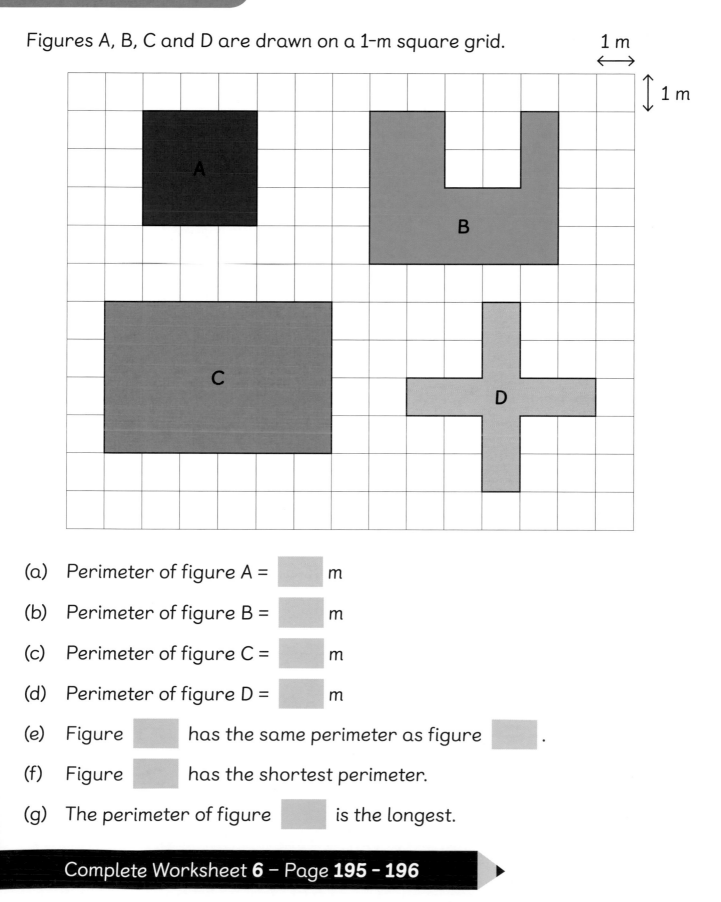

(a) Perimeter of figure A = ☐ m

(b) Perimeter of figure B = ☐ m

(c) Perimeter of figure C = ☐ m

(d) Perimeter of figure D = ☐ m

(e) Figure ☐ has the same perimeter as figure ☐.

(f) Figure ☐ has the shortest perimeter.

(g) The perimeter of figure ☐ is the longest.

Complete Worksheet 6 – Page 195 – 196

Calculating Perimeter

In Focus

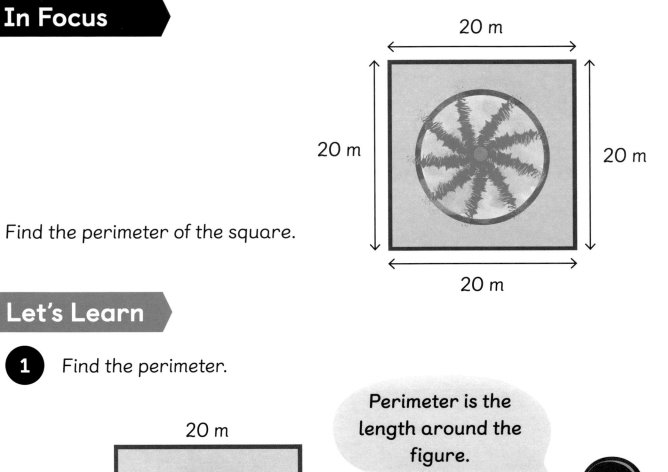

Find the perimeter of the square.

Let's Learn

1 Find the perimeter.

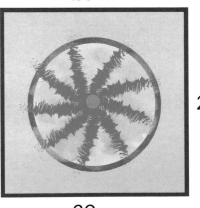

Perimeter is the length around the figure.

Perimeter = 20 m + 20 m + 20 m + 20 m
= 80 m

2 Find the perimeter of the square.

20 m

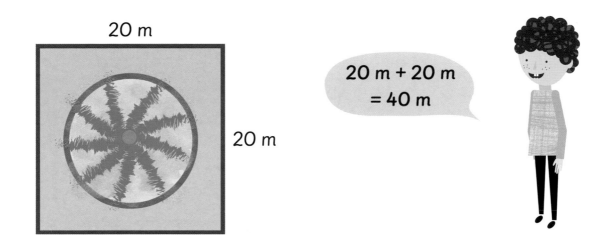

20 m

20 m + 20 m = 40 m

How can we use the 40 m to calculate the perimeter?

Perimeter = [ ] × 40 m

= [ ] m

3 Find the perimeter of the square.

20 m

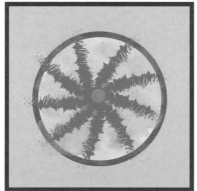

I think that is all you need to know.

Explain if Ruby is correct.

Perimeter = [ ] × 20 m

= [ ] m

Guided Practice

Find the perimeter.

Add the length of each side to find the perimeter.

1

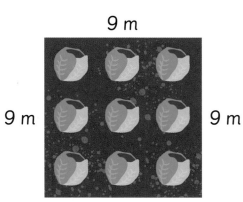

24 m

13 m   13 m

24 m

24 m + 13 m + 24 m + 13 m = ⬜ m

The perimeter of the field is ⬜ m.

2

9 m

9 m   9 m

9 m

9 m + 9 m + 9 m + 9 m = ⬜ m

⬜ × ⬜ = ⬜ m

The perimeter of the vegetable plot

is ⬜ m.

3

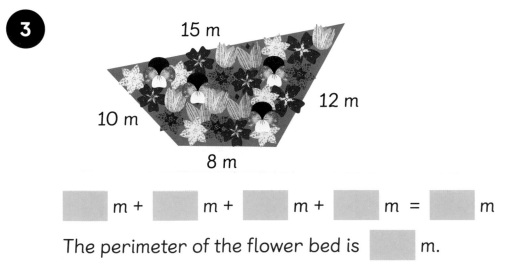

15 m

10 m   12 m

8 m

⬜ m + ⬜ m + ⬜ m + ⬜ m = ⬜ m

The perimeter of the flower bed is ⬜ m.

4 Find the perimeter of each figure.

(a)

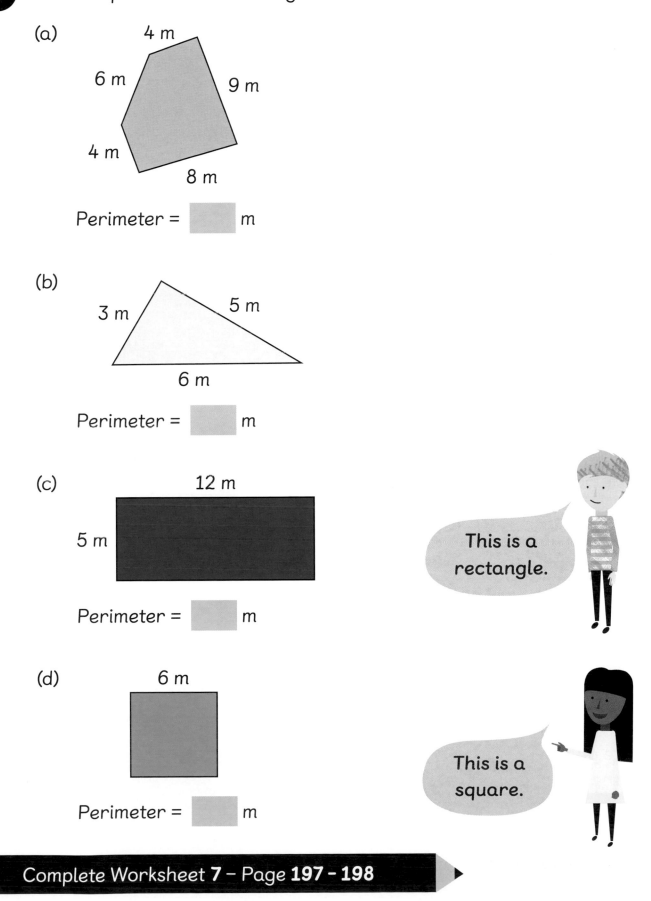

4 m

6 m

9 m

4 m

8 m

Perimeter = ☐ m

(b)

3 m

5 m

6 m

Perimeter = ☐ m

(c)

12 m

5 m

Perimeter = ☐ m

This is a rectangle.

(d)

6 m

Perimeter = ☐ m

This is a square.

Complete Worksheet **7** – Page **197 – 198**

Calculating Perimeter

In Focus

A rectangular carpet is used to cover the floor of the room.
The carpet has a length of 19 m and a width of 8 m.
What is the perimeter of the carpet?

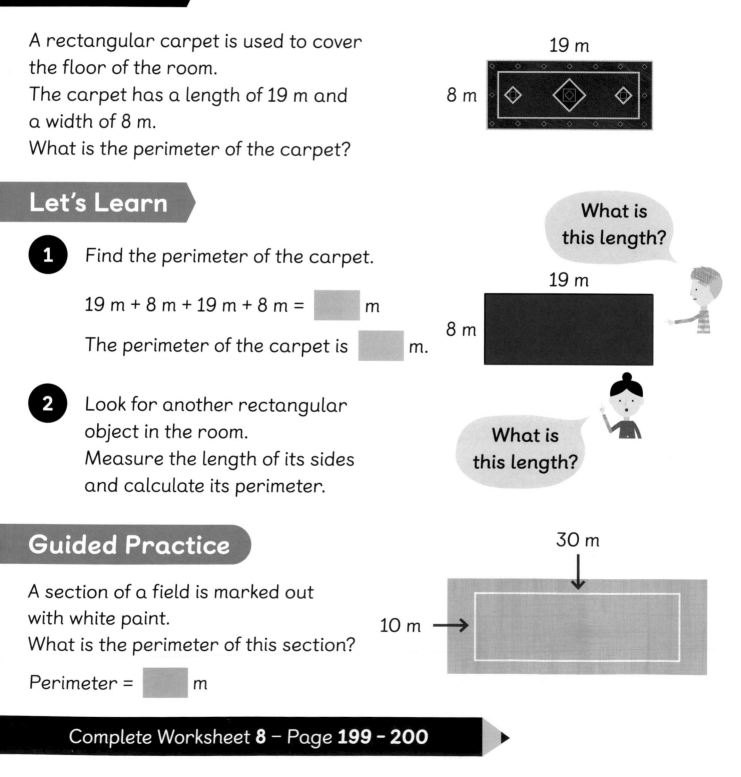

19 m

8 m

Let's Learn

1 Find the perimeter of the carpet.

19 m + 8 m + 19 m + 8 m = [   ] m

The perimeter of the carpet is [   ] m.

What is this length?

19 m

8 m

2 Look for another rectangular object in the room.
Measure the length of its sides and calculate its perimeter.

What is this length?

Guided Practice

A section of a field is marked out with white paint.
What is the perimeter of this section?

Perimeter = [   ] m

30 m

10 m →

Complete Worksheet 8 – Page **199 – 200**

Calculating Perimeter

In Focus

Sam builds a fence around a square garden.
The length of the sides of the square is 7 m.

What is the length of fence used?

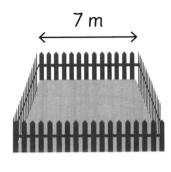

7 m

Let's Learn

Find the perimeter of the garden.

How do we know the length of this side?

7 m

Since the fence is built around the garden, we find the perimeter of the square garden.

7 m + 7 m + 7 m + 7 m = 28 m
The length of fence is 28 m.

Guided Practice

The rectangular land shown is surrounded by a fence.
What is the length of the fence?

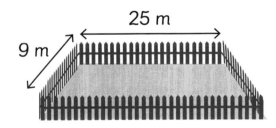

25 m

9 m

Perimeter = ☐ m

Complete Worksheet 9 – Page 201

Calculating Perimeter

In Focus

A rectangular piece of paper had a length of 24 cm and a width of 8 cm.
A square with 5 cm sides was cut out from the piece of paper.

24 cm

8 cm

5 cm

What was the perimeter of the remaining piece of paper?

Let's Learn

1   Amira did it this way.

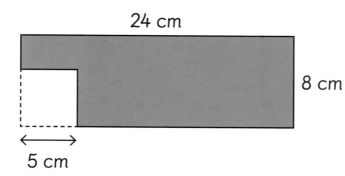

24 cm

8 cm

5 cm

Perimeter of the rectangle
= 24 cm + 8 cm + 24 cm + 8 cm
= 64 cm

Perimeter of square
= 5 cm + 5 cm + 5 cm + 5 cm
= 20 cm

$$
\begin{array}{r}
24 \\
+\quad 8 \\
\hline
32
\end{array}
\qquad
\begin{array}{r}
32 \\
+\quad 32 \\
\hline
64
\end{array}
$$

Perimeter of remaining piece
= 64 cm – 20 cm
= 44 cm

4 × 5 = 20

Amira is wrong.
Show the correct way to do it.

2 Charles did it this way.

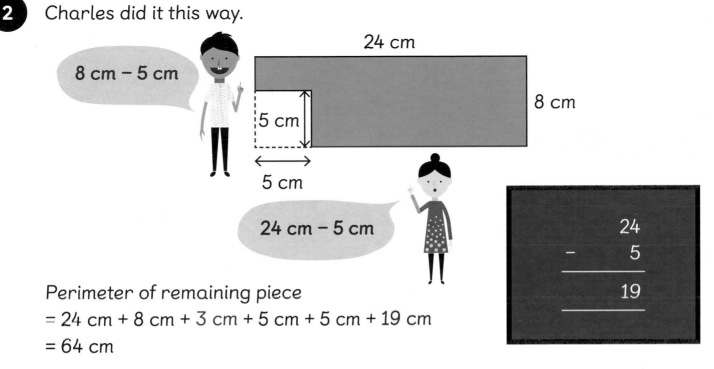

8 cm – 5 cm

24 cm

8 cm

5 cm

5 cm

24 cm – 5 cm

```
    24
 -   5
   ___
    19
   ___
```

Perimeter of remaining piece
= 24 cm + 8 cm + 3 cm + 5 cm + 5 cm + 19 cm
= 64 cm

The perimeter of the remaining piece is 64 cm.

Guided Practice

Find the perimeter of the remaining piece when ⬚ ↕ 2 cm squares

10 cm

are cut from   6 cm.

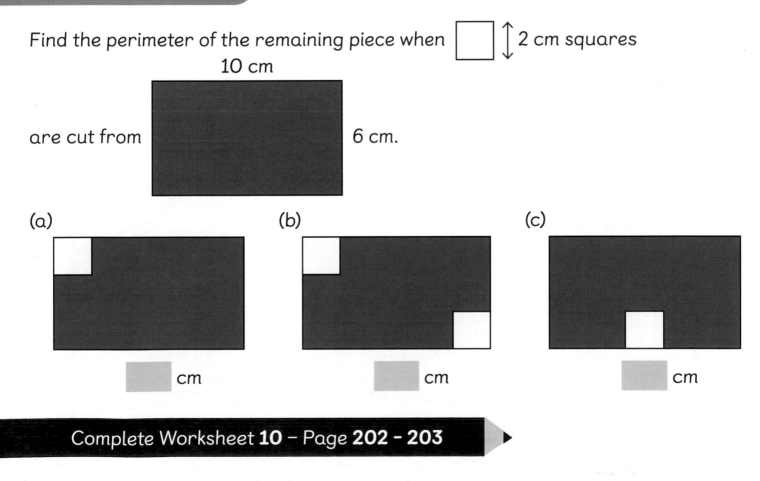

(a)

☐ cm

(b)

☐ cm

(c)

☐ cm

Complete Worksheet **10** – Page **202 - 203**

Lulu cuts a rectangular piece of paper into two identical pieces.

10 cm

4 cm

A   →   B   C

She says that the perimeter of B and C is the same as the perimeter of A. Do you agree? Why or why not?

Write a note to a friend to explain to him or her how to find the perimeter of a rectangular card.

Happy Birthday

I know how to...

☐ measure the total length around a shape.

☐ find the perimeter of figures using a square grid.

☐ find the perimeter of figures in cm and m.

☐ find the perimeter of squares and rectangles.

Self Check